CHINA'S LEGAL S

China Today
Creative Industries in China, Michael Keane
Urban China, Xuefei Ren
China's Environmental Challenges, Judith Shapiro

CHINA'S LEGAL SYSTEM —

Pitman B. Potter

polity

First published in 2013 by Polity Press

Polity Press
65 Bridge Street
Cambridge CB2 1UR, UK

Polity Press
350 Main Street
Malden, MA 02148, USA

ISBN-13: 978-0-7456-6268-8
ISBN-13: 978-0-7456-6269-5(pb)

A catalogue record for this book is available from the British Library.

Typeset in 11.5 on 15 pt Adobe Jenson Pro
by Toppan Best-set Premedia Limited
Printed and bound in Great Britain by Clays Ltd, St Ives plc

The publisher has used its best endeavours to ensure that the URLs for external websites referred to in this book are correct and active at the time of going to press. However, the publisher has no responsibility for the websites and can make no guarantee that a site will remain live or that the content is or will remain appropriate.

Every effort has been made to trace all copyright holders, but if any have been inadvertently overlooked the publisher will be pleased to include any necessary credits in any subsequent reprint or edition.

For further information on Polity, visit our website: www.politybooks.com

For my students, from whom I have learned so much

Contents

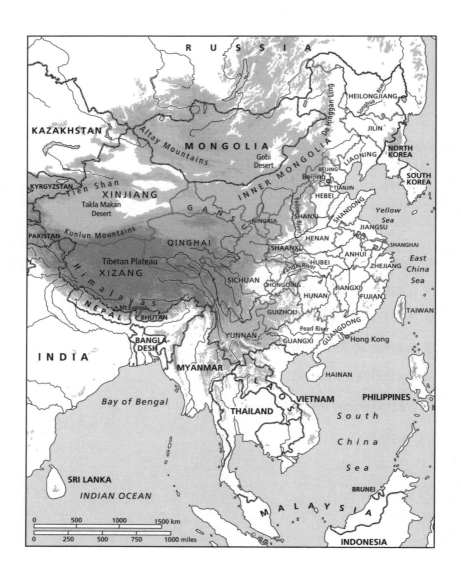

Tables and Figures

Chronology

1894–5	First Sino–Japanese War.
1904–11	Imperial Law Commission (Shen Jiaben). Influence of Japanese and German advisors. Influence of German civil law. Enactment of Company Law (1904); Court Organization Law (1909); Criminal Codes (1911); drafting of Trade Law, Trademark Law, Civil Procedure Law; Civil Code.
1911	Fall of the Qing dynasty. Republic of China (ROC) established under Sun Yat-sen.
1919	May 4th Movement, ideological and patriotic awakening for many who later joined the Communist movement.
1921	Founding of Communist Party of China.
1923	First United Front: Alliance of Nationalist Party (Guomindang – GMD) and Communist Party of China (CPC) against warlords.
1927	Split between GMD and CPC; civil war begins.
1927–37	"Nanjing Decade" – consolidation of ROC rule. Legislation on Civil Code (1929); Company Law (1929); Criminal Code (1935); Civil Procedure Law (1935); Trademark Law (1936).
1928–35	Jiangxi Soviet (CPC Base Area).
1934–5	Long March: CPC evades GMD encirclement. Mao Zedong becomes CPC leader.

1936–7	Marco Polo Bridge Incident, Japanese Invasion of China.
1937–45	Xian incident, 2nd United Front (GMD/CPC alliance against Japan); Nanjing Massacre (December 1937); Communist forces establish Jin Cha Ji/Shen Gan Ning Border Areas.
1945–9	Defeat of Japan (1945). Civil war between GMD and CPC resumes.
1949	People's Republic of China (PRC) founded (October); ROC removed to Taiwan.
1950–3	Korean War.
1950–4	CPC law and policy focused on state building. Enactment of Marriage Law (1950), Land Reform Law (1950), Constitution (1954). First meeting of National People's Congress. Political consolidation through campaigns such as San-Fan and Wu-Fan (1951–2).
1953–7	First Five-Year Plan; PRC adopts Soviet-style economic planning.
1956–7	Hundred Flowers Movement, CPC permits limited political debate. Anti-Rightist Movement, retaliation against critics of CPC leadership.
1958–60	Great Leap Forward: An effort to transform China through rapid industrialization and collectivization.
1959	Tibetan Uprising in Lhasa; Dalai Lama flees to India (March).
1960–2	Three Hard Years, widespread famine with tens of millions of deaths. Mao influence wanes.
1963–5	Socialist Education Campaign: Mao reasserts authority.

1966–76	Great Proletarian Cultural Revolution; Retaliation against Mao opponents (real and perceived). Mao personality cult.
1972	President Richard Nixon visits China; "Shanghai Communiqué" pledges normalization of US–China relations (February).
1976	Tangshan earthquake kills hundreds of thousands (July). Death of Mao Zedong (September). Ultra-Leftist Gang of Four (includes Mao's wife Jiang Qing) arrested (October).
1978	Deng Xiaoping assumes power; launches legal and economic reforms (3rd Plenum of 11th CPC Central Committee) (November–December). One-child family planning policy introduced.
1979	Democracy wall movement suppressed. Wei Jingsheng imprisoned. China enacts "Seven Laws," first legislation of the post-Mao legal reforms – includes Criminal Law; Criminal Procedure Law; Organization Laws for People's Courts, People's Procuratorates, Local People's Governments and Congresses; Election Laws; and Joint Venture Law. US and China establish formal diplomatic ties; Deng Xiaoping visits Washington. China announces rehabilitation for victims of 1957 Anti-Rightist Campaign.
1981	CPC Resolution on Party History repudiates Cultural Revolution. Trial of Gang of Four.
1982	Census reports PRC population at more than one billion.
1984	Margaret Thatcher co-signs Sino–British Joint Declaration agreeing to return Hong Kong to China in 1997 (December).

1986–7	Student demonstrations in Fall 1986 lead to dismissal of reform-minded CPC General Secretary Hu Yaobang in early 1987 and launch of "Anti-Bourgeois Liberalism Campaign." CPC General Secretary Zhao Ziyang speech to 13th National CPC Congress asserts China in preliminary stage of socialism (October 1987).
1988	Economic crisis (inflation, runs on local banks, CPC Special Politburo meeting to cut government spending affects urban employment).
1989	Tiananmen Square protests in Beijing and sympathetic protests across China culminate in June 4 military crackdown and subsequent period of repression and policy conservatism.
1992	Deng Xiaoping's Southern Inspection Tour re-energizes economic reforms.
1993–2002	Jiang Zemin is president of PRC and CPC General Secretary; economic growth agenda continues.
2001	PRC accession to the WTO (November).
2002–3	SARS outbreak in PRC and Hong Kong.
2003–12	Hu Jintao is president of PRC and CPC General Secretary; introduces policies of "harmonious society" to counter challenges of rapid economic growth.
2008	Sichuan earthquake kills tens of thousands (May). Summer Olympic Games in Beijing (August). Dissident Liu Xiaobo arrested for "Charter 08," calling for political and legal reform (December).
2010	Shanghai World Exposition; Liu Xiaobo awarded Nobel Peace Prize while in prison.

2012   CPC 18th National Congress sees Xi Jinping appointed Party General Secretary. New Politburo Standing Committee reflects influence of Jiang Zemin and decline of Hu Jintao influence.

2013   12th National People's Congress appoints Xi Jinping President.

Acknowledgments

I would first like to thank Polity Press for their invitation and particularly David Winters for his steadfast support for the preparation of this volume. Research for this volume was supported by the Major Collaborative Research Initiative (MCRI) program of the Social Sciences and Humanities Research Council of Canada (SSHRC), for which I am deeply thankful. Several graduate students at UBC contributed significantly to the success of this project, including Erika Cedillo-Corral, Maggie Juan Li, Liu Huan, Liu Yue, Matthew Nickelmann, and Hanna Yang. I offer my deepest thanks to two anonymous readers, as well as to Alison Bailey, Timothy Cheek, Stanley Lubman, and Sophia Woodman for reviewing and commenting on the manuscript. The Faculty of Law at UBC has been unfailingly supportive of this project, for which I remain sincerely grateful. In particular, I would like to thank Rozalia Mate and Abbey Barley at the Faculty of Law for their ongoing administrative assistance. I would also like to thank my colleagues at Borden Ladner Gervais LLP for their long-standing encouragement and support. For those whom I may grievously have neglected to mention, I can only offer my apologies and deepest thanks. Naturally I remain responsible for the errors and omissions that no doubt remain.

Pitman B. Potter
Vancouver, Canada
February 2013

Author's Note

This text concerns the legal system of the People's Republic of China (PRC), and does not examine the laws of Taiwan, Hong Kong, or Macao. While these jurisdictions are considered part of "Greater China" and in the cases of Hong Kong and Macao are within the territorial boundaries of the PRC, common international usage generally equates China with the PRC. Accordingly, we have elected to use the term "China" in the title of this volume to denote the People's Republic of China.

Introduction

The legal regime is a key element of governance in the People's Republic of China (PRC) today. Law in China remains very much a contested domain of conflicting concepts, policies, and practices. Scholars of Chinese legal studies have generated broad understanding of the PRC legal system and offered useful perspectives on its origins and operation. Jerome Alan Cohen's pioneering work on the PRC criminal justice system and many other topics combined with the work of Stanley Lubman, R. Randall Edwards, and William Jones to provide a scholarly foundation for understanding law in the early PRC.[1] Their work continues to influence studies of contemporary Chinese law. Stanley Lubman, for example, has been a key participant in a broad debate over whether the PRC legal system satisfies the criteria of objectivity and autonomy required for the rule of law, or whether it matches notions about a "thin rule of law."[2] With greater possibilities for living, working, and doing research in China, China law scholars have been able more easily to study the operation of the PRC legal system at the local level.[3] Detailed studies of many areas of China's civil and commercial law, property, contracts, criminal law and procedure, judicial institutions, international trade and investment, and many other areas have vastly expanded international understanding of the PRC legal system.[4] As well, the burgeoning community of PRC scholars conducting research and analysis on China's legal system has contributed to our knowledge in many important ways.[5] This volume is informed by much of this work.

Set against an historical tradition where law in China was an instrument of state rule and punishment, law in the PRC today serves primarily as an instrument of rule for the Communist Party of China (CPC). The PRC legal system is aimed first and foremost at protecting the power of the Party/State – that expansive network of bureaucratic and political organs responsible for administration and governance even as they remain subject to the leadership of the CPC. Other priorities include protection of private civil relationships of contract and property, supporting economic development, safeguarding of social interests and human rights, supporting further engagement with international institutions, and international trade and investment relations. The operation of law in China can be understood largely in light of tensions between these priorities and the imperative of Party/State power.

As well, students of law in the PRC need to be aware of the important gaps between laws and regulations on the books and in action. As a policy instrument, law in China is constantly subject to interpretation and intervention by central and local level officials of the Party/State. The application of legal and regulatory requirements to individuals and enterprises often depends on political priorities and relationships rather than on the text of the law itself. Whether in the area of constitutional rights, economic regulation in matters such as contracts and property, or social development issues of labor relations and environmental protection, the realities of legal performance often differ substantially from the content of laws and regulations. The courts too are affected by the political environment in which law operates – judicial decisions are often reviewed and amended by committees chaired by Party officials (so-called "Adjudication Committees") before going into effect. Local enforcement of laws and regulations enacted for national application is often inconsistent, as local political and policy priorities affect interpretation and implementation. Just as China's interaction with international rule of law standards reflects dynamics of interpretation and application based on local conditions, so too is local implementation of central government edicts (including laws and regulations) subject to variation according to local imperatives. With these complexities in mind, this research and learning guide will provide a general introduction to the PRC legal regime, focusing on opportunities and challenges that change in China brings for the rule of law.

What began in December 1978 as a tentative legal reform program to re-establish government authority following the chaos of the Cultural Revolution (1966–76) has developed into a complex array of legal forms and organizations. The operation of law in China is affected by the fact that many aspects of the PRC legal regime are borrowed from European and North American legal models and yet also are suffused with local legal norms and culture. The legal regime remains heavily instrumentalist – a tool of Party and state policy. As the policy goals to which socialist law is applied have expanded, so too has the legal regime grown in reach and complexity. Law in the PRC remains a work in progress, subject to a range of policy priorities associated with China's socio-economic and political transformation and influenced by competing local and international norms.

The PRC legal system is worthy of study for many reasons. First is the intrinsic value of understanding legal norms and institutions in the most populous and soon to be largest economy in the world. As well, China's expanding trade and investment relations around the world lend practical value to the study of PRC law. In addition, understanding the structures and performance of the PRC legal system is important for its potential to strengthen understanding of other legal systems from a comparative perspective. Finally, China presents a case study of the development of "socialist law" as a category of legal system distinct from the Continental/civil and Anglo-American/common law models. China's "socialist rule of law" system reveals practices of adaptation and hybridization in response to engagement with the civil and common law models of Europe and North America. China's socialist legal system also reveals important dimensions of the relationship between ideals about the rule of law and imperatives of governance. This in turn invites consideration of notions about independence and autonomy of legal systems generally, and with regard to China in particular. For these reasons at least, the legal system of the People's Republic of China is a compelling focus for study by advanced undergraduate and graduate students in law, political science, and related disciplines.

This research and learning guide aims to provide students with basic information about the PRC legal system and to invite consideration and debate around foundational questions about law in China. Readers should be mindful that the specific content of particular laws and regulations will change over time, as will the organizational arrangements for China's legal institutions. By developing a basic understanding of the foundations of the PRC legal regime, readers of this volume can adapt to future changes in particular rules and organizations.

With these goals in mind, the volume opens with an historical overview and discussion of influences on PRC law today. The historical antecedents for the PRC legal system provide essential context for the current operation of law in China. Attention is given to the legal regime of the Qing Dynasty (1644–1911), where Confucian relational standards of socio-economic and political harmony were combined with punitive legalist doctrines of rigid enforcement and punishment. The legal system of the Republic of China (founded in 1911, removed to Taiwan in 1949) is also addressed, largely as an institutional context for the subsequent emergence of law in the PRC. The historical overview also examines legal arrangements in the CPC revolutionary base areas (particularly Jin Cha Ji Border Area), which provided a foundation for many of the laws of the early years of the PRC. The early history of the PRC is discussed as a source for law in the post-Mao era. With the post-Mao legal reforms of the Deng Xiaoping leadership after 1978, PRC law was linked increasingly with political control and economic and social development.

Accordingly, the book then turns to three thematic challenges that confront the PRC today, namely political stability, economic prosperity, and social development. The chapter on political stability focuses on the role of the PRC legal regime in ensuring and protecting the political authority of the Party/State. This combines normative issues of Party ideology with legislative and operational structures around criminal law and administrative control. The chapter on economic prosperity examines the ways in which the PRC legal regime supports expanded autonomy for commercial activities while still imposing a modicum of state regulatory intervention, as an alternative to the state-planned economy in which economic actors were wholly subordinate to state direction. Applied to the economy, the legal system of the PRC reflects development policies that have shifted from an emphasis on state planning to a qualified emphasis on market relations. This in turn supports a transition in the role of the government over economic affairs from one of direction to one of facilitation, even while reserving certain strategic sectors (e.g. security and defense, natural resources, telecommunications, and infrastructure) to the prerogatives of the Party/State. The chapter on social development examines the ways in which the PRC legal regime facilitates the transition in the policy imperatives of the Party/State from leading social transformation to providing social services. Touching on examples of health policy, education, labor, women's rights, and treatment of minorities, this chapter examines the emerging role of the Party/State as a protector of social wellbeing rather than a leader of revolutionary change.

Underlying all three sectors is the importance of the legal regime as an instrument for policy implementation and in providing legitimacy to the rule of the Party/State. These three thematic chapters explore tensions around dynamics of control and autonomy in local political, economic, and social relations, particularly in the relationship between the imperative of political stability and the needs of economic prosperity and social development. The PRC legal system is an important arena where these tensions are expressed and efforts to resolve them attempted.

Reflecting the expanded presence of China in the world, the final chapter examines issues of China's international engagement. The complex phenomenon of globalization presents opportunities and challenges for China's increased influence in the world. The opportunities to borrow, internalize, and adapt legal norms and institutions have been seized by China's leaders to develop a legal system that on the surface appears generally compatible with international standards and the legal systems of other countries. However, challenges emerge also, particularly as norms of liberalism (particularly standards of liberal democracy) challenge the monopoly on political power held by the Party/State. Many of China's official explanations of the direction of its legal development are grounded in assertions about the non-applicability of international liberal standards of governance. China's closer integration with the world political economy involves tensions between the standards that inform the global system and the prerogatives of the PRC Party/State.

This book is intended to serve as a research and learning guide for university-level audiences with general but non-specialized knowledge about China. The book relies on primary and secondary literature (a reference section is provided at the end of the volume) as well as the author's own experience and research. Included in the text are excerpts from Chinese laws and other legal materials, offered to illustrate points made in the main text and also to invite readers to begin grappling with the challenges of documentary analysis. Readers are encouraged to parse these documents with care to identify underlying elements of ideology, policy, and interest. Each chapter also includes discussion questions and suggestions for further reading.

1   Development of the Socialist Legal System _____

The contemporary PRC legal system reflects a range of historical and contemporary influences. Domestic influences provide the foundation for Chinese law, beginning with the traditions of the imperial period. Legal initiatives under the Republic of China (est. 1911), during the revolutionary period, and after the 1949 Communist Revolution, reflected tensions between domestic concerns with increased international influence. The launching of legal reforms in 1978 signaled a new effort at building a legal system, although there have been numerous changes and challenges since then. Understanding the PRC legal system today requires an appreciation for its historical antecedents and contemporary contexts.

I. HISTORICAL FOUNDATIONS FOR PRC LAW

The PRC legal system reflects the influences of historical conditions and changes affecting China over the past several centuries. Particular elements of this include Chinese legal tradition and the law code of the Qing Dynasty (*Da Qing Lü Li*) that used formal rules and institutions of punitive law (referred to in Chinese as "*fa*") to enforce moral principles of Confucian propriety ("*li*"). This dichotomy between moral education and formal legal punishment continued to influence the development of law under the Republic of China and later in the PRC.

While much of the Qing Code focused on criminal punishments for errant social behavior, many kinds of ordinary social and economic activities were also addressed, including commercial law, contracts, and property.[1] As well, the handling of disputes in local practice under the Qing suggested that the guidance of formal legal codes was aimed primarily at expressing ideals of governance while local practice tended to reflect local priorities around relationships and community socialization.[2] Features of the Qing Code (and the Ming Code before that), such as severity of punishment; the privileged status of officials; reliance on magistrates as judge, jury, and executioner; and the general lack of attention to formal legal education, were grounded in Confucian norms of hierarchy, propriety, and relational justice.

Confucian foundations of Qing law included notions of "relational justice," by which the application of law depended on hierarchical relations in society that privileged officials, men, and elders over commoners, women, and youth. Thus, criminal punishment applied not only to conventional crimes such as murder, assault, and theft, but also to behavior that would be classified as civil rather than criminal in many legal systems today, such as breach of agreement, harm to reputation, and interference with commercial relationships As well, the severity of punishment varied according to the relationship between the perpetrator and the victim – punishment was more severe if the act was deemed to violate a Confucian relationship in society.

Traditional perspectives of Qing law also included the notion of "catch-all statutes," by which officials were granted discretion to implement legal rules. Under this system, officials were indoctrinated in Confucian classics prior to being appointed, and so were presumed to possess the virtue and propriety needed to govern society – whether through law or through other mechanisms of governance. As a result, application of law tended to be flexible and dependent on the discretionary judgment of officials, whose technical training (often acquired on the job or through personal vocation) was considered less important than their Confucian rectitude. This "amateur ideal," by which government officials were expected to make decisions not based on technical expertise in the subjects of administration but reliant instead on Confucian virtue and propriety, influenced subsequent approaches to law under the Republic of China and later the People's Republic of China.[3]

During the later years of the Qing Dynasty, the government attempted a range of legal reforms, including establishment in 1904 of the Imperial Law Commission. Under the leadership of Shen Jiaben, the Commission was tasked with compiling information on legal models in other countries – particularly Japan and Germany, and drafting legislation for application in China. This process was one of several initiatives taken by the declining Qing government to utilize foreign knowledge and technology while preserving the essence of Chinese values and identity. The tension over how to adapt foreign techniques to China without jeopardizing China's culture has often been referred to as the debate between *ti* (preserving China's essence) and *yong* (utilizing foreign knowledge).[4] This dilemma had played a strong role in the various processes of China's opening to the outside world, at the end of the Qing Dynasty, during the Republican Period (1911–49), and under the PRC, particularly in the post-Mao era.

The work of the Qing Imperial Law Commission included preparation of a Company Law (1904), drafting of an Administrative Court Organization Law (1909) and a Criminal Code (1911), and included efforts to complete legislation in the areas of foreign trade, trademarks, civil procedure, and a Civil Code. These efforts represented an important shift away from practices and principles of discretionary rule that had characterized the Confucian model of law and governance in traditional dynastic China. The Civil Code embodied a transition from punishment to rights as the basis for socio-economic relations, while distinguishing these relationships from criminal acts punishable under the Criminal Code was also a significant step away from traditional practices. While the decaying Qing government was far too weak to ensure the implementation of these laws, many of those working on law reform in the late Qing period continued this work under the Republic of China government.

The establishment of the Republic of China (ROC) in 1911 marked the end of traditional dynastic rule and a major watershed in the transition to modern government. Inspired by the philosophy of Dr Sun Yat-sen, the Nationalist Party of China (*Guomindang* or GMD) attempted to establish a parliamentary system of governance. Under the doctrine of "political tutelage," the GMD established a dual system of governance by which state institutions such as legislatures, courts, and administrative agencies operated under the guidance of a parallel structure of supervisory GMD organs. This pattern of dual party and state rule was replicated later by the Communist Party of China (CPC). During the period of ROC rule (1911–49), recurring economic and political crises inhibited efforts to establish an effective national government. Nonetheless, during the ten years of relative peace between 1927 and 1937 (the so-called "Nanjing Decade"), the ROC saw an impressive record of law making. Significant efforts included a Civil Code (1929) that combined civil and commercial regulation following the model of Swiss law, a Company Law and Negotiable Instruments Law (1929), a Criminal Code (1935), a Civil Procedure Law (1935), and a Trademark Law (1936).

Several aspects of law under the Republic of China are noteworthy. The transition away from the "relational justice" norms of Qing China toward more objective treatment of legal actors was embodied in the ROC Civil Code. The introduction of the concept of "legal persons" (individuals) and "natural persons" (associations, companies, and the like) was derived from civil law arrangements of continental Europe and made little if any reference to social relationships as the basis for legal status. In a reversal of Qing orthodoxy, the ROC legal system combined objectivity in the treatment of legal actors with subjectivity in the analysis of legal acts. Thus, ROC law included the role of intent as the basis for juristic acts, in contrast to the more rigid provisions of the Qing Code where every act brought legal (and often punitive) consequences based simply on the act and its presumed effects on the social relationships between the actors involved, rather than the subjective intent of the perpetrator. ROC law also entrenched the distinction between public and private law such that obligations such as contracts were considered private even when enforcement was subject to public institutions. Here again, this was a departure from the patterns of the Qing Code, which tended to conflate public and private relationships such that private disputes and offenses were often subject to criminal punishment.

These developments in ROC law remain influential. In Taiwan today, court decisions issued under the Republic of China beginning in 1911 continue to serve as legal precedent. As well, legal institutions and practice under the Republic of China influenced drafting and interpretation of law in the PRC during its early years and during the legal reform of the post-Mao era. Thus, while ROC law applied effectively only in a few cities along the Yangtse River owing to the relative political and military weakness of the government, legal doctrines and ideals continued to serve as a foundation for the legal arrangements that emerged under the PRC and in Taiwan.

II. TRANSITION TO LAW IN THE PRC

When the People's Republic of China was established in 1949, the leaders of the Communist revolutionary movement already had significant experience with legal institutions and regulatory processes. Even as they carried out their commitment to revolution, China's new leaders drew upon their own past experience with governance and regulation.

A. Law in the Revolutionary Base and Border Areas

Soon after the founding of the CPC in Shanghai in 1921, the movement was driven out into the rural area of southeast Jiangxi province where it established a Revolutionary Base Area (the "Jiangxi Soviet Republic"). Institutions of law and governance were established along with codes of formal law and regulation on matters such as family relations, land reform, and taxation.[5] Later, after near-defeat by Nationalist encirclement campaigns, the CPC embarked on the Long March to northwest Yan'an in Shaanxi province in 1934–5 and established the Shaan-Gan-Ning (Shaanxi-Gansu-Ningxia) and Jin-Cha-Ji (Shanxi-Chahar-Hebei) Border Areas to continue resistance to GMD/ROC rule and to confront Japanese invasion. In each of these areas, the CPC established organizations for governance and legal administration, and enacted laws and regulations on such diverse matters as criminal law, taxation, elections, marriage, labor, and land reform. As shown in table 1.1, many of these laws served later as the basis for legislation and regulation after the founding of the PRC.

The transition from revolution by the CPC to governance under the People's Republic brought significant challenges. With the defeat of Japan in 1945 and the CPC victory in the civil war in 1949, what had been largely a rural revolutionary movement faced tasks of national governance that required significantly greater institutional capacity than had been needed either in the Jiangxi Soviet or in the northern Border Areas. Whereas the revolutionary experience had largely been one of popular mobilization and military conflict, governing the country required systematic processes for government organization and control. In the short term, this meant continued reliance on the GMD/ROC law codes whose structure and content continued to influence the shape and operation of law in the early years of the PRC, even as they were publicly repudiated by the new CPC-led regime. The new PRC government also relied initially on legal specialists from the

Table 1.1   Comparison of Jiangxi Soviet, Jin Cha Ji Border Region, and PRC Laws

Chinese Soviet Republic, Jiangxi 1927–34	Jin Cha Ji Border Region 1936–49	People's Republic of China, est. 1949
Constitution 1931	Governance Outline 1940	Constitution 1954
Land Law 1931	Land Law 1947	Land Reform Law 1950
Labor Law 1933	Regulations on Safeguarding Labor Hiring in Rural Areas 1944	Regulations on Labor Insurance 1951
Election Law 1933	Election Regulations 1943	Election Law 1953
Regulations on Suppression of Counterrevolutionaries 1934	Special Regulations on Traitors Who Voluntarily Surrender 1938	Regulations on Punishment of Counterrevolutionaries 1951
Marriage Law 1934	Marriage Regulations 1943	Marriage Law 1950

Sources: William E. Butler, ed., *The Legal System of the Chinese Soviet Republic 1931–34* (New York: Transnational Publishers, 1983); Lan Quanpu, *Jiefangqu fagui gaiyao* [Outline of laws and regulations in the liberated areas] (Beijing: Masses Publishers, 1982); Han Yanlong and Chang Zhaoru, eds, *Zhongguo xin minzhuzhuyi geming shiqi genju di fazhi wenxian xuanbian* [Collection of legal documents from the base areas during China's new democratic revolution] (Beijing: Chinese Academy of Social Sciences Press, 1981).

former ROC regime, although this was largely halted with a 1952 campaign to remove former GMD judges.

B. Socio-economic and political transformation

Legal development in the early years of the PRC, particularly between 1949 and 1954, was influenced by contradictions between continuing revolution and institution-building. After attaining national political power, the CPC addressed challenges of transforming the traditional Chinese economy and society through laws that changed the foundations for land and family relations.

The Land Reform Law was developed on the basis of land reform laws and regulations developed in the Jiangxi Soviet Base Area, and continuing in the Shaan-Gan-Ning and Jin-Cha-Ji Border Areas. Departing from the collectivization model urged by their Soviet Russian advisors, the Chinese Communists adopted programs of land redistribution. This had caused significant disagreement between the Chinese communist leadership and their Soviet supporters during the time of the Jiangxi Soviet and the northern Border Areas. Nonetheless, the land reform campaign, which stretched from the later revolutionary period into the early years of the PRC, revealed a commitment to redistribution of land rather than collectivization. The 1950 PRC Land Reform Law[6] espoused policy goals of redistribution of land through confiscation from landlords and allocation to poor peasants through the local village peasant associations. The law reflected the Marxist ideology underpinning CPC policy, addressing land as part of the means of production and calling for landlords to work (land ownership alone not being considered as labor):

> *Article 10*: All confiscated or expropriated land and other means of production except that to be nationalized as set forth herein shall be taken over by the township peasants association and then allocated in

a unified fair and reasonable way to the poor peasants with a lack of land or without land or other means of production and to the landlords as well allowing them to maintain their life by working on their own and improve themselves at work.

Policy debates over land reform continued, however, such that by 1952 policies of collectivization emerged that would later be entrenched in the 1955–6 "high tide of collectivism."

Just as the Land Reform Law challenged traditional economic arrangements, the 1950 PRC Marriage Law[7] challenged traditional social arrangements, specifically abolishing "the feudal marriage system including marriage through arbitrary decision by any third party, marriage based on compulsory arrangements, the supremacy of men over women, and the disregard of the interests of children" (Art. 1). In addition to being subjected to practices of footbinding, arranged marriages involving child brides, and the pervasiveness of polygamy, women had also been formally excluded from the legal system – lacking property rights, inheritance rights, or legal personhood. The Republic of China had introduced reforms to family law relations under the ROC Civil Code (1929) and the ROC Marriage Law (1930), particularly in expanding inheritance rights for women and enshrining the principle of voluntary marriage. Nonetheless, traditional practices remained – as indicated in part by the preservation of certain aspects of concubinage as matters of "custom" protected under the ROC Civil Code.

The CPC regime aimed to go farther still in reforming conditions of the family – not only for ideological reasons born of Marxist approaches to gender equality, but also to further broader social transformation. The Marriage Law challenged traditional family arrangements, putting in place a "new democratic marriage system based on the freedom of choosing partners, monogamy, equal rights for men and women and the protection of legitimate rights and interests of women and children" (Art. 1). The Marriage Law granted women nominal rights to choose a spouse (arranged marriages had heretofore been standard). The Marriage Law allowed women greater freedom of divorce (albeit subject to agreement of both spouses), and provided for more equitable distribution of property upon dissolution of marriage, rights that previously had been severely restricted under conventional social practices. The Marriage Law also supported the right of women to take employment and to participate in social and political life.

In addition to efforts at economic and social transformation, the new regime also used law and regulation to further its immediate governance priorities. Shortly after taking power, the government embarked on what became known as the *Sanfan* ("three anti's") and *Wufan* ("five anti's") campaigns, aimed at curbing corruption among newly recruited CPC officials and at suppressing class enemies such as business owners and former ROC government officials. These political efforts were aimed not only to attack perceived ills both within the officialdom and in society at large, but also to bolster the power and authority of government and CPC organs in charge of enforcement. While these campaigns emerged from CPC decisions and directives and were not subject to much in the way of formal legal restraint, administrative reviews on the conduct of these campaigns often led to regulations governing future activities.

Throughout this process, law and regulation were used to entrench the policy preferences of the regime. The typical pattern for rule-making involved CPC leadership decisions on key policy priorities, whether in social and economic reform or political control, which would then be followed by experimentation through campaign-style mobilization efforts. Both the Marriage Law and the Land Reform Law, for example, were informed by CPC policy decisions and tested through experimentation in Jiangxi and the northern Border Areas. The contours of the *Sanfan* and *Wufan* campaigns emerged from the pattern of political mobilization and anti-corruption efforts of the civil war period. The results of these efforts then were formalized into legal and regulatory provisions, which served to articulate ideals for future behavior rather than to limit the authority of enforcing agencies.

The early years of the PRC saw debates over policy priorities, as well as contending approaches to implementation through either formal regulation or informal management and campaigning. The institutional formality of legal regulation conflicted with the flexibility and expediency of political campaigns. This tension continued through the early years of the PRC, as institutions and officials of the Party/State attempted to achieve policy goals of socio-economic and political transformation in ways that were both organizationally robust and also able to mobilize popular support. The close relationship between law and policy that characterized the initial years of the PRC has continued throughout the history of contemporary China, as debates over policy preferences were reflected in the dynamics of law making and institution building.

C. Constitutional change and conflicts over formalization of law and governance

The experience of reforms in land and family relations together with the apparent successes of the political consolidation through the *Sanfan, Wufan,* and other campaigns paved the way for enactment of a formal constitution. The 1954 Constitution of the PRC represented a culmination of sorts in the process of revolutionary consolidation. Following a rather conventional institutional pattern whereby constitutions serve as foundational documents for the organization of the state, the 1954 Constitution contained provisions on the structure of government, jurisdictional boundaries between departments, and the relative roles of legislative, judicial, and administrative organs.[8] The

Constitution also contained provisions on the rights and duties of citizens.

The 1954 Constitution had its origins in the 1949 Common Program of the Chinese People's Political Consultative Conference (CPPCC).[9] The CPPCC itself served as the provisional agency for public representation in government in the early years following the establishment of the PRC. As a proto-legislature, the CPPCC aimed to fulfill the political ideals of the Communist Party to expand representation in government by recruiting elements of society such as peasants, workers, and soldiers, who had previously been marginalized in traditional and Republican (1911–49) China.

The "Common Program" set forth organizational principles for the newly formed PRC government after completion of the 1949 revolution, revealing the CPC's ideological orientation through terms such as "bureaucratic capital" (property held by private interests supported by state institutions), "feudal" (reflecting an historical approach positing a transition from feudalism to capitalism and then to socialism and communism), "class" (noting the preference given to workers, peasants, and petty and national/patriotic bourgeoisie and the suppression of counter-revolutionaries and reactionaries), and "political change" (the reference to "new democracy" reflecting the inclusion of workers and peasants and the exclusion of oppressive capitalist classes):

> *Article 3*: The People's Republic of China must . . . confiscate bureaucratic capital and put it into the possession of the people's state. It must transform the feudal and semi-feudal land ownership system into a system of peasant land ownership in a systematic way; it must protect the public property of the state and of the cooperatives and must protect the economic interests and private property of workers, peasants, petty bourgeoisie and national bourgeoisie. It must develop the people's economy under our new democracy and steadily transform the country from an agricultural into an industrial one.

Article 7: The People's Republic of China shall suppress all counter-revolutionary activities, severely punish all Guomindang counter-revolutionary war criminals and other leading unrepentant counter-revolutionary elements who collaborate with imperialism, who commit treason against the motherland and who oppose the people's democratic cause. Feudal landlords, bureaucratic capitalists and reactionary elements in general, after they have been disarmed and have had their special privileges abolished, shall also be deprived of their political rights in accordance with law for a required period. At the same time, however, they are to be provided with some means of livelihood and shall be compelled to reform themselves through labor so as to become new people. If they continue their counter-revolutionary activities, they will be punished severely.

Alongside its ideological and policy preferences, the Common Program also contained familiar arrangements for the organization of state administrative structures as well as general principles of governance.

Shortly after the enactment of the Common Program, the new regime embarked on a process of drafting a formal constitution that would enshrine the governance principles of the CPC. The drafting committee was chaired by Deng Xiaoping, while Peng Zhen played a key role. The first constitution of the PRC was enacted in 1954 and articulated principles of governance for the new regime. Particularly noteworthy in the Preamble are ideological references to the transition from feudalism and capitalism to socialism and the attendant class struggle against counterrevolutionaries, even while noting the legal equality of citizens (a restrictive term excluding class enemies from legal protection):

Preamble: . . . This is a period of transition from the founding of the People's Republic of China to the establishment of a socialist society.

The general tasks of the state during the transition period are, step by step, to realize the socialist industrialization of the country and, step by step, to accomplish the socialist transformation of agriculture, handicrafts and capitalist industry and commerce. In the past few years our people have successfully carried out the reform of the agrarian system, the war to resist United States aggression and aid Korea, the suppression of counter-revolutionaries, the recovery of the national economy, and other large-scale struggles, which thereby prepare the necessary conditions for planned economic construction and the gradual transition to a socialist society.

. . .

Article 19: The People's Republic of China safeguards the system of people's democracy, suppresses all treasonable and counter-revolutionary activities and punishes all traitors and counter-revolutionaries.

. . .

Article 85: All citizens of the People's Republic of China are equal before the law.

The 1954 Constitution also contained provisions for establishment of a national legislature (the National People's Congress), and executive (the State Council), a court system and systems for public prosecutions and public security. These key institutions remain central to the governance structure of the PRC today.

While the "Common Program" was primarily a program of guidance for a political advisory body (the CPPCC) with little genuine political power, the 1954 Constitution was presented as the authoritative foundational law for the PRC, with significant implications for enforcement of policy preferences. In the context of tensions between flexible, campaign-style governance and formal institutional rule, the 1954 Constitution indicated a strong orientation toward the latter. Under

Marxist theory, law served as a tool of oppression by the ruling class, oppressive of the working classes under capitalist bourgeois leadership but under communist leadership a mechanism for empowering the proletariat. The formalization of rule under the Constitution suggested that the revolutionary initiatives of political campaigns and other efforts at consolidation of CPC political power on behalf of the proletariat had largely completed the work of class struggle.

These perspectives were reflected in the constitutional principle that "all citizens are equal before the law" (Art. 85). The principle of legal equality reflected political and ideological conclusions that, with completion of the revolution and seizure of political power by the CPC, legal equality of citizens was a justifiable expression of the victory of class struggle. Later, during the political conflicts of the Cultural Revolution, the principle of legal equality would come to be criticized explicitly as contrary to China's revolutionary ideals and the needs for continuation of class struggle. But in the mid-1950s, the new government felt sufficiently comfortable about its hold on power and its policy priorities that formalizing the notion of legal equality seemed generally non-controversial.

Following enactment of the 1954 Constitution, the government continued efforts at institution building, such that the period from 1954 through 1957 is often seen as a period of institutional formalization.[10] Among the many developments during the mid-1950s was the effort to draft a Civil Code – particularly important because of its role in regulating private social and economic relationships. As well, the establishment and expansion of police, prosecutorial offices, and courts formed a basic framework for the criminal justice system, with the Ministry of Justice serving as the State Council agency with broad responsibility for legal system administration. All of these measures reflected efforts to entrench policy preferences of particular political actors within the Party/State who favored increased formalization of governance.

Despite the constitutional arrangements of 1954, the political leadership of the PRC was not fully unified around policies of class struggle and continuing revolution, and the operational issues that stemmed from them. Formalization of law and governance was offset by ideological concerns over maintaining the course of revolutionary transformation through political campaigns on issues such as land, family, and commercial relations. While some in the political leadership such as Liu Shaoqi and Peng Zhen were concerned primarily with state-building and establishment of institutions of governance, others led by Mao Zedong pressed for continued ideological campaigns and for continued political flexibility in governance.[11] Mao himself challenged the usefulness of formal law as a basis for regulation, noting instead the importance of moral cultivation through CPC leadership:[12]

[Chairman:] [We] can't rule the majority of the people by relying on law. The majority of people [can be ruled only] by relying on the cultivation of [good] habits. The army's reliance on rule by law didn't work; what's actually worked has been the 1,400-man conference. Who could remember so many clauses of a civil code or a criminal law? I participated in the formulation of the Constitution, even I can't remember [it]. Han Feizi advocated rule by law; later the Confucianists advocated rule by men. Each of our draft resolutions is law; Holding conferences is law, too. Observing public security regulations is possible only when people have cultivated good habits. [If this] becomes public opinion [and] everyone becomes conscious [of it], then communism is achievable. The great majority, 90 percent, of our rules and regulations are created at the departmental and bureau [level]. Essentially we do not rely on these; mainly we rely on resolutions, holding conferences – four held annually – and not a civil code or a criminal law to maintain social order. The National People's Congress and the State Council in conference have their ways, and we rely on our ways. This has to do with the superstructure.

The political competition between advocates of formalization of rule and those who emphasized continued social transformation had not yet crystallized into what later came to be called "factions," but rather represented a changing, sometimes conflicted, often overlapping set of policy priorities that often gave rise to ad hoc decision making veering between each extreme.[13]

Expanded formal legal arrangements were seen by supporters as necessary for stability and to consolidate the achievements of the revolution, but by opponents as improperly limiting the scope of Party-led revolutionary transformation. The drafting of a Civil Code, for example, was never completed due to ideological conflict, despite its importance for social relations and economic development. The potential for a Civil Code to clarify rights and obligations ranging from contracts to property and inheritance was well understood by legal specialists in the 1950s, many of whom were familiar with the ROC Civil Code. However, formalizing legal rights and relationships was seen to have potential to entrench social and economic inequities and to inhibit class struggle, and so was opposed by those whose primary concern remained the task of revolutionary transformation.

Similarly, the establishment of the People's Courts of the PRC as formal sources of judicial decision making was tempered by provisions requiring court decisions to be made not simply by judges but also through participation by "people's assessors," laypersons selected from the local community. The operation of police and prosecutorial departments was augmented by the role of neighborhood, village, and street committee participation and by the authority of local Party cadres, most of whom lacked formal education or legal training. Recruiting local activists was an important element in the success of the CPC in establishing mechanisms of rule at the local level. Mediation, for example, served not only as an informal, community-based method for dispute resolution, but also as an instrument for political control as members of local communities and the disputes in which they were involved were subjected to oversight by the Party/State.

Land reform remained a contentious issue. While the 1954 Constitution entrenched principles of state and public ownership of land, debate over specific policies continued. The collectivization campaign of 1955 (foreshadowed in 1952) signaled a final departure from the land redistribution model associated with the Revolutionary Base Areas and the Land Reform Law. The Great Leap Forward (GLF) policy of 1957–8 saw further entrenchment of collectivization with the establishment of the People's Communes, while the resulting economic crisis and famine saw a relaxation of collectivization programs and the return to private farming on a limited basis. This continued tension between policies of collectivization and policies supporting limited private farming continued through the 1960s and was not fully resolved until well after the Cultural Revolution (1966–76). Similar policy conflicts emerged in areas like education and health policy, industrial development, and agricultural management, such that operation of the legal system and the regulatory apparatus of the Party/State reflected the outcome of political debates over formalization and continuing revolution.

D. Themes of law and governance

During the Maoist era, legal development reflected a number of important themes that continue to influence the shape of law in China today. Law was used as a tool of policy administration. Law was not the basis for private rights, but rather served as an instrument through which the government implemented its policy choices. Law and formal regulation was used as an instrument for socio-economic transformation, exemplified by the Marriage Law and the Land Reform Law. Formal law and regulation also played a role in the implementation of economic policy – contract regulations in the early 1950s were aimed to rebuild economic activity following the disruption of the revolution and civil war and in the early 1960s to facilitate recovery from the economic disaster and famine brought on by the Great Leap Forward.[14]

On the other hand, maintaining social order and carrying out CPC policies on suppression of "class enemies" was largely the province of political campaigns and occasional administrative regulations, such as the "Security Administration Punishment Act" and arrangements for "reform through labor," which gave security departments extensive powers to detain and punish offenders. Despite constitutional language on "equality before the law," treatment of citizens under the legal system was determined largely according to their class backgrounds. People from landlord families and families of business operators were discriminated against while children from preferred class backgrounds such as peasants, workers, and soldiers were given preference.

The first decade of legal development under the PRC exhibited parallels with patterns of law during the Qing and the Republic of China. Qing traditions were evident in PRC practices around the codification of rules, the emphasis on public law, the role of officials as non-technical but ideologically reliable amateurs (echoed in debates over whether officials should be appointed according to criteria of being "red or expert"), and the role of "relational justice" through class labeling. Yet there were also differences. The early years of the PRC saw formal establishment of a national economy, whereas under the Qing the economy was not subject to meaningful national regulations. As well, governance at the local level was subject to the organization and authority of the CPC with little intermediation by local elites as had been the case under the Qing.[15] The early years of the PRC also bore resemblance to some aspects of GMD/ROC rule. For example the PRC relied expressly on many laws borrowed from the ROC, even while repudiating them publicly, and on judges and other legal officials from the former ROC government, who later would be criticized as well. Institutional patterns under the PRC, including the dual

Party–State administrative structure, whereby state agencies such as the courts, the procuracy, and the police were subject to direction by local Party departments and officials, also reflected GMD influences.

Of course, there were important differences. Deliberate efforts to change the social structure through land and family law, the general repudiation of private rights, and the emphasis on class were distinctive features of the PRC. Law in the early years of the PRC also bore close resemblance to legislative and regulatory experience in the revolutionary Base Areas and Border Areas, expressing ideals of transformational governance while providing flexible templates for bureaucratic organization.

III. LAW AND POLITICAL CONFLICT

By the late 1950s, increased political conflict had grown to crisis levels between those in the leadership who favored stable formal institutional government (commonly associated with Liu Shaoqi and Peng Zhen) and those (often linked with Mao Zedong) who favored informal campaign-based governance. Political conflict contributed to the so-called "Hundred Flowers" campaign of 1957 that encouraged public comment and debate on CPC policy, and the "Anti-Rightist" campaign that followed and penalized critics of CPC leadership. The result was generally to sideline approaches focused on formal, institutional governance. Among the targets for the "Anti-Rightist" campaign were lawyers and judges (many of whom had been holdovers from the GMD/ROC regime who had escaped the 1952 campaign against ROC legal personnel). Many of these were sent to the countryside or to prison for decades – the last victims released did not see freedom until after 1979.

The tumultuous years following the Anti-Rightist Campaign saw a campaign of radical collectivization and grass-roots industrialization (the "Great Leap Forward") that nearly bankrupted the country and led to the starvation of tens of millions of people. The "Socialist Education Campaign" of the early 1960s imposed ideological require- ments on virtually all forms of education and professional life. These political events culminated in the so-called "Great Proletarian Cultural Revolution" (GPCR, 1966–76), which saw legal organizations dis- mantled, legal specialists killed and imprisoned, and the role of law condemned as contrary to China's revolutionary requirements. While the "Campaign to Criticize Lin Biao and Confucius" beginning in 1973 extolled the virtues of ancient legalists like Han Feizi, this was driven primarily by parochial political ambitions rather than a commitment to the legal system. Regulations continued to be issued, but largely in the service of attacking political enemies, explained by reference to class struggle and the dictatorship of the proletariat:[16]

> The public security organs are an important tool of the dictatorship of the proletariat. They must adapt to the needs of the situation and progress of the Great Proletarian Cultural Revolution, take appropriate measures, strengthen dictatorship over the enemy, safeguard the demo- cratic rights of the people, and protect the normal progress of the full and frank airing of views, big-character posters, debate, and exchange of revolutionary experience.

The enactment in 1975 of a new constitution – often referred to as the "Cultural Revolution Constitution" – signified a high point in the repudiation of formal legal arrangements.[17] Not only were formal insti- tutions of governance (including legal institutions) diminished, but campaign-oriented principles such as the right to strike and the "Four Big Freedoms" (speaking out freely, airing views fully, holding great debates, writing big-character posters) were given formal recognition:

> *Article 13*: Speaking out freely, airing views fully, holding great debates and writing big-character posters are new forms created by the masses of

the people to carry on socialist revolution. The state shall protect the right of the masses to use these forms to create a political situation in which there are both centralism and democracy, both discipline and freedom, both unity of will and personal ease of mind and liveliness, to thereby help consolidate the leadership of the Communist Party of China over the state and consolidate the dictatorship of the proletariat.

The death of Mao and the ending of the Cultural Revolution in 1976 saw a limited political retrenchment that was reflected in a new constitution enacted in 1978.[18] This was a compromise document that retained many elements of Maoism even while backing away from some of the extremes of the Cultural Revolution. References to concluding the Cultural Revolution and starting a new stage of development, struggling for production and modernization, and protecting property, labor discipline, and public order all speak to the policy imperative of curbing the excesses of the Cultural Revolution:

Preamble: The triumphant conclusion of the first Great Proletarian Culture Revolution has started a new stage of development of our country's socialist revolution and construction. According to the basic line of the Communist Party of China for the entire socialist history, the general task for the people of the whole country in this new period is: to carry on revolution under the dictatorship of the proletariat, to carry forward the three great revolutionary movements including class struggle, the struggle for production and scientific experiment, and to establish our country to be a great and powerful socialist country with modernization of agriculture, industry, national defence and science and technology by the end of the century.

Article 57: Citizens must take care of and protect public property, observe labor discipline, observe public order, respect social public morality, and safeguard state secrets.

The final repudiation of Cultural Revolution policies was expressed at the 1978 3rd Plenum of the 11th Central Committee and in the 1981 CPC "Resolution on Party History."[19]

This lengthy period of political conflict, ranging roughly from 1957 through 1976 had significant and harmful effects on the legal system. There was a general repudiation of legal organizations – first through the attacks against "Rightists" in 1958, continuing through the Socialist Education Campaign of the mid-1960s, and culminating in the GPCR through 1976. There was also significant decay in the prestige and legitimacy of the ruling CPC. The national economy suffered, such that China's economic weakness was a major factor leading to Deng Xiaoping's call for policies of economic and legal reform at the 3rd Plenum of the 11th CPC Central Committee in November–December 1978.

The excesses of the Cultural Revolution and the political campaigns that preceded it led many in China to crave stability as a fundamental imperative – one that continues to characterize regime claims to legitimacy today. The Cultural Revolution also instilled in China's political elite an abiding fear of losing the Party/State's monopoly on the use of force. The experience with Red Guards and Revolutionary Militias defying orders and directives from established government agencies left Cultural Revolution survivors with an abiding commitment to ensuring that the institutions of rule remained under Party/State control. This tended to direct the energies of political conflict toward control of formal political and legal organizations, marginalizing (ultimately eliminating) the informal popular arrangements such as the Red Guards and People's Militia that Mao and his followers had used during the Cultural Revolution (largely because they had been denied access to formal organizations by political opponents). The consequences of the Cultural Revolution were far-reaching, even bringing China to the brink of war with the Soviet Union. Chairman Mao's death in September 1976 was followed by the arrest of his closest followers in October and the ending of the Cultural Revolution.

IV. POST-MAO LEGAL REFORM
UNDER DENG XIAOPING

At the 3rd Plenum of the 11th CPC Central Committee in November–December 1978, the post-Mao leadership announced a series of tentative legal and economic reform measures.[20] Changing the regime's policy focus from revolution to economic development with specific reference to the priority given the forces of production over the relations of production, the Plenum noted:

> Realizing the four modernizations requires that we significantly heighten productive forces, which will inevitably require many changes in the relations of production and the superstructure that are not suited to the development of productive forces, and require changes in all unsuitable management styles, styles of activity, and modes of thought.

The Plenum also called for a commitment to legal reform, noting the linkage with economic reform and stressing the importance of judicial independence (not from the Party but from unauthorized social forces as had occurred with the abuses by Red Guards during the Cultural Revolution):

> The meeting held a serious discussion on the issue of democracy and the legal system. The meeting held that socialist modernization requires collective and unified leadership and must strictly carry out various rules and regulations and labor discipline. . . . In order to safeguard the people's democracy, we must strengthen the socialist legal system, cause democracy to be systematized and legalized, and cause these systems and laws to have stability, continuity, and great authority so that we have

law to rely on, law that we must rely on, enforcement that is strict and investigation of violations of law. From now on we need to place law-making work on the important agenda of the National People's Congress and its Standing Committee. The Procuratorates and judicial organs must be sure to have independence; and must be faithful to law and order, to the people's interests, and to the actual situation; they must ensure that the people are equal before their own laws and not permit anyone to be above the law.

Legal specialists were rehabilitated and brought back from prison and internal exile, and directed to prepare a range of new laws to support these reform measures. Law drafters were encouraged to examine China's past – particularly the legislative and regulatory record of the 1950s – and also to borrow from abroad. This repudiated Maoist orthodoxy that tended to reject reliance on past practice and to resist international influences, while also echoing the *"ti-yong"* dynamic from earlier eras that had called for preserving the essence of China's traditions while also utilizing foreign knowledge.

Many of the new laws enacted early in the post-Mao era were aimed at restoring the Party/State's monopoly on the legitimate use of force, which had been eroded if not destroyed during the Cultural Revolution. Among the first laws enacted after the Cultural Revolution were a new criminal law and criminal procedure law, as well as organizational laws for the People's Courts and the People's Procuratorate (public prosecutors). While these measures offered little in the way of procedural protections for accused criminal defendants, they nonetheless under-scored the role of organs of the Party/State as the sole agencies author-ized to impose criminal punishments.

The post-Mao regime also directed law and legal institutions toward policy goals of economic development. A foreign investment (joint venture) law was among the first items of legislation following the 1978 3rd Plenum. Shortly thereafter, in 1980, a draft civil procedure law was enacted. China's first contract law was enacted in 1981. A preliminary civil code (termed the "General Principles of Civil Law") was enacted in 1986 that allowed broader rights in civil matters such as property and contract relations. A wide range of foreign business laws was enacted governing trade, investment, foreign exchange, and other issues, as well as legislation on taxation, and intellectual property. All of these measures reflected policy preferences and political compromises of the senior CPC leadership under Deng Xiaoping.

Consistent with earlier patterns of legal system development, ideological and policy preferences were a key determinant in the development of law and legal organizations. From the earliest years of the PRC, the ideological question of class struggle had been central to policies on economic development and the legal system provisions established to support them. Much of Mao's critique of formalization of law was grounded in ideas about continued class struggle and the need for permanent revolution. The conclusion of the 3rd Plenum of the 11th CPC Central Committee that class struggle would continue but had been largely resolved indicated an important step away from Maoist orthodoxy.

During the post-Mao era of the 1980s, Party policy continued to diminish the importance of class struggle, which in turn permitted greater support for private social and economic relationships. Releasing formal law and regulation from the ideological dilemma of class oppression allowed for increased privatization in the economy. Laws on matters such as investment, property rights, corporations, and contracts, which would have been almost unheard of during the Maoist period, were enacted in quick succession under the Deng Xiaoping regime. Aside from formal legislation, significant numbers of regulations came to be issued on a routine basis by government ministries and regulatory agencies on issues ranging from business registration and taxation to employment and health, and encompassing a wide range of sector-specific measures on agriculture, industry, transportation, and commerce. At the 13th National Party Congress in 1987, General Secretary Zhao Ziyang held forth the principle that China was in the "preliminary stage of socialism," suggesting that from the class struggle point of view, China had progressed yet further from the time of the 1978 3rd Plenum when class struggle was said to persist for some time to come.

To a very large extent, the 1980s saw a concerted effort to shift the mechanisms of government from reliance on political and ideological directives to use of formal law and regulation in managing socio-economic relations. However, greater attention to legal regulation often brought with it questions about governance capacity as untried laws and regulations were an imperfect substitute for the often crude but effective methods of political and ideological campaigns. By the late 1980s, economic crises had created significant social unease regarding the capacity of the Party/State to govern effectively. Economic expansion policies resulting from the decisions of the 13th CPC Congress Plenum in late 1987 led to inflationary pressures which in turn contributed to a run on the Chinese banks during the summer of 1988. That fall, an emergency meeting of the CPC Politburo directed cutbacks in government spending. This resulted in the closing of many construction projects and the downsizing of state-owned factories, many of which had employed migrant workers from the countryside who could no longer return home. Conditions of economic uncertainty contributed significantly to the political demonstrations that emerged following the death of Hu Yaobang in spring 1989.[21] The student demonstrations in Beijing's Tiananmen Square and in other locations across China captured the attention of the world, but were brutally suppressed by the regime. As a result of the Tiananmen crisis and the policy divisions that had given rise to it, economic and legal reform efforts stalled.

In 1992, Deng Xiaoping led an inspection trip to Southern China. Deng, who had masterminded initial efforts at legal and economic reforms after the 1978 3rd Plenum and who had also overseen the brutal repression of democracy demonstrators in 1989, was by then 85 years old and in frail health. His dreams of a strong and unified China, seemingly so attainable during the heady days of reform of the 1980s, had been sidelined as a result of political conflict around the 1989 crisis – particularly the resurgence of more conservative policy positions emphasizing collective economic ownership and limiting the possibilities for independent market activity and social freedoms. True to the stubborn and persistent temperament that had characterized his entire career, Deng emerged from seclusion to lead the 1992 Southern Tour. China's official media use the term *nanxun* to describe the event – borrowing the term used to describe similar tours by the Qing emperor Qianlong.[22]

Deng Xiaoping's Southern Tour of 1992 galvanized those elements in the political and governance leadership that supported intensified market reforms, and likely reflected that a consensus around what was called "deepening reform" had already emerged. Within the next few years China embarked on a wide-ranging legislative effort – bringing in laws on corporations and securities regulation, and making significant improvements to existing laws on other economic matters such as taxation. A new law on contracts was enacted in 1999, while foreign investment laws were expanded considerably. Intellectual property laws saw expanded protection for patents, trademarks and copyrights (including protection of computer software), with new measures to protect trade secrets. These measures and the policies that underpinned them helped encourage expansion of the finance and service sectors in China's economy.

Increased reliance on formal law and regulation as instruments for policy enforcement was accompanied by greater attention to administrative law and process. The Administrative Litigation Law (1990) provided for limited judicial review of bureaucratic decisions, while new laws on administrative reconsideration and compensation for administrative wrongs provided additional, albeit limited, protections for those harmed by bureaucratic wrong-doing.

Deng Xiaoping's direct involvement in political leadership continued to diminish during the 1990s, leading to his chosen successors Jiang Zemin and later Hu Jintao assuming the mantle of government and Party leadership. The peaceful transition of the senior Party/State leadership was an important Deng legacy, and one that depended on building a broad consensus across the Party/State not only concerning candidates for leadership positions but also on major policy issues of China's development. During the post-Deng period of coalition leadership, China's legal system reflected several important themes, including the continued supremacy of Party leadership, the influence of tradition, and influence of globalization.

V. LOCAL AND GLOBAL CONTEXTS FOR CHINA'S SOCIALIST LEGAL SYSTEM

The socialist legal system of the PRC reflects a range of local and global influences. Domestically, the policy imperatives of the CPC Party/State as well as traditional perspectives drawn from earlier periods of Chinese history have a significant impact. As well, China's increased engagement with the world has introduced normative and institutional influences around issues of trade, human rights, and legal education and practice.

A. *Party leadership and policy choice*

Submission to the leadership of the Communist Party has remained a central tenet of the PRC legal system under Jiang Zemin and Hu Jintao. Deng Xiaoping's famous "Four Basic Principles" (*sixiang jiben yuanze*) had underscored the importance of Party leadership, along with fealty to the socialist system, dictatorship of the proletariat, and

Marxism-Leninism–Mao Zedong thought. These principles cast important ideological restrictions on the possibilities for moving law toward a genuine rights-based system in which individuals and groups in society could enjoy significant autonomy from government control. The supremacy of the Party was expressed through the continued role of Party committees across the judicial system and in particular the role of Party secretaries in chairing the Adjudication Committees in the People's Courts that review and approve judicial appointments and decisions. The immunity of Party decisions from the scope of judicial review under the Administrative Litigation Law signified the extent to which the Party was not subject to constraint by the legal system. These developments had significant implications for issues of judicial independence, autonomy of legal relationships, and the consistent enforcement of the rule of law.

The role of the PRC legal system in supporting Party leadership also involves the connection with policy choices as these emerge from the complex process of inner-Party political debate, competition, and compromise. A useful example is the emphasis on economic development as the primary goal of policy and law, and resistance to political reform. Acutely aware of the conditions that led to the fall of the Soviet Union, attributed in China to attempts at political reform in the absence of economic prosperity, the PRC leadership continued to focus on political and social stability as the bases for economic development. Thus, laws and regulations aimed to building economic growth remain subservient to the leadership and direction by the Party/State and the maintenance of stability. In the wake of problems borne of rapid economic expansion such as disregard of labor rights, environmental decline, and corruption, the government has attempted reforms in labor law (especially the Labor Contract Law), environmental law, and taxation policy. At the same time, the imperative to preserve stability has led to expansion of domestic security, surveillance, and administrative and judicial punishment systems. The regime continues to resist political reform, interpreting rule of law ideals as guides for government administrative procedures for policy implementation, but not in terms of imposing on government standards of accountability to society. Thus, the role of law has been focused on supporting substantive dimensions of economic development rather than building institutions and procedures that constrain the power of the Party/State.

B. Socialist law in local context

Examples of criminal law, family relations, land use, and environmental protection are emblematic of the ways that law in the PRC reflects the influence of local traditions and practices.

1. Criminal Law

The Criminal Law of the PRC was one of the first laws published after the 1978 3rd Plenum of the 11th CPC Central Committee, and continues (as we shall see in chapter 2) to serve as a primary mechanism for social control. Discretion remains a key element in criminal prosecution and sentencing – reflecting the approach of traditional and Republican China that ideologically reliable officials should be empowered to use discretion in the service of the state. As well, parallels between current criminal law and the criminal codes of the Imperial dynasties are evident in the relationship between the so-called "catch-all statutes" of the Imperial era, by which judges were empowered to impose penalties for offenses that are not specifically identified in the criminal code, and the "rule of analogy" enshrined in the 1979 Criminal Law of the PRC, which allowed judges to impose punishments for an offense not covered in the criminal code by reference to the closest analogous provision. Even after the rule of analogy was removed in the 1997 revisions to the Criminal Law, a 1998 Supreme Court interpretation of the PRC Criminal Procedure Law allowed criminal punishment to be imposed based on provisions of the criminal law that are deemed applicable even if not included in the formal prosecutorial complaint.

Criminal law is augmented by numerous administrative detention regulations for punishing social disorder and political dissent, which allow punishment of offenses without the defenses available under criminal procedure. While reliance on administrative rules may represent some measure of formalization in the process of state punishment in comparison to the campaign-style processes of the past, it also reflects traditional approaches to ensuring that those who are considered to have offended against society or state norms are punished with little regard to the rights of the accused. While criminal law specialists – particularly law professors and judges – have attempted to bring more objectivity and consistency to the imposition of criminal sanctions, China's criminal justice system still reflects traditional practices of discretion and flexibility.

2. Land Use

In China's agrarian tradition, land-use practices were embedded in local social conditions. The *dian* system in Imperial China allowed limited private control over land, subject to the overall authority of the emperor's titular ownership. Expansion of private land ownership under the ROC beginning in 1911 entrenched the authority of local aristocracies who served (much like they had under the Qing) as agents of the central government. The Land Reform movement that began under the CPC in the Jiangxi Soviet was intended to root out the political economy of landlord domination that characterized much of South China. During the civil war period, the CPC imposed rent and interest reduction strategies in the North, such as those enacted in Jin Cha Ji Border Area, aimed at challenging local power holders and liberating small landholders. During the Maoist period, while collectivization of land ownership remained a key policy priority, there were times when quasi-private control over land use (so-called "private plots") were permitted subject to the approval of the Party/State.

As we shall see in chapter 3, current arrangements on land rights reflect PRC traditions on public ownership, with modest ad-hoc adjustments to land-use rights that suit local conditions. Rather than beginning with a presumption of individual rights to private owner- ship of property in land, the PRC system proceeds from the assump- tion that the state holds the basic rights of ownership, and that all subsequent uses, transfers, etc., depend on state approval. The Constitution and the General Principles of Civil Law provide that ownership of land remains the exclusive province of the state and the collective. While the state is identified through its administrative agen- cies such as the Land Administration Bureau, the 'collective' is identi- fied generally by reference to the village and township committees that serve as government agencies at the local level. The Land Administration Law (1986) underscored constitutional principles of public ownership of land and clarified the jurisdictional arrangements for land adminis- tration. Land-use rights (as opposed to ownership rights) are increas- ingly granted to private farming and business operations in rural and urban areas, and remain a key feature of the property rights regime under the PRC's socialist legal system. Thus, land law in the PRC reflects long-standing efforts at land reform by the Party/State, even as economic changes challenge the effectiveness of these traditional approaches.

3. Family Relations

As we shall see in chapter 4, family relations remain a key element of social regulation in the PRC, calling to mind the legacy of the 1950 Marriage Law and its challenge (tentatively begun under the GMD/ ROC) to traditional norms and practices in family relations. These early efforts were aimed to emancipate women from the rigid patriarchy present in traditional society and encouraged by Confucian norms.

Revisions to the 1950 Marriage Law in 1980 and again in 2001 saw expansion of rights for women in matters such as no-fault divorce without consent of the other spouse. Property distribution rights for women were also expanded, such that joint property can now be disposed of by agreement between the parties or by court order in the absence of an agreement – in contrast to the 1950 Marriage Law provision that pursuant to divorce, the wife received only the property that was hers prior to the marriage. Nonetheless, family relations in China today remain affected by Confucian traditions of patriarchy, even as the formal ideals of China's Marriage Law reflect historical efforts by the Party/State to improve the status of women. Socio-economic changes have put additional pressure on society and government to achieve true justice for women.

4. Environmental Protection

During the Republican period (1911–49) and earlier, in Imperial China, the environment was subject to human domination. Despite literary and artistic traditions extolling the beauty of the natural world, deforestation and destruction of wetlands and other natural habitats overseen by various dynastic governments were widespread.[23] During the Maoist period, the environment was seen as a tool for development that could be mobilized in the service of socialist revolution.[24] This long-standing orientation toward state control over the environment provides historical context for policy debates today over the relative priority to be accorded to economic development and environmental stewardship.

As discussed in chapter 4, after the 1980s, as China's economic growth trajectory brought with it increased environmental harm, stewardship of resources and the environment was compromised by institutional conflicts over the priority given to economic growth as well as the challenges of regulatory administration of an environmental protection system that is seen to increase costs of production and to threaten employment. Traditional norms and practices extolling human control of the environment are also evident in current policy terminology such as "environmental construction" (*huanjing jianshe*) that find expression in law.

The examples of criminal law, family relations, land use, and environmental protection reveal the ways in which China's modernizing legal system reflects domestic historical influences. While these influences should not be overstated, traditional norms of legal regulation provide important context for understanding the PRC legal system today.

C. Globalization and China's rise

The China of the early 2000s is more internationalized than perhaps at any other time in Chinese history – the cosmopolitan Tang Dynasty (618–907 CE) offering a useful comparison. As discussed in chapter 5, China's increased interaction with the world has seen international influences become increasingly evident in the PRC legal system. Two areas are particularly noteworthy, namely international trade and human rights. As well, international effects on legal education and practice are noteworthy.

1. International Trade

The 1990s saw the acceleration of China's effort to resume its seat at the General Agreement on Tariffs and Trade (GATT) and to join the World Trade Organization (WTO). Joining the GATT and the WTO posed significant challenges for China's economic and business policies and for the laws and institutions established to implement them. Under the "Protocol of Accession to the WTO," China undertook to make significant reforms in its regulation of foreign business, financial markets, foreign exchange, and other areas. Many of the international assessments of China's trade policy are critical of alleged protectionism and mercantilism,[25] although it is important to appreciate the positive effects that China's greater participation in the world economy has had for legal reform and legal institutions in the PRC. Whether we examine China's evolving property law regime, securities regulations, or government procurement rules, we find significant efforts to incorporate international standards in the regulatory system.

However, as we have seen during earlier periods of the PRC, reliance on imported regulatory mechanisms has not always been fully effective. Recurring problems of disregard of intellectual property rights, recurring securities fraud, and continued protectionism in government procurement programs, to name but a few, suggest that China's application of international legal and regulatory standards for trade and commerce will continue to face challenges of interpretation and implementation.

2. Human Rights

China's experience with globalization has also seen increased interaction with international standards on human rights. Human rights have become a focus of much discussion during the early post-Mao period and particularly following the political repression of 1989. Beginning in the 1990s, criticism by international human rights groups of conditions in China became a regular occurrence. In response, human rights research and analysis have been increasingly supported by the PRC government and in many cases used to support its domestic policy initiatives, as well as responses to international human rights criticism.

China has signed both the International Covenant on Economic, Social and Cultural Rights (ICESCR) and the International Covenant on Civil and Political Rights (ICCPR), and has ratified the ICESCR, subject to reservations that preserve China's policy preferences on labor rights. International standards on economic, social, and cultural rights in areas such as labor, health, housing, and living standards are echoed in PRC domestic laws, but are still subject to limitations on enforcement. Political and civil rights remain highly controversial. Amendments to the PRC Constitution in 2004 included the provision that "the State respects and protects human rights," although enforcement continues to depend on a political orthodoxy that emphasizes stability and proscribes challenges to the authority of the Party/State.

3. Legal Education and Practice

Internationalization has had significant, albeit uneven, effects on legal education. Law faculties are filled to capacity with many of China's best students, driven by the prospect of lucrative employment to study a field that for all intents and purposes did not exist 30 years ago. At elite law schools, legal education has been modeled after examples in Europe, North America, and Japan – becoming more rigorous and professionalized, with classes and seminars demanding increased student analysis and discussion. At lower tier institutions, where engagement with international standards is less direct, rote learning of statutory texts and formulaic recitation of principles is more common. Distance education is widely used, relying on globalized information technology to offer training and education to students in remote locations. Bookstores in Beijing, Shanghai and other major cities are well stocked with books on law, and crowded with prospective purchasers. Similarly with other professional service sectors, Chinese law firms are active across the country and internationally – many with branch offices in major cities in North America, Europe, and Japan.

Table 1.2 Judicial Case Loads in 2010

Supreme People's Court 2010
  Cases Dealt With: 12,086 (down 6.99% from 2009)
  Cases Concluded: 10,626
Local Courts
  Cases Dealt With: 11.7 million (up 2.82% from 2009).
  Cases Concluded: 10.999 million
Types of Cases
  Criminal cases concluded: 779,641 (up 1.68% from 2009).
    – Severe crimes (including homicide, kidnapping, robbery, attacking
      school children and undermining national security): 265,397
      (down 0.7% from 2009).
    – Financial crime (including embezzlement, bribery and
      malfeasance): 27,751 (up 7.1% from 2009).
  Administrative cases concluded: 129,806 (up 7.7% from 2009).
  Foreign business and maritime affairs cases concluded: 20,258
    (up 0.83% from 2009).
  Family law cases (including divorce, child raising, inheritance and other
    marriage and family related matters) cases concluded: 1.428
    (up 3.45% from 2009).
  Contract cases concluded 3.239 million (up 2.71% from 2009).
  Financial cases concluded 578,919 (up 11.63% from 2009).
  Merger and acquisition and bankruptcy cases concluded; 14,694
    (up 56.9% from 2009).
  Intellectual property cases concluded: 48,051 (up 32.96% from 2009).
  Environmental pollution compensation cases concluded 12,018
    (up 2.83% from 2009).

Source: "Highlights of Work Report of Supreme People's Court" (March
11, 2011) http://www.chinadaily.com.cn/china/2011npc/2011-03/11/
content_12157831.htm (accessed October 25, 2012).

Judicial caseloads have been increasing steadily such that judges in
China's courts are handling multiple cases each day. As indicated in
tables 1.2 and 1.3, the number of disputes resolved through mediation
and arbitration continues to rise.

Throughout this process, the content and operation of PRC law
continue to be informed by China's relations with the world. Law

Table 1.3   CIETAC Arbitral Case Loads – Cases Accepted by
CIETAC (Foreign-Related and Domestic)

Year	CIETAC Beijing	CIETAC Shanghai (Shanghai Sub-Commission)	CIETAC Shenzhen (South China Sub-Commission)
2011	668	523	21
2010	672	476	182
2009	650	610	216
2008	598	427	204
2007	630	332	156
2006	495	306	180
2005	462	304	213
2004	453	238	159
2003	373	205	131
2002	401	174	109
2001	420	173	138

Source: 2011 Quanguo zhongcai gongzuo nianhui zai Guiyang zhaokai
[2011 National Arbitration Annual Meeting will be held in Guiyang] (July
26, 2011. Source: Xinhua Net), http://www.chinanews.com/df/2011/07-
26/3210754.shtml (accessed October 25, 2012).

reviews at Chinese law schools increasingly address comparative and
international law questions, while also reflecting the influence of international standards on legal scholarship. Legislative and regulatory
drafting processes increasingly reflect the influence of international
standards, while judicial and arbitral dispute settlement processes and
decisions incorporate ever more widely the influence of international
legal discourses. China is increasingly active in international legal institutions. Whether directly through representation at the GATT/
WTO, the UN Human Rights Council, or other international agencies, or indirectly through participation and leadership of legal offices
in regional and global financial institutions and development agencies,
China's professional and scholarly legal community is increasingly
active in the world.

In sum, the PRC legal system reflects a combination of influences from local traditions and international engagement. The process of globalization has brought China ever closer into the world community and made it more subject to international standards on a wide variety of issues of legal regulation. Yet traditional legal norms about socio-economic relationships and the domination of the Party/State remain powerful, and continue to influence the ways in which international standards are received and incorporated into the PRC legal system.

SUMMARY

The socialist legal system of the PRC emerged out of the tumult of revolution but remained influenced by pre-revolutionary practices and norms. In the early years of the PRC, the legal system reflected policy priorities of state building, while also revealing policy conflicts over the relative importance given to priorities of formalization of rule and continuing revolution. Political conflict borne of these policy conflicts led to the breakdown of legal institutions, which were re-established only after 1978.

China's law reform program began at the 3rd Plenum of the 11th CPC Central Committee in late 1978. The Plenum reflected a tentative policy consensus about the need to reform the state-planned economy and build a legal system that would support economic growth and restore for the regime the monopoly on legitimate coercion that had been lost during the Cultural Revolution. While it is tempting to view the history of legal reform in China as an uninterrupted process of policy consensus, in fact the post-Mao period was marked by much contention and disagreement. Certainly, the post-Mao era saw a rapid development of legal institutions and processes in response to compelling socio-economic and political needs. Yet the political crisis surrounding the Tiananmen massacre of 1989 raised the prospect that both legal and economic reform would be halted. Deng Xiaoping's 1992 Southern Tour secured momentum for stronger links between legal and economic reform. The subsequent acceleration of market-oriented economic policies supported expanded efforts at law-building in areas that supported economic development and political stability. Following China's accession to the GATT/ WTO, the globalization of China's economy and society has brought with it significant challenges for social order and economic justice, which in turn have led to a reconsideration of many of the directions of legal reform in China.

The role of law in China today remains conflicted. On one hand, the Chinese government and society at large have accorded significant importance to the role of law in socio-economic relations. Hundreds of pieces of legislation have been enacted at the national level alone since 1979, not to mention the multitude of administrative regulations and provincial and municipal enactments. And through this steady litany of legislation, administrative regulations, and policy pronouncements, the government continues to extol the Party's leadership over socialist law.

But herein lies the rub – as fealty to Party control under the rubric of "socialism" unavoidably qualifies, and in the view of many diminishes, the capacity for law to serve as an independent source of restraint on government behavior. Problems with law enforcement in practice are abundantly evident. Issues of corruption, piracy of intellectual property, uncertain enforcement of contract and property rights, weak and often politicized enforcement of administrative regulations, and ongoing repression of those whose views are deemed heretical by the ruling Party, suggest significant obstacles to establishing a functional system of legal rule. These and many other contradictions are the source of ongoing debate among scholars, policymakers, jurists, and other observers. The chapters that follow are aimed to enable readers to develop their own understanding of the PRC legal regime.

DISCUSSION QUESTIONS

1. What have been the elements of continuity and change in the development of the PRC legal system?

2. What effects did political and policy debates during the 1950s and 1960s have on the PRC legal system?

3. Discuss the significance of the following events for the PRC legal system:

   a) 3rd Plenum of the 11th CPC Central Committee

   b) Deng Xiaoping's 1992 inspection tour

   c) China's accession to the WTO.

4. How has the PRC government used law to implement its policy priorities?

SUGGESTIONS FOR FURTHER READING

Bodde, Derk and Clarence Morris, *Law in Imperial China* (Philadelphia, PA: University of Pennsylvania Press, 1967).

Cohen, Jerome A., *The Criminal Process in the People's Republic of China* (Cambridge, MA: Harvard University Press, 1968).

Lubman, Stanley B., *Bird in a Cage – Legal Reform in China after Mao* (Stanford, CA: Stanford University Press, 2000).

MacFarquhar, Roderick, ed., *The Politics of China, 1949–1989* (Cambridge: Cambridge University Press, 1993).

Vogel, Ezra F., *Deng Xiaoping and the Transformation of China* (Cambridge, MA: Belknap Press of Harvard University Press, 2011).

2   Political Stability

The PRC legal system is intended in significant part to maintain political stability. To a large extent this involves protecting the domination of the Communist Party of China (CPC). Yet the mechanisms for maintaining political stability have both expanded and challenged the role of law. From an ideological point of view, the PRC Party/State has justified legal reform and the authoritarian role of the CPC through reconsideration of questions about class struggle and development. Operationally, legal reform has been seized as an instrument of rule whereby policy decisions by the Party/State are implemented through formal rules and organizations.

I. THE CENTRALITY OF PARTY LEADERSHIP

Revealing the policy instrumentalism of law in the PRC, China's Constitution enshrines Deng Xiaoping's "Four Basic Principles" as imperatives of governance. First articulated by Deng Xiaoping in 1979, the Four Basic Principles include (i) upholding socialism; (ii) upholding the people's democratic dictatorship; (iii) upholding the leadership of the CPC; and (iv) upholding "Marxism-Leninism Mao Zedong Thought."[1] Beneath what may appear to many as ideological jargon lie important policy priorities. References to "socialism" refer to the importance of public ownership in the economy and Party/State leadership over development – giving rise to questions about the proper role of private property, market forces, and private enterprise. References to the "people's democratic dictatorship" involve claims that the Party/ State is the revolutionary representative of the majority of Chinese people and is authorized to exercise dictatorship over political opponents – giving rise to questions around protection of individual civil and political rights. References to the "leadership by the CPC" is widely seen as the most fundamental of the Four Basic Principles, and speaks to the monopoly of Party leadership over governance activities and institutions – inviting discussion on judicial independence and the rule of law. As Peng Zhen noted in his remarks introducing the 1982 Constitution for approval by the National People's Congress Standing Committee:[2]

> What is most important in adherence to the four basic principles is adherence to socialism and to the leadership of the Communist Party. It has been proved by the facts of the past that in China no victory of the revolution will be gained without the leadership of the Communist Party armed with Marxism-Leninism and Mao Zedong Thought, and thus no success in adherence to socialism will be achieved.

Finally, references to "Marxism-Leninism Mao Zedong Thought" involve policy commitments linking the class analysis of Marxism and the hierarchical politics of Leninism with Mao's interpretation of China's needs and conditions – limiting challenges to ideological orthodoxy and barring review of policy mistakes of the Maoist era.

Although material conditions in China have changed considerably since the Four Basic Principles were first announced, they continue to be applied as justification for CPC rule – even if in amended form. Thus, the socialist system is seen as embracing market forces and private property ownership, even as the Party/State remains firmly in control of policy decisions and direction. On the question of class struggle, the people's democratic dictatorship has replaced dictatorship of the proletariat as the guiding ideal, confirming the decline of class struggle, but inviting concern on the process and methods for governance. The proletariat (working) class is now defined to include mental and service workers – thus allowing professional elites to join laborers as the social base for political leadership as powers of authoritarian dictatorship remain with the Party/State. The commitment to Party leadership remains a central tenet of the socialist rule of law. The provision on Marxism-Leninism Mao Zedong Thought has been expanded to include the market-oriented economic reform policies of Deng Xiaoping, the proposals for broader social inclusion under Jiang Zemin's "Three Represents," and Hu Jintao's theory of "scientific development." These changes suggest that the basic tenets of governance may well evolve, but subject always to the will of the Party/State.

A key question in this ideological dynamic is the question of the transition to socialism. Under classical Marxist theory, economies make transitions from capitalism to socialism to communism as the working class exercises ruling power. A key indicator of this process is the condition of class struggle, such that at earlier stages of development (e.g. capitalism), class struggle between proletariat workers and bourgeois capitalists was seen as an intense socio-economic conflict that engenders political change. With socialism and later communism, class struggle would gradually die out and the focus on building prosperity could begin. A key tension therefore is between the dynamics of class struggle, also referred to as the "relations of production," and the requirements of economic development, often referred to as the "forces of production." During periods of capitalism and to a lesser extent socialism, relations of production (class struggle) remain the key challenge for the Party. Beginning with the stage of socialism and continuing into the phase of communism, however, the key task for Party leadership becomes one of building material prosperity (building the forces of production).

The debate between these two priorities characterized much of the early post-Mao period and continues today. The Preamble to the 1982

Constitution[3] asserted the completion of socialist transformation, which justified the emphasis on modernization over class struggle:

> The socialist transformation of the private ownership of the means of production was completed, the system of exploitation of man by man eliminated and the socialist system established. . . .
>
> The basic task of the nation in the years to come is to concentrate its effort on socialist modernization. . . . The exploiting classes as such have been eliminated in our country. However, class struggle will continue to exist within certain limits for a long time to come.

Twenty years later, Party Chairman Jiang Zemin's theory of the "Three Represents" contained similar comments on the importance of productive forces:[4]

> Our Party must always represent the development requirements of China's advanced productive forces. The theory, line, program, principles, policies, and all-round work of the Party must endeavor to comply with the law of development of productive forces, must continuously promote the requirements of the liberation and development of social productive forces, and in particular, must reflect the requirements of the development of advanced productive forces and continue to improve the people's living standards.

Questions about class struggle point directly to the role of the CPC as a vanguard party claiming to lead China's progress towards socialism. As class struggle dies away and socialism approaches, the role of the Party shifts from promoting class struggle to promoting development. The key question then involves the relationship between the Party's political authority and the conditions of China's development, as the Party's legitimacy depends significantly on how effectively it redresses socio-economic inequalities (relations of production) and promotes prosperity (forces of production). Particular challenges for regime legitimacy have arisen when the Party/State gets the balance wrong. For example, during the Cultural Revolution preoccupation with issues of class struggle brought political chaos and economic decay, while in recent years attention to economic growth has given rise to disparities of wealth as well as declining conditions for education, labor relations, and the environment.

Questions about class struggle and the progress toward socialism have important implications for the rule of law. The juxtaposition of class struggle and legal reform had been brought into sharp relief during the Maoist period. During the 1958 Anti-Rightist Campaign, for example, proponents of legal reform were criticized and purged for departing from Mao's priorities on class struggle. During the political tumult of the Cultural Revolution, formal law was considered antithetical to both the dictatorship of the proletariat and to the Party's leadership of class struggle. Formal law was criticized by Maoists as limiting the scope of revolution and the leadership of the Party. With the decline of class struggle, however, the ruling Party could more easily justify reliance on increasingly formal legal rules for the management of society. Whereas during the Maoist period, the concept of rule of law was criticized as a counterrevolutionary restraint on the Party and people, during the post-Mao era, law became an essential component of the rule of the Party/State.

A key element of the policy decisions made at the 1978 3rd Plenum of the 11th CPC Central Committee involved the issue of class struggle. The Plenum communiqué stated that large-scale class struggle in society had "basically been resolved," and used this conclusion to justify a wide range of economic reforms permitting private businesses and foreign investment. The announcement at the 13th CPC Central Committee in 1987 that China had reached the "preliminary stage of socialism" offered an authoritative interpretation that supported further diminution of class struggle and greater attention to economic growth.

Policy decisions at the time to reduce direct CPC leadership over day-to-day administration and business (*dang-zheng fenkai*) reflected ideological conclusions about the Party's changing role under socialism.

Each of these important decisions combined reduced attention to class struggle and increased attention to development with continuing calls for legal reform. As class struggle receded to the deep background, Party policy priorities turned increasingly to development and the forces of production. The 15th National CPC Congress in 1997 saw reductions in Party control of economic activity in favor of private ownership and legal regulation, while the 17th National CPC Congress in 2007 emphasized President Hu Jintao's notion of "scientific development," which saw legal regulation placed at the service of the social development goals of the Party/State. The 18th Party Congress of 2012 continued the policy emphasis on forces of production with some attention to managing the attendant social costs.

Changing perspectives on relations and forces of production (class struggle and development) have had an impact on the content of law as well. In the criminal law area, for example, crimes were defined increasingly according to behavior rather than class. During the Cultural Revolution, individuals from "bad" class backgrounds were punished and often killed solely on the basis of their class status (a label conferred by local Party cadres often for reasons of personal animus rather than revolutionary fervor). Beginning in 1980 with the Criminal Law and Criminal Procedure Law of the PRC, however, criminal punishment attended to behavior instead. Criminal defendants were still referred to as class enemies during the post-Mao era, but this label derived from their actions in violation of criminal law rather than their socio-economic or political status.

As well, legal rights began slowly to be focused on the individual rather than the collective. Thus, under the 1986 General Principles of Civil Law, individuals were granted expanded rights to enter into contracts and to own property. These patterns continue in the current period and are expressed across the broad range of PRC legislation. However, such rights under law remained limited to those specifically granted by the Party/State – either through its law-making process or through the exercise of regulatory authority and policymaking. As the political leadership came increasingly to a consensus on the decline of class struggle, the Party/State began to use formal law as an instrument of rule. An important example of Party/State's articulation of political authority through law involves China's Constitution.

II. CONSTITUTIONAL ARRANGEMENTS

As discussed in chapter 1, the PRC Constitution has a rich and varied history reflecting conflicting and evolving policy priorities of the political leadership on issues of class struggle (relations of production) and economic development (forces of production) with resulting implications for formalization of law and governance. The current Constitution was enacted in 1982,[5] based on work by a drafting committee headed by Peng Zhen. Consistent with the principles of economic development and legal reform adopted by the Third Plenum of the 11th CPC Central Committee, the 1982 Constitution provided for development of a formal legal system, emphasizing its role in supporting economic development:

Article 5: The State upholds the uniformity and dignity of the socialist legal system.

No laws or administrative or local regulations may contravene the Constitution.

All State organs, the armed forces, all political parties and public organizations and all enterprises and institutions must abide by the Constitution and other laws. All acts in violation of the Constitution or other laws must be investigated. No organization or individual is privileged to be beyond the Constitution or other laws.

. . .

Article 28: The State maintains public order and suppresses treasonable and other counter-revolutionary activities; it penalizes criminal activities that endanger public security and disrupt the socialist economy as well as other criminal activities; and it punishes and reforms criminals.

The 1982 Constitution incorporated the 1954 Constitution principle of equality before the law, which had been deleted from the 1975 and 1978 versions. The 1982 Constitution also addressed important elements of government organization, incorporating many of the provisions of the 1954 Constitution on the structure of the state and the institutions of legislation (National People's Congress), executive (State Council), and judiciary (People's Courts and People's Procuracy). The Constitution enshrined the principle of judicial independence by insulating courts from interference by administrative agencies, public organizations, or individuals. Of note, however, is the fact that this did not necessarily preclude interference by Party organs (although Peng Zhen had inveighed specifically against direct Party interference in judicial decision making[6]). The 1982 Constitution also deleted provisions on the right to strike and the "four big freedoms" that had been enshrined in the 1975 and 1978 versions. The 1982 Constitution continues to condition the granting of rights upon citizens upholding various duties to the Party/State, and on rights enforcement not infringing on the rights of others. The 1982 Constitution also entrenched the "Four Basic Principles" associated with Deng Xiaoping.

The 1982 Constitution has been amended several times over the past decades.[7] In 1988, amendments were incorporated to reflect the decisions of the 13th CPC Congress on China achieving the initial stage of socialism and the decline of class struggle. Specifically the 1988 amendments recognized the role of privately owned businesses in complementing the publicly owned socialist economy. In 1993 the Constitution was amended yet again to reflect and accommodate increasingly market-oriented economic growth policies in the wake of the "deepening of reform" following Deng Xiaoping's 1992 Southern Tour. The communes that had been established during the Great Leap Forward (1958–60) were abolished. State enterprises that formerly had been the mainstay of the economy, were now to be referred to as "state-owned enterprises" to contrast them from the privately owned enterprises that were emerging as a result of economic reform policies. This transition had significance for the social welfare role that state enterprises had played previously in providing education, healthcare, and other social services for workers. By re-labeling state firms as "state-owned enterprises" and drawing parallels with privately owned companies, the new constitutional arrangements diminished the social welfare component of industrial employment. The 1993 constitutional amendments diminished the role of state planning in the economy in favor of market forces. In part this reflected the general direction of economic policy, but it also bore the influence of China's application to join the General Agreement on Tariffs and Trade (GATT), which required participants to pursue market policies.

The Constitution was amended yet again in 1999. Of particular importance was the addition of a provision on the "socialist rule of law." While this amendment entrenched the ideal that China would be a country run by law, the proviso for "socialist" law reveals continued fealty to the "Four Basic Principles" and particularly the dominance of Party rule. The 1999 amendments also formalized the role of non-public, private businesses in the socialist market economy, once again reflecting the direction of economic reform policies. Provisions for reliance on Deng Xiaoping's theory were also included, entrenching flexible ideals about "socialism with Chinese characteristics."

A further set of amendments was enacted in 2004. Private property was specifically protected, although it did not achieve the same level of protected status accorded to public property. The private property provision was a compromise amendment that had been attempted in 1999 without success. The 2004 amendments to the Constitution also included a provision on respect for human rights, although here again the amendment that was accepted was considered by many to fall short of the proposal on the unconditionality of human rights enforcement. Also included in the 2004 amendments was a reference to the "Three Represents" theory of Jiang Zemin, which underscored the importance of productive forces and embraced expanded market reforms and greater participation of professional and business elites in government.

China's Constitution remains an instrument for expressing and entrenching Party policy. Constitutional norms around the rule of law, human rights, the market economy and private property reflect the outcome of political deliberations around policy priorities of the Party/State. The legal terminology of international constitutional usage takes on a different meaning when interpreted and applied in the context of China. As well, the policy significance of constitutional provisions means that each of the amendments and the processes around them reflect intense political debates about policy priorities. Constitutional amendments also have implications for the organizations and institutions of governance, as amendments around the rule of law and other issues affect the authority and tasks of political and legal institutions. China's changing Constitution reflects the continued interplay between politics and policy and their expression through formal law.

III. LEGAL INSTITUTIONS

Informed by an instrumentalist approach to the rule of law, the CPC has established institutions aimed at formalizing and enforcing Party policy through legal forms. Of particular importance are the National People's Congress (NPC), the administrative law system, and institutions for dispute resolution.

A. *The NPC: legislation as formalization of policy*

Under the 1982 PRC Constitution, the NPC's legislative duties extend to enacting basic statutes of national application, as well as passing amendments to the Constitution and reviewing decisions by the State Council and the NPC's own Standing Committee (NPC-SC). The 1982 Constitution expanded the powers of the NPC Standing Committee to include not just enactment of law but also supervision of the work of the State Council and other administrative bodies. Efforts to strengthen the role of the NPC-SC were continued in the 1990s by NPC Chairman, Qiao Shi, who emphasized the importance of legislative institutions lending a degree of permanence to law making, so as to insulate it from the whims of particular leaders. Qiao also supported the supremacy of law over CPC members, and the authority of the NPC and its Standing Committee to supervise enforcement of the Constitution, legislation, and the work of state organs. Differences between Qiao Shi and CPC General Secretary Jiang Zemin on questions about Party leadership over the lawmaking and law enforcement processes led ultimately to Qiao's loss of his Politburo seat and of his Chairmanship of the NPC Standing Committee.

The NPC system has undergone a number of important changes. While the NPC Legislative Affairs Committee continues to dominate the processes of legislative drafting and consultation, experimentation with more open rule-making processes has led to wider use of a system of legislative hearings that permitted an increasingly broad spectrum of (mainly elite) society to comment on successive drafts of legislation.[8] Limits remain, however, to the potential expansion of

NPC authority. As affirmed in the 2008 government White Paper on the rule of law, NPC legislation remains subject to constitutional provisions on Party leadership.[9] The legislative process for key policy areas is generally initiated by a decision of the Politburo and its Politics and Law Committee, while draft laws remain subject to review and approval by the Politburo and its Standing Committee. All important NPC decisions are made initially by the NPC-SC, whose membership of senior Party members is determined by the Party Politburo. Hu Jintao's efforts to ensure Party leadership over legal regime development suggest a continued commitment to the NPC remaining an instrument of Party policy.[10] The official functions of the NPC are set forth in table 2.1, in an excerpt from an official PRC website.

B. Administrative agencies: instruments of governance

Administrative bureaucracies under the State Council have long dominated the process of governance in China, to the extent that administrative decision making often eclipses the law-making authority of the NPC system. As indicated in table 2.2, administrative agencies of the State Council have responsibility for a wide array of activities.

The influence of the State Council in the processes of legal change in China is also evident through its increasingly active use of White Papers to formalize expressions of government policy.[11] For domestic audiences, these White Papers serve to entrench policy positions so as to influence administrative decisions around regulatory enforcement. For example, the White Paper on Labor and Social Security (2002) expressed commitments by the government to institute labor contract systems as well as systems for retirement, medical, and unemployment insurance well before formal legislation on these systems went into effect.[12] However, the international audience is also important, as

Table 2.1   NPC Organization

1. The NPC: the highest organ of state power with five years of each term. The plenary session of the NPC is held once every year or at any time under special circumstances. Deputies to the NPC are members forming the highest organ of state power to be elected from the provinces, autonomous regions, municipalities directly under the Central Government and the armed forces.
2. The Standing Committee of the NPC: the permanent organization of the highest organ of state power consisting of the chairman, vice chairmen, secretary-general and members who shall not assume any posts in the state administrative organ, judicial or prosecuting organs. The term of office is also five years. The chairman and vice chairmen shall not serve more than two consecutive terms. Normally the Standing Committee is convened once every two months.
3. The Meeting of the Chairmen of the Standing Committee: Participated by the chairman, vice chairmen and secretary-general to deal with major routine work of the Standing Committee.
4. Special committees: permanent committees of the NPC, they are composed of the chairman, vice chairmen and members. Under the leadership of the NPC, special committees are guided by the Standing Committee of the NPC when the latter is not in plenary session. The special committees study, review and draft motions and bills.
5. Deputy Credential Examination Committee: permanent organ of the NPC Standing Committee for examining the credentials of NPC deputies. The specific job of the committee is to examine the credentials of deputies emerged from by-elections of the present session and the newly elected deputies for the coming session. The committee is composed of the chairman, vice chairmen and members, all nominated from among the members of the Standing Committee and by the Meeting of the Chairman of the Standing Committee, to be agreed upon by the plenary session of the Standing Committee for a term of five years.
6. The General Affairs Office, Legislative Work Committee and Budget Committee: permanent organs of the NPC Standing Committee for serving the plenary session of the NPC, meetings of the Standing Committee and sessions of the Meeting of the Chairmen of the Standing Committee; for serving the deputies of the NPC and members of the Standing Committee in their execution of functions and powers according to law and for serving the development of socialist democracy and improvement of the socialist legal system.

Source: http://www.china.org.cn/features/state_structure/2003-05/16/content_1064763.htm (accessed October 3, 2012).

Table 2.2 State Council/Administrative Agencies

Organs Composing the State Council		

Ministries		Commissions
Agriculture 农业部	Foreign Affairs 外交部	National Development and Reform Commission 国家发展和改革委员会
Civil Affairs 民政部	Health 卫生部	Commission of Science, Technology and Industry for National Defense 国防科学技术工业委员会
Commerce 商务部	Information Industry 信息产业部	State Ethnic Affairs Commission 民族事务委员会
Communications 交通部	Justice 司法部	State Population and Family Planning Commission
Construction 建设部	Labor and Social Security 劳动和社会保障部	中国人口与计划生育委员会
Culture 文化部	Land and Resources 国土资源部	State Owned Assets Supervision and Administration Commission 国务院国有资产监督管理委员会
Education 教育部	Science and Technology 科技部	
Finance 财政部	State Security 安全部	
	Supervision 监察部	
	National Defense 国防部	
	Water Resources 水利部	

Other
People's Bank of China 中国人民银行
National Audit Office 国家审计署

Organs Directly Under the State Council 国务院直属机构	Institutions Directly Under the State Council 国务院直属事业单位	Working Organs of the State Council 国务院办事机构
General Administration of Customs 中国海关总署	Xinhua News Agency 新华通讯社	Overseas Chinese Affairs Office of the State Council 国务院侨务办公室
State Administration of Taxation 国家税务总局	Chinese Academy of Sciences 中国科学院	Hong Kong and Macao Affairs Office of the State Council 国务院港澳事务办公室
State Administration for Industry and Commerce 国家工商行政管理总局	Chinese Academy of Social Sciences 中国社会科学院	Legislative Affairs Office of the State Council 国务院法制办公室
State Environmental Protection Administration 国家环境保护总局	Chinese Academy of Engineering 中国工程院	Economic Restructuring Office of the State Council 国务院经济体制改革办公室
General Administration of the Civil Aviation of China 中国民航总局	Development Research Center of the State Council 国务院发展研究中心	Research Office of the State Council 国务院研究室
State Administration of Radio, Film and Television... 国家广播电影电视总局	National School of Administration 国家行政学院	Taiwan Affairs Office of the State Council... 国务院台湾事务办公室
State General Administration of Sport 国家体育总局	China Seismological Bureau... 中国地震局	Information Office of the State Council 国务院新闻办公室
National Bureau of Statistics 国家统计局	China Meteorological Administration 中国气象局	Office of the Leading Group for Western Region Development of the State Council 国务院西部开发领导小组办公室
State Forestry Administration 国家林业局	China Securities Regulatory Commission 证券监督管理委员会	
State Drug Administration 国家药品监督管理局		

Table 2.2 Continued

Organs Directly Under the State Council 国务院直属机构	Institutions Directly Under the State Council 国务院直属事业单位	Working Organs of the State Council 国务院办事机构
State Intellectual Property Office 国家知识产权局	China Insurance Regulatory Commission 中国保险监督管理委员会	State Council Informatization Office 国务院信息化工作办公室
National Tourism Administration 国家旅游局	National Council for Social Security Fund 全国社会保障基金理事会	
State Administration of Religious Affairs 国家宗教事务局	National Natural Science Foundation of China 国家自然科学基金委员会	
Counselors' Office of the State Council 国务院参事室	State Electricity Regulatory Commission 国家电力监管委员会	
Government Offices Administration of the State Council 国务院机关事务管理局	China Banking Regulatory Commission 中国银行业监督管理委员会	
State General Administration for Quality Supervision and Inspection and Quarantine 国家质量监督检验检疫总局		
General Administration of Press and Publication 中国新闻出版署		
National Copyright Administration 国家版权局		
State Administration for Work Safety (State Administration of Coal Mine Safety) 国家安全生产监督管理局 (国家煤矿安全监察局)		

Source: Congressional Executive Commission on China (CECC), "China's State Organizational Structure," http://www.cecc.gov/pages/virtualAcad/gov/state/struct.php (accessed July 3, 2012).

indicated in the 2008 White Paper on the rule of law, which highlights the achievements of the Chinese legal regime, while attempting to rebut criticisms.

The first major piece of legislation governing China's administrative regulatory system was the Administrative Litigation Law (ALL) enacted in 1989. Aimed at curtailing the power of bureaucratic agencies, the ALL formalized the authority of the People's Courts to review administrative agency decisions imposing fines; restricting or infringing on property rights; intervening in business operations; denying licenses; and a number of other matters. The judicial review provisions of the ALL were augmented by those of the 1994 State Compensation Law (SCL), which permitted awards of compensation to individuals and organizations harmed physically or financially by unlawful bureaucratic action. The SCL was revised in 2010 to expand the scope of compensable injury and to reduce the requirements for exhaustion of administrative remedies with the offending department, to recover damages even in cases of lawful but negligent misconduct, and to recover for psychological injury.

The ALL and the SCL are not without their limitations, however. The SCL excludes the possibility of compensation for harm by officials acting outside the scope of their duties, where the complainant has caused harm through its own acts, or "under other circumstances prescribed by law." The ALL does not permit review of discretionary decisions, which are commonplace in light of the textual ambiguities of Chinese laws and regulations. In addition, ALL review does not extend to the lawfulness of the underlying regulations upon which administrative decisions are based, which in effect permits administrative agencies to make rules immunizing their decisions from ALL review. The ALL's provisions on exhaustion of administrative remedies were expanded and formalized in the 1999 Administrative Reconsideration Law of the PRC, further shielding administrative decisions from judicial review. Finally, the ALL does not extend to

Party decisions, thus prohibiting judicial scrutiny of the most funda-mental activities of PRC governance.

The pattern of ALL litigation suggests that its effects have been limited. Political intervention to thwart the application of the law – particularly in cases reviewing police misconduct – as well as efforts to secure exemptions from judicial review through legislation have com-bined to weaken the ALL's potential impact. While the judicial review system has introduced an element of legal accountability to the process of governance, the ALL and the SCL do not impose meaningful limits on the Party/State.

Attempts to formalize rule-making processes, such as the early reform period "Tentative Regulations on the Procedure for Enacting Administrative Laws and Regulations" and the Legislation Law of the PRC (2000), purport to establish limits on the rule-making authority of administrative offices and departments based on their relative ranking in the bureaucratic hierarchy. Administrative regulations (*xingzheng guiding*) are issued by the State Council and its affiliated organs and have national application. Local People's Congresses may enact "local regulations" subject to reporting to the NPC Standing Committee "for the record."

The Administrative Supervision Law (1997) authorized superior-level agencies to require subordinate units to amend or annul their regulations where inconsistent with superior laws and regulations. However, the statute offered little support for the subjects of adminis-trative action to challenge bureaucratic rule making. The Administrative Procedure Law (1998) helped to address this question by specifying processes for administrative actions, including formal rule making. However, supervision of the rule-making practices of bureaucratic agencies remains largely confined to the authority of superior level departments, and the Party still exercises leadership over gov-ernment rule making in the State Council's regulatory process.[13] The Administrative Licensing Law (2004) sets forth substantive and procedural standards for application and issuance of licenses by bureaucratic agencies. The Administrative Enforcement Law (2012) attempts to strengthen the capacity of administrative agencies to enforce their decisions.

Augmenting these formal administrative processes, the "Letters and Visits" (*xinfang*) system affords citizens opportunities to petition the government for redress – most often over practical matters such as unpaid wages and benefits, rather than abstract human rights claims. Yet this system has been under threat from those who encourage broader use of the formal legal regime for redress of popular grievances.[14] Ideals about strengthening legal restraints on Party and State power notwithstanding, such formalization of the process may ultimately work to exclude those without the resources to participate effectively in the legal regime.

C. Courts: symbols of the socialist rule of law

China's court system involves primarily the People's Courts, although there are also military courts and courts associated with the national railway system. The People's Courts are structured pursuant to the Court Organization Law of the PRC (1979, rev. 1983), one of the first laws enacted after the Cultural Revolution. The Supreme People's Court (SPC) operates at the national level and has general administrative responsibility over the operations of courts at lower levels. The SPC also has appellate jurisdiction over decisions issued by provincial-level courts. Below the SPC are the people's courts at the administrative levels of *Province* ("Higher Level People's Courts"), *Prefecture* ("Intermediate Level People's Courts"), and *County* ("Basic Level People's Courts"). Generally, jurisdiction is established by geographic location, such that the vast majority of cases originate at the county level and are heard by the Basic Level People's Courts. However so-called "large and complex" cases may be filed originally with the

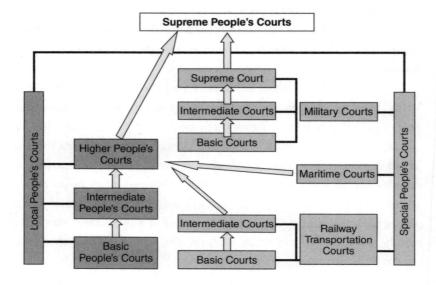

Note: the arrows point to the next superior courts, while the lines denote the components.

Figure 2.1 Court Structure
Source: Jiahong Yang, "Report From China: Supreme People's Court," http://www.thecourt.ca/2007/03/27/report-from-china-supreme-people's-court/ (accessed September 13, 2012).

Intermediate Level People's Courts of the prefecture level. Cases involving foreigners are generally filed at this level as well. Significant cases that have province-wide significance may be filed as a matter of first instance with the provincial level Higher Level People's Courts. The SPC hears cases on appeal from the provincial level Higher Level People's Courts, although this is discretionary rather than mandatory except in death penalty cases. The structure of the court system is illustrated in Figure 2.1.

The revised Civil Procedure Law (1991), building on the earlier 1982 draft, signaled an effort to give the courts greater authority to resolve an increasingly large and complex array of private disputes. Expanding the system whereby the People's Courts were initially subdivided into specialized criminal, economic, and civil trial divisions, new divisions were added for foreign economic relations, intellectual property, and administrative law. Revisions in 2007 reflected further efforts to improve judicial performance in areas of retrials and enforcement of judgments. Further revisions to the Civil Procedure Law in 2012 reinstated the importance of mediation and provided for expedited litigation procedures.

The People's Courts also have responsibility for recognizing and issuing orders to enforce foreign arbitral awards under the New York Convention on the Recognition and Enforcement of Foreign Arbitral Awards, to which China acceded effective in 1987. The Supreme People's Court's "Rules on Certain Issues Relating to Jurisdiction over Proceedings of Foreign-Related Civil and Commercial Cases" (2001) contributed to greater certainty in the enforcement of foreign arbitral and judicial awards. Increased attention has also been paid to training judges, first under the Supreme Court's Senior Judges Training Centre and later at the PRC Judicial Institute. The Judges Law of the PRC (1995) imposed education and testing requirements for judges, in an effort to improve quality.

Unfortunately, the Chinese court system has been hampered by the generally low level of political status, and lacks the authority of formal legal institutions of the Western legal tradition. China's courts lack the practical capacity to compel production of evidence and enforce awards. The often-parochial view (referred to as "local protectionism") taken by local courts resisting enforcement of judicial awards from outside their area of jurisdiction reflects ingrained traditions of localism and the centrality of personal relations as the basis for behavior. Judicial processes of internal and informal fact-finding and decision making often leave disputants vulnerable to abuses of power and political connections by their adversaries. As well, the Party continues to play a dominant role through the "Adjudication Committees" that are attached to each court and which in effect review and approve judicial decisions notwithstanding official directives ordering that the intervention of adjudication committees be curtailed.[15] These committees are generally chaired by the Party Secretary of the court for which they sit and are comprised of senior judges virtually all of whom are Party members and subject to Party disciplinary controls. Adjudication Committees often work closely with local Party political–legal committees. Judicial corruption remains a serious problem. Local funding of the courts has long meant their potential subservience to local political imperatives, although recent proposals to centralize court funding may help alleviate this problem.

The People's Courts are generally not authorized to interpret the meaning of legislation, which is reserved under the Constitution for the NPC-SC. Nonetheless, the Supreme People's Court has taken to issuing "Opinions" on various issues of implementation of particular laws, such as the Contract Law, Property Rights Law, Criminal Procedure Law, etc. [16] Since these "Opinions" ostensibly address issues of implementation, they do not conflict with Constitutional provisions on NPC-SC interpretations of legislation. Nonetheless, the Supreme People's Court "Opinions" have important influence on the interpretation and implementation of law.

While courts are not supposed to engage in Constitutional analysis, local judges have on occasion offered opinions on the meaning and constitutional validity of local legislation. The well-known "seeds case" in Henan (2003) and the Qi Yuling case in Shandong (2001) reveal the possibility for judicial review of local legislation and regulations, although in each of these the judges involved were castigated for exceeding their nominal authority.[17] Constitutional adjudication still remains beyond the reach of court authority, although proposals for a formal constitutional review mechanism continue to circulate among legal academics and professionals.

D. Legal practice

Legal practice is subject to the regulatory authority of Party/State through the Ministry of Justice and the All China Lawyers' Association of the CPC's United Front Work Committee. Building on a set of regulatory pronouncements aimed at curbing legal representation for collective disputes and protesters, the revised Lawyers Law (2007) underscored efforts to restrict the use of law to challenge policies and practices of the Party/State.[18] These restrictions are reiterated in turn under the "Lawyers' Code of Practice" of the All China Lawyers Association, which imposes requirements for "lawfulness" in law practice that in effect require loyalty to the Party/State.[19]

By virtue of their training and licensing, lawyers have the training and authority to engage in interpretation and advocacy around the very laws through which the Party/State implements its authority. For the first 20 or so years following the beginning of legal reform in 1978, lawyers remained a more-or-less passive sector, constrained by tradition and regulation from challenging policy initiatives of the Party/State. Law schools remained small and underfunded, while law graduates were not in particularly high demand. With the burgeoning growth of the Chinese economy, however, legal specialists have come to be in great demand – leading to higher salaries, better funding for law schools, and more competition for admission. As indicated in table 2.3, the number of lawyers (200,000) and law firms in China relative to a population of 1.3 billion is modest (1:7,500). Canada, by contrast, has approximately 80,000 lawyers for a population of approximately 35 million (1:438).

As well, the energetic efforts of international organizations and the agencies of foreign governments to promote legal education exchanges saw a generation of PRC lawyers receive advanced training and experience in law in Europe, Japan, and North America. One consequence of this is a gradually increasing level of professionalism.

Table 2.3   Licensed Lawyers in China

Domestic Law Firms		
Year	Lawyers	Law Firms
2011	200,000	17,000

Cases		
Litigation	Non-Litigation	Legal Assistance
6.24 million	1.65 million	6.4 million

Foreign Law Firms			
Year	Firms	Countries	Offices in China
2011	242	21	314

Source: All China Lawyers Association, "Licensed Lawyers number 200,000 in China" (December 26, 2011), http://www.china.org.cn/china/ 2011-12/26/content_24249504.htm (accessed September 16, 2012).

An important dimension of this process has been the emergence of a new category of lawyers known as "rights defenders," who take on public interest cases on behalf of poor and marginalized clients.[20] However, the government has aggressively tried to suppress the use of law to protect rights of which it does not approve, even when these are articulated in specific legislation and regulatory enactments. The abuse of blind public interest lawyer Chen Guangcheng, including detention, harassment, and physical abuse, is emblematic of the ways in which officials have attacked lawyers for challenging their authority. Chen gained notoriety initially by representing victims of forced abortion and sterilization, and later became a vocal and effective advocate for marginalized people such as AIDS victims, unpaid military pensioners, and people suffering from environmental harm.

Nonetheless, the rights defenders movement has expanded steadily. The growing trend of public citizens using the law to enforce their rights against government abuse and against abuse by privileged citizens suggests a new and dramatic phase in China's legal development. This poses a significant dilemma for the governing regime, which has to a large extent based its legitimacy on a commitment to the rule of law. If the legitimacy of the regime comes to be compromised to the extent that it fails to deliver on commitments regarding the rule of law, an entirely new calculus of political authority may emerge. Although the Party staffing and discipline systems are powerful mechanisms for ensuring compliance by judges and lawyers, the regime's ability to control outcomes is weakened to the extent that the law becomes part of the public domain.

IV. PROTECTING STABILITY: LAW AND SOCIAL CONTROL

The PRC legal system is an important instrument for ensuring stability through social control. From an ideological point of view, this involves questions about class struggle as well as the requirements for economic development. Thus, while class struggle is seen to have diminished, social stability remains critical to China's pursuit of economic development. As behavior replaces class as the criterion for legal treatment by the regime, criminal law has taken on important significance. As well, administrative detention serves as a supplement to criminal justice processes.

A. *Criminal justice and protection of stability*

Social control and the preservation of political stability are primarily the province of the criminal justice system. Through an enumeration of criminal offenses that includes economic and political crimes as well as crimes against persons and property, the Criminal Law of the PRC serves as a main instrument for social control. The Criminal Procedure Law of the PRC ensures that the institutions of the criminal justice system operate in conformity with the imperatives of the Party/State.

1. Criminal Law

Driven to re-assert a monopoly on legitimate use of force for social control following the excesses of the Cultural Revolution, and mindful of the need to build legitimacy through law, the post-Mao regime enacted the Criminal Law and the Criminal Procedure Law in 1979. The purpose of the criminal justice system was expressed simply as punishing crime and protecting the people, although the specific tasks of the PRC Criminal Law[21] reflected the policy priorities of the regime around regime security, class dominance by the proletariat, public ownership, property protection, and development:

> *Article 2*: The tasks of the PRC Criminal Law are to use punishment struggle against all criminal acts to defend national security, the political power of the people's democratic dictatorship, and the socialist system; to protect state-owned property and property collectively owned by the laboring masses; to protect citizens' privately owned property; to protect citizens' right of the person, democratic rights, and other rights; to maintain social and economic order; and to safeguard the smooth progress of the cause of socialist construction.

The Criminal Law provided specifically that only acts defined as criminal by the law are subject to punishment (Art. 3) – a significant departure from the ideological flexibility that accompanied the use of force under the class-based system of the Maoist era. As well, the

Criminal Law incorporated the principle of equality before the law (Art. 4) that had been articulated initially in the 1954 Constitution, criticized during the Cultural Revolution, and then was restored under the 1982 Constitution. While this reflected the general transition from class to behavior as the basis for criminal punishment, the definition of crimes remains quite broad, including offenses against state interests, public ownership, and property and development interests:

> *Article 13*: All acts that endanger the sovereignty, territorial integrity, and security of the state; split the state; subvert the political power of the people's democratic dictatorship and overthrow the socialist system; undermine social and economic order; violate property owned by the state or property collectively owned by the laboring masses; violate citizens' privately owned property; infringe upon citizens' rights of the person, democratic rights, and other rights; and other acts that endanger society, are crimes if according to law they should be criminally punished.

The Criminal Law applies to PRC citizens who commit crimes specified in the law, whether within or outside the territory of the PRC (Art. 7). Foreign nationals are also subject to punishment under the Criminal Law for criminal acts committed in the territory of the PRC, and outside where the applicable punishment is not less than three years imprisonment, but not if the act is not punishable according to the law of the place where it is committed (Art. 8). Criminal responsibility attaches for both intentional and negligent crimes (Arts. 14 and 15). The minimum age for attachment of criminal responsibility is 18 years, and may attach to persons as young as 14 for serious crimes such as murder, rape, robbery, drug trafficking, and arson (Art. 17). Criminal responsibility does not attach to acts by the mentally ill who at the time are unable to recognize or unable to control their conduct, although compulsory medical treatment by the family or the government may be required (Art. 18). This provision has been subject to abuse as incarceration of political dissidents at mental hospitals has been reported.[22] Preparation to commit crimes and criminal attempt are also punishable under the PRC Criminal Law (Arts. 22 and 23).

Punishments under the PRC Criminal Law include control (surveillance), criminal detention, fixed-term imprisonment, life imprisonment, and the death penalty (Art. 33). Legislation aimed at reforming the prison system was enacted in 1994, symbolizing an effort to regularize the administration of prisons and labor camps, and articulating ideals about the treatment of prisoners.[23] Although China has been widely criticized for the excessive use of the death penalty, ongoing efforts by criminal justice reformers have resulted in recent decisions to reduce the application of the death penalty and to subject it to greater appellate review.[24] In addition to the primary penalties under the PRC Criminal Law, a range of supplemental penalties also apply, including fines, deprivation of political rights, and confiscation of property (Art. 34). The deprivation of political rights includes deprivation of: (a) the right to vote and to stand for election; (b) the right to freedom of speech of the press, of assembly, of association, of procession, and of demonstration; (c) the right to hold a position in state organs; and (d) the right to hold a leading position in a state-owned company, enterprise, or institution or people's organization (Art. 54). These provisions are a vestige of the class orientation of China's socialist ideology – presuming that criminals are class enemies (albeit based on behavior rather than socio-economic status) and therefore should be deprived of the opportunity to participate in political and economic affairs. Punishment of political dissidents routinely includes deprivation of political rights in addition to other penalties such as fixed-term imprisonment.

Revisions to the Criminal Law in 1997[25] reflected an effort to reduce the potential for arbitrary punishment. The revision provided that an act is not criminal unless specifically stated in the law – thus eliminating the "rule of analogy," which under the 1980 law had permitted criminal conviction for acts not expressly identified as criminal, by reference to the most closely analogous provision of the law. Nonetheless, the revisions to the Criminal Law also strengthened the Party/State's monopoly on political authority to suppress critics of the government. While eliminating the crime of counter-revolution, the revised law used instead the crime of endangering state security, which is not limited by the intent requirement that informed the counter-revolution provisions of the past. Absent the requirement to prove intent, the state may now determine without restriction whether it is endangered by an act with which it disagrees. While the intent requirement may have been of little practical significance, its elimination sends a powerful message that the Party/State will tolerate no threats, intended or not, to its monopoly on political authority. The use of these provisions to repress the defenders of civil rights and critics of regime policy is testament to the intent of the Party/State to use law to support authoritarian rule.

2. Criminal Procedure

The Criminal Procedure Law of the PRC provides direction on the institutions and processes for implementation of the Criminal Law.[26] The purposes of the Criminal Procedure Law emphasize the role of law in protecting state interests, public order, property and development through application of law and punishment:

> ensur[e] correct enforcement of the Criminal Law, punishing crimes, protecting the people, safeguarding State and public security and maintaining socialist public order (CPL Art. 1)

and

> to ensure accurate and timely ascertainment of facts about crimes,
> correct application of law, punishment of criminals and protection of
> the innocent against being investigated for criminal responsibility; to
> enhance the citizens' awareness of the need to abide by law and to fight
> vigorously against criminal acts in order to safeguard the socialist legal
> system, to protect the citizens' personal rights; their property rights,
> democratic rights and other rights; and to guarantee smooth progress
> of the cause of socialist development. (CPL Art. 2)

Here again, we see the policy priorities of the Party/State incorporated into formal legal instruments, such that the CPL is aimed not only at implementing provisions of the Criminal Law, but also at safeguarding state security, maintaining socialist public order, and guaranteeing smooth progress of the cause of socialist development. These policy imperatives play a role in the ways that officials in the courts and the public prosecutions department (People's Procuratorate) interpret and apply the law.

The CPL formalizes the respective roles of the public security organs to investigate crimes, the People's Procuratorates to prosecute them, and the People's Courts to adjudicate cases (CPL Art. 3). This specialization of functions reflects not only the commitment to formalizing the separate roles of judicial institutions, but also allows for greater professionalism within the separate domains of investigation, prosecution, and adjudication. The investigatory functions of the public security organs are augmented by the role of the Ministry of State Security in investigating crimes that endanger state security. Consistent with constitutional provisions, the People's Courts and the People's Procuratorates are granted authority to exercise judicial power independently (CPL Art. 5), although the People's Procuratorates also exercise legal supervision over criminal proceedings (Art. 8). As with the Criminal Law, the CPL applies to foreigners (CPL Art. 16).

China's criminal procedure system allows for two instances of adjudication – trial and appeal (CPL Art. 10), and provides for public trials of cases unless otherwise provided (CPL Art. 11). Adjudication is made by the People's Courts, using a panel comprised of two judges and one lay "people's assessor" (*peishen yuan*) – another vestige of China's socialist ideology that combines specialized professionals with representatives of society at large. In practice, however, the "people's assessors" tended simply to follow the instructions given by the trained judges on the panel. Recent experiments have seen the use of "people's juries" (*peishen tuan*) to bring local community views into the judicial process more effectively.[27]

Consistent with provisions of the Organization Law for the People's Courts, jurisdiction is based on geographic conditions combined with a few substantive elements. Thus the county-based "Basic Level People's Courts" have jurisdiction as courts of first instance over ordinary criminal cases falling within their territory, while the prefecture-based "Intermediate Level People's Courts" have jurisdiction over cases involving counter-revolutionary cases and cases endangering state security; ordinary criminal cases punishable by life imprisonment or the death penalty; and criminal cases in which the offenders are foreigners (CPL Art. 20). Provincial "Higher Level People's Courts" have jurisdiction as courts of first instance over major criminal cases that pertain to an entire province (CPL Art. 21) and the Supreme People's Court has jurisdiction as the court of first instance over major criminal cases that pertain to the whole nation (CPL Art. 22). In instances of "major or complex" cases, the People's Court at a higher level than where the case arose may handle the case, and higher level courts have authority to direct their subordinates to transfer cases as necessary (CPL Arts. 23–26).

Criminal defendants are entitled to a defense (CPL Art. 11). Criminal defendants may entrust as defenders either lawyers, persons represented by a public organization or the unit to which the criminal suspect or defendant belongs, or guardians, relatives or friends of the criminal suspect or defendant (CPL Art. 32). Non-lawyer criminal defenders acting with permission of the People's Court are authorized to "consult, make abstracts of or reproduce the indictment and technical appraisal materials of the case, may meet and correspond with the crime suspect in custody" once the People's Procuracy begins to examine and prosecute the case (CPL Art. 36).

Public prosecutions departments (People's Procuratorate) are obliged to inform criminal defendants of their right to entrust a legal defender, and the People's Courts may (but are not required to) appoint legal defenders (CPL Arts. 33 and 34). Criminal defenders have the right and obligation to present evidence proving the innocence of the defendant (CPL Art. 35), although criminal defense lawyers have been punished for purportedly introducing unreliable evidence in criminal proceedings under CPL Article 38, which provides:

> Defense lawyers and other defenders shall not help the criminal suspects or defendants to conceal, destroy or falsify evidence or to tally their confessions, and shall not intimidate or induce the witnesses to modify their testimony or give false testimony or conduct other acts to interfere with the proceedings of the judicial organs.[28]

This provision combines with Article 306 of the Criminal Law, which provides punishments of up to three years' imprisonment for legal defenders who induce submission of false evidence and testimony, to impose a "big stick" for intimidating defense counsel.[29]

There has been widespread criticism that criminal defenders are routinely denied access to the facts and documentation supporting the prosecution's case against their client defendants.[30] Police have long been empowered to detain (*juliu*) accused defendants for up to 37 days before filing a formal arrest (*daibu*) (CPL Art. 69), which often delays the process of "examination and prosecution," which starts the time when the defendant's legal rights to receive information and evidence begin to take effect. Amendments to the Criminal Procedure Law effective in 2012 allow for detention of persons suspected of crimes related to national security or terrorism in a designated location of the agencies' choice for up to six months. Notice must be given to relatives within 24 hours (unless police deem this would impede the investigation). The location of the detention is not required to be disclosed, and police may deny the detained person access to defense counsel, further eroding the possibilities for effective criminal defense.

Evidence is defined as "all facts that prove the true circumstances of the case," including verified material and documentary evidence, witness testimony, victim statements, statements and exculpations of criminal suspects or defendants, expert conclusions, records of inquests and examination, and audio-visual materials (CPL Art. 42). Judges, prosecutors, and investigators are legally obligated to collect evidence to prove guilt or innocence, but also are prohibited from extracting confessions by torture and from collecting evidence by threat, enticement, deceit, or other unlawful means (CPL Art. 43). China has faced recurring criticism from the UN Special Rapporteur on Torture, who has concluded that the problem of torture continues.[31] The People's Courts, People's Procuratorates, and public security organs have authority to compel appearance of criminal suspects, generally through arrest approved by the People's Procuratorate or People's Court, although provisions allow for criminal suspects who post appearance bonds to remain free from detention (CPL Arts. 56–59).

Following an investigation by the public security organs and prosecution by the People's Procuratorate, judgment by the People's Court is to be made based on the evidence, allowing three types of verdict – guilty, innocent, and innocent for lack of evidence:

The collegial panel shall conduct its deliberations and, on the basis of the established facts and evidence and in accordance with the provisions of relevant laws, render one of the following judgments:

(1) if the facts of a case are clear, the evidence is reliable and sufficient, and the defendant is found guilty in accordance with law, he shall be pronounced guilty accordingly;

(2) if the defendant is found innocent in accordance with law, he shall be pronounced innocent accordingly;

(3) if the evidence is insufficient and thus the defendant cannot be found guilty, he shall be pronounced innocent accordingly on account of the fact that the evidence is insufficient and the accusation unfounded. (CPL Art. 162)

Judgments are to be made in writing (CPL Arts. 163 and 164). Appeals (referred to as "procedures of the second instance") to the next highest level of People's Court are allowed as a matter of right (CPL Art. 180 *et seq.*).

Revisions to the Criminal Procedure Law in 1996[32] and again in 2012 reflect efforts to improve the criminal justice system in response both to international criticisms and to domestic pressures. Revisions to the Criminal Procedure Law not only dispensed with unregulated administrative detention measures, but also did away with many provisions of the 1980 law that were seen as improperly strengthening the power of the prosecution at the expense of defendants' rights. Criminal defense counsel were granted earlier access to prosecution evidence. The determination of criminal liability was reserved exclusively for the courts, thus doing away with the Procuracy's previous powers to determine guilt or innocence. The revisions also impose on prosecutors the burden to produce reliable and ample (*queshi, chongfen*) evidence of the guilt of the accused – a far cry from the "presumption of innocence" trumpeted by some optimistic observers, but a significant step nonetheless.[33]

Clarity in judicial decision making on criminal cases was underscored by the Supreme People's Court in its Interpretation on the Criminal Procedure Law, which also included the possibility of a verdict of acquittal for lack of evidence, along with conventional verdicts on guilt and innocence:[34]

Article 176: The People's Court shall render a verdict depending on actual conditions of the case.

1. In cases where the accused is found guilty as prosecuted on the basis of facts being clear and evidence being objective and sufficient in accordance with the law, a guilty verdict shall be rendered.
2. In cases where the accused is found guilty as prosecuted on the basis of facts being clear and evidence being reliable and sufficient, the offence that he has been prosecuted for is different from that ascertained in the trial of the People's Court, a guilty verdict shall be rendered.
3. In cases where the accused is found innocent on the basis of facts being clear and evidence being reliable and sufficient in accordance with the law, a guiltless verdict shall be rendered.
4. In cases where a charge of crime fails due to insufficient evidence to affirm that the accused is guilty as prosecuted, the accused shall be acquitted for lack of evidence.
5. In cases where facts of the case are partly clear and evidence is reliable and sufficient, a guiltless or guilty verdict should be rendered legally with doubtful charges of crime and unreliable evidence rejected legally.

This did not necessarily ensure procedural rigor in the criminal process, however, as the Supreme Court Interpretation allowed criminal convictions for acts for which the defendant is not charged, but which are punishable under other provisions of Criminal Law.

While many have noted the weaknesses of China's criminal justice system in practice,[35] China has faced particular criticism for the use of criminal law for political purposes. Dissident intellectual Liu Xiaobo was imprisoned for his role in the drafting and distribution of the human rights manifesto "Charter 08," and was sentenced to 11 years' imprisonment after a closed trial.[36] The challenge posed by Charter 08 for the regime is made even more intense by Liu Xiaobo's conduct throughout his trial and imprisonment, where he adopted the bearing of a patriotic critic of an unjust regime.[37]

The award of the Nobel Peace Prize to Liu in October 2010 did little to dampen the government's hostility to Liu and Charter 08. The government attempted to intimidate the Nobel Prize Committee prior to the award being announced, and after the award was announced, Beijing termed it a desecration and aired all manner of bullying criticism against the award. After the prize was announced, the government started rounding up associates of Liu Xiaobo and blocked his family and colleagues in China from attending the award ceremony.

The question of public trials and the application of the Criminal Procedure Law to foreign-related matters have also been troublesome, such as in the Stern Hu/Rio Tinto case involving charges of corruption around the awarding and pricing of supply contracts for iron ore. Stern Hu, an Australian citizen, and three other Rio Tinto employees were subjected to a closed trial at which diplomatic representatives from Australia were excluded.[38] In 2012, politically sensitive trials of Wang Lijun and Bogu Kailai reflected the extent to which application of the Criminal Procedure Law is often modified accordingly to Party dictates.[39]

B. *Administrative measures*

The Criminal Law allows for non-criminal punishment for acts where "the circumstances are clearly minor and the harm is not great" (Art.

13), thus allowing for administrative punishments. Achieving political stability through administrative measures includes the role of administrative detention.[40] Emerging from a tradition of extra-judicial and often politicized detention of class enemies under the Maoist system, China's administrative detention system is aimed at achieving efficiencies in the punishment of minor offenses. The Criminal Law of the PRC permits administrative detention to be imposed in lieu of criminal sanctions where the circumstances of a person's crimes were deemed to be minor and not requiring criminal punishment (Art. 37). Often, however, this results in the diminution of procedural protections for defendants.

Under the Regulations of the PRC on Security Administration and Punishment (1957, rev. 1986, rev. 1994), administrative detention was commonly applied against individuals who committed acts not considered serious enough to constitute criminal offenses. The more severe administrative system for "reform through labor" (*laogai*) involves what many have described as a prison camp system, but which is described by Chinese authorities as an effort to change criminals through persuasion.[41] China's "re-education through labor" (*laojiao* or RETL) was established pursuant to regulations issued by the State Council in 1957, which were continued under new rules enacted in 1979 and again in 1982.[42] The Ministry of Justice, "Detailed Regulations on Administration of Education Through Labor" (1992) provide further detail on implementation and structure of the RETL system. Following the 18th CPC Congress in 2012, calls for the abolition of the RETL system raised hopes that this legacy of the Mao era would finally be put to rest.

The administrative punishment system generally denies offenders whatever protections might have been available under the formal criminal justice system, such as relative certainty of sentencing. Under the re-education and reform through labor systems, those whose terms had expired could be detained for longer periods if they were without employment or had served their sentences in sparsely popu-lated areas and were needed in the area.[43] In addition, the process of "shelter for investigation" (*shourong shencha*) authorized discretionary arrest and detention of suspicious individuals with little if any legal restrictions imposed. With revisions to the Criminal Procedure Law in 1996, "shelter and investigation" was nominally eliminated, although many of the flexible provisions of the process were incorpo-rated into the revised statute.[44] Related to "shelter for investigation" is the process of "shelter for repatriation" (*shourong qiansong*) by which people lacking local registration documents are detained pending return to their registered places of residence. The death in custody of Sun Zhigang, a college-educated office worker, prompted widespread criticism of the practice of "shelter for repatriation," which was abol-ished in 2003.[45]

The Administrative Punishment Law (1996) was intended to unify the procedures for administrative organs imposing penalties ranging from fines to detention in response to legal and regulatory violations. Rather than simply displacing prior regulations on administrative pen-alties, the new law provides only that prior provisions incongruous with the new law should be revised by December 31, 1997. Despite these reforms, however, administrative detention remains a common instrument for political repression against religious adherents, political dissidents, and minority activists, which is often imposed without any legal sanction.

In sum, social control remains a high priority for the PRC regime. Motivated in part by the need to maintain stability as a precondition for economic growth and reflecting the lessons of the past when politi-cal divisions led to a breakdown in the institutions of governance, the PRC regime has come to rely heavily on the institutions of criminal justice and administrative detention to punish offenders and deter others. While the greater institutionalization of social controls reflects important developments toward a more rules-based system of governance, the control that the Party/State exerts over the content of law and its application tends to minimize whatever rights protections might be embedded therein. The abuse of the criminal justice system for political purposes – whether in the case of suppression of political dissidents such as Liu Xiaobo, or other targets (minorities and religious adherents, for example) – tends to undermine the legitimacy of the system as a whole. Nonetheless, China's mechanisms for maintaining political stability continue to develop along the lines of formal institutionalization. In comparison with the excesses of the Maoist period of political mobilization and class struggle, this is a marked change. Much more will be needed before a truly rights-based system emerges.

SUMMARY

Following the upheaval of the Cultural Revolution, China's leaders embarked on a complex process of legal reform aimed at providing institutions and rules for implementation of the policies of the Party/State, particularly around economic development and political stability. Resurrecting a constitutional structure established in 1954, the PRC regime used formal legal rules and institutions to articulate and protect the authority of legislative institutions (such as the NPC), administrative agencies (such as the ministries under the State Council), and judicial institutions (such as the courts). As an instrument of building political stability, PRC criminal law and procedure has served to protect the Party/State's legitimate monopoly on the use of force, while also providing a modicum, inadequate perhaps but improving, level of procedural protections for criminal defendants. Administrative detention remains an important mechanism for ensuring control over society and while many of the most egregious abuses have been curtailed, the potential for misuse remains. While the pursuit of stability resonates with many people in China – particularly those who experienced the Cultural Revolution – the purpose of stability remains to protect the power and privileges of the ruling Party/State. Nonetheless, the emergence of law and legal institutions as a fully legitimate mechanism for governance has opened new avenues for participation by an ever-widening proportion of society.

DISCUSSION QUESTIONS

1. How do the Four Basic Principles influence legal rights in China?

2. How does the legislative process reflect the relationship between law and policy in China?

3. What is the role of administrative agencies in policy and law making in China?

4. How does the PRC legal regime operate to ensure social control by the Party/State?

SUGGESTIONS FOR FURTHER READING

Amnesty International Country Report – China (2009) (http://report2009.amnesty.org/en/regions/asia-pacific/china).

China Quarterly, "Developments in Chinese Law: The Past Ten Years" (2007).

Columbia Journal of Asian Law, "Special Issue: Celebrating the Work of Stanley Lubman," vol. 19, no. 1 (Spring–Fall 2005), pp. 1–29.

Congressional-Executive Commission on China, *2011 Annual Report* (http://www.cecc.gov/pages/annualRpt/annualRpt11/AR2011final.pdf).

Fu Hualing and Richard Cullen, "Weiquan (Rights Protection) lawyering in an authoritarian state: toward critical lawyering," *The China Journal*, vol. 59, no. 111 (2008) http://papers.ssrn.com/so13/papers.cfm?abstract_id=1083925 (accessed October 31, 2012).

Human Rights Watch, "World Report 2012 – China" (http://www.hrw.org/world-report-2012/world-report-2012-china).

Beginning with the 3rd Plenum of the 11th CPC Central Committee in 1978, the PRC Party/State has pursued policy imperatives of strengthening China's economy, supported by ideological conclusions about the decline of class struggle and the importance of strengthening the forces of production. The PRC legal system has been directed in large part toward supporting this process. Understanding the role of law in supporting economic prosperity in China involves developing an appreciation for contending approaches to law and development as well as building knowledge about specific aspects of China's legal and regulatory regimes for contracts, property, and other dimensions of economic regulation. Local conditions for economic life are an essential context for the application of legal regulation.

I. LOCAL CONDITIONS AND PRACTICES

The role of law in supporting economic prosperity depends significantly on local features of China's economy. Two important characteristics of China's economy have been described in terms of "corporatism"[1] and "clientelism."[2] Corporatism involves a situation of shared interests and cooperative relations between regulatory officials and economic actors, while clientelism speaks to the dynamic of personal relationships between patrons and clients as the dominant feature of economic and social organization. These dynamics have important implications for China's legal system. The use of law in managing the economy is directed primarily at protection and promotion of particu-lar relationships and interests – either systemic (corporatist) or per-sonal (clientelist). Thus, organizational and personal relationships tend to determine conditions of regulatory enforcement. While the legal system remains instrumentalist, in the sense of being an instrument for achieving policy goals, its operation remains dependent on relation-ships among individuals operating within the system. Economic policy directives may inform legal protections for private contract and prop-erty rights and support for autonomous business relations, but consist-ent enforcement depends on relational priorities (organizational, personal, and otherwise) of the Party/State and its members.

This begs the question whether law is the most effective mechanism for building economic growth through mechanisms for predictability and risk management. In the absence of empirical data, observers of law and development in China and elsewhere should be cautious about expecting causal relationships between formal legal institutions and economic growth. Common occurrence does not necessarily mean causal occurrence. The Chinese tradition has often been characterized as involving informal obligations to a greater extent than formal legal requirements.[3] This suggests that informal relationships (*guanxi*) may be more effective in lending predictability and reducing risk and com-mercial transactions than formal legal arrangements, and indeed the pervasive role of *guanxi* in contemporary China tends to confirm this.[4] Nonetheless, as indicated by the legal development programs of many European and North American governments, investments in China's legal development have been justified by reference to expectations about economic development and political reform.[5]

II. APPROACHES TO LAW AND DEVELOPMENT

The post-Mao development of China's commercial legal system also involves questions about contending approaches to law and development[6] and the application of conflicting regulatory models drawn from abroad. Recall that during the reform period of the late nineteenth century, the abiding issue for intellectuals in China was the question of which technologies from the West could be used in China while still preserving the essence of Chinese culture and values (the so-called *ti-yong* debates). China's effort to build legal norms and structures supporting economic development echo the *ti-yong* dilemma facing reformers of years past.

Approaches to economic development that focus on the need for equitable distribution of resources and income are often associated with Marxist and neo-Marxist discourses,[7] and were more or less the norm in PRC policy prior to the post-Mao legal reform effort that began in 1978. While Marxist ideology accepts the potential for law to further economic development,[8] attention to equity and class relations remains a key focus. This dimension is reinforced through the discourse of "dependency theory," a perspective suggesting that elites in developing economies protect their own privileged status while also entrenching the subordinate position of their national economies by importing legal and economic institutions associated with the developed West.[9]

China's engagement with international regulatory standards also involves consideration of neo-classical approaches to economic development that tend to give primacy to dynamics of accumulation and consumption.[10] Much of the rationale underlying commercial legal regimes of contract and property in Europe and North America, from which China has borrowed liberally in developing its own legal system since 1978, concerns the role of law in strengthening predictability and reducing risk in autonomous commercial transactions.[11]

As we have seen in the context of constitutional change and political authority, the tension between developing relations of production and forces of production has been a key ideological issue for the PRC Party/State with important policy consequences. Contending priorities around the relations and forces of production also have an impact on the role of law and regulation in managing the economy. Attention to relations of production has been expressed in part through legal and regulatory provisions ensuring that economic transactions remain subject to the ideological and policy priorities of the Party/State. Attention to developing the forces of production is expressed in part through legal and regulatory approaches aimed at facilitating increasingly autonomous economic transactions.

The contest between relations and forces of production is often reflected in the relationship between "economic law" and "civil law" models of legal regulation. The "economic law" discourse in China owes much to the jurisprudence of Evgeny Pashukanis, a Soviet jurist who posited the notion that law could serve as an instrument for control over the economy by the Party/State.[12] In this view, law represented the formalization of policy, thus at once empowering the state to regulate economic behavior while also limiting the discretion of state officials. While Pashukanis' theories were discredited in the USSR and he was executed under Stalin, his conceptions had significant influence on the development of socialist law in China. The economic law discourse involves primarily, if not exclusively, a vertical hierarchical relationship between the Party/State and the society/economy. Under this approach economic policy is determined by the Party/State and then formulated into legal rules for matters such as contracts and property. Economic law too serves as an instrument for controlling economic actors, who have little if any autonomy in the conduct of their commercial affairs. This suited the needs of the planned economy in Maoist China.

Supporting autonomous private transactions in the economy has often been expressed through the discourse of civil law. In contrast to the economic law discourse, the discourse of civil law posits a facilitative role for law in support of relatively autonomous social and economic interactions.[13] Civil law serves as an instrument for policy implementation by the Party/State, but would be deployed in support of policies affording economic actors greater autonomy to manage their affairs. The tension between the discourses of the economic law and civil law in the development of the PRC legal system has been particularly evident in China's contract and property law regimes.

III. SUPPORT FOR DEVELOPMENT: CONTRACT AND PROPERTY LAW

In keeping with the policy instrumentalism that characterizes law in the PRC, law serves as an important mechanism for achieving policy goals of development through protection of contract and property relationships. In many ways these are the foundation for most economic activity – contract law imposing standards on the formation and performance of agreements around market activities; property law imposing standards on relationships between market actors in respect to things, land, ideas, and business interests.

A. Contract law

Following the policy decisions to embark on economic reforms through greater reliance on market forces, China has given considerable attention to developing contract laws to support domestic and foreign business activities. The Economic Contract Law (ECL) was enacted in 1981 for domestic transactions, providing limited rights for transacting parties but still subjecting contracts to the requirements of state planning.[14] Enacted largely in response to pressures of the international business environment, the 1985 Foreign Economic Contract Law (FECL) offered contracting parties broader freedom to determine issues such as which laws will govern interpretation and enforcement of contracts and which institutions and rules will apply in the course of dispute resolution.[15] This signaled a partial resolution to various ideological and policy debates around the application of liberal notions of contract autonomy and socialist principles of state control. Nonetheless, the FECL still affirmed the authority of regulatory agencies to impose contract approval requirements and imposed catch-all proscriptions against contracts deemed in violation of State and social interests. Under both the ECL and FECL, contract validity depended on whether the parties had the requisite administrative approvals to engage in the contracted transaction and on whether state agencies approved of the transaction.[16]

While the ECL and the FECL embodied a state-centric approach to contract under the rubric of "economic law," the 1986 General Principles of Civil Law (GPCL) reflected a more facilitating approach to contract transactions under the rubric of "civil law."[17] The GPCL codified a number of important contract principles, including ideals of party equality and autonomy and principles of private compensation for non-performance:

Article 3: Parties to a civil activity shall have equal status.

Article 4: In civil activities, the principles of voluntariness, fairness, making compensation for equal value, honesty and credibility shall be observed.

Article 5: The lawful civil rights and interests of citizens and legal persons shall be protected by law; no organization or individual may infringe upon them.

Yet the General Principles also include provisions protecting the power of State interests and policies:

Article 6: Civil activities must be in compliance with the law; where there are no relevant provisions in the law, they shall be in compliance with State policies.

Article 7: Civil activities shall have respect for social ethics and shall not harm the public interest, undermine State economic plans or disrupt social economic order.

This tension between regulation and facilitation tended to run parallel to debates over the respective roles of state planning and the market as the policy foundations for economic activities.

A new comprehensive Contract Law of the PRC (UCL) was enacted in 1999. The UCL echoed many of the provisions of the still-effective GPCL, while also harmonizing provisions in the ECL and FECL, which were replaced by the UCL. The UCL also incorporated some provisions of China's Technology Contracts Law that had applied to technology transfers by Chinese units operating within China. The UCL echoed policy tensions between private rights and state control that had been evident in the ECL and the GPCL, while also under-scoring prior themes of equality of the parties, compliance with law, and enforcement of contract obligations:

Article 1 Purpose: This Law is formulated in order to protect the lawful rights and interests of contract parties, to safeguard social and economic order, and to promote socialist modernization.

Article 3 Equal Standing of Parties: Contract parties enjoy equal legal standing and neither party may impose its will on the other party.

Article 4 Right to Enter into Contract Voluntarily: A party is entitled to enter into a contract voluntarily under the law, and no entity or individual may unlawfully interfere with such right.

Article 7 Legality: In concluding or performing a contract, the parties shall abide by the relevant laws and administrative regulations, as well as observe social ethics, and may not disrupt social and economic order or harm the public interests.

Article 8 Binding Effect: Legal Protection: A lawfully formed contract is legally binding on the parties. The parties shall perform their respective obligations in accordance with the contract, and neither party may arbitrarily amend or terminate the contract. A lawfully formed contract is protected by law.

The UCL is divided into General Principles (Chapters 1–8) and Specific Provisions (Chapters 9–23). The General Principles section combines approaches reflecting foreign legal principles with regulatory norms inherent to China's socialist legal system. The section on Specific Provisions addresses various different types of contracts, and applies in the absence of contrary provisions either in the contracts themselves, or in other laws and regulations. While the UCL reflects a general orientation toward greater contract autonomy and market orientation in economic life, debates over policy and practice continued to affect implementation.

1. Policy Compromise

Compromise between principles of contract autonomy and state control are particularly evident in the UCL's "General Provisions" (Arts. 1–8), which support the "lawful rights and interests of contract parties" as well as goals to "preserve social and economic order and promote socialist modernization" (UCL Art. 1). Protecting "rights" and "interests" involves a distinction between legal rights that are granted in law and the operational interests of particular legal actors, which in turn are qualified by policy goals of preserving social and economic order. UCL Article 7 for example, includes prohibitions against disrupting social and economic order and undermining the public interests of society along with provisions on compliance with applicable law and regulation, while Article 52(5) invalidates contracts deemed in violation of law or administrative regulations.[18]

The UCL appears to resolve a long-standing policy debate over whether contracts represent an economic or a civil law relationship, in other words whether contract law is an exercise in state direction over the economic transactions or an exercise in state facilitation of private relationships among economic actors. Article 2 of the UCL provides that contacts are agreements that establish, modify, and terminate civil rights. This orientation toward a civil law model of contracts is underscored by provisions on equality of contracting parties (UCL Art. 3) and non-interference by outside parties (UCL Art. 4). Yet the economic law model is also present, as contracting parties must still comply with laws and administrative regulations even where these permit State agencies to intervene in contract formation and performance.

Policy compromises are also evident in provisions on administration, choice of law, dispute resolution, and various gap-filling measures in Chapter 8 (Ancillary Provisions, Arts. 123–129). Thus, the UCL requires that contract provisions in other laws must be observed (UCL Art. 123). Thus, provisions of other laws will govern even where in conflict with those of the UCL. These provisions ensure that the wealth of PRC law and regulation related to contracts will remain in force.[19]

2. Interpretation and Application

Chapter 8 of the UCL provides for interpretation of contracts according to factors such as contract language; pertinent contract terms, purposes of the contract, business practice, and the principles of honesty and good faith (UCL Art. 125).

The Ancillary Provisions modify provisions from the ECL and FECL on choice of law (UCL Art. 126). Contracts formed pursuant to the ECL had been governed and interpreted according to Chinese law. Under the FECL, however, parties to foreign-related contracts were permitted to choose the law used to interpret their agreements in cases of dispute, except in cases of equity and cooperative joint venture contracts and contracts for the exploration and exploitation of natural resources. The FECL provisions on choice of law were included in the UCL, but the exception for foreign investment and natural resource contracts was narrowed somewhat by the provision that Chinese law must be selected to govern these contracts where performed within the territory of the PRC. This permits foreign law to govern joint venture and natural resource contracts performed outside of China. On the other hand, there is a further provision in the UCL that was not contained in the FECL to the effect that the parties' choice of law might otherwise be restricted by Chinese law. While the FECL required compliance with general laws and regulations of the PRC, the new UCL raises explicitly the possibility that laws may be enacted or interpreted so as to preclude or limit choice of law by the contracting parties. Article 126 states further that in the absence of party selection, the national law of the jurisdiction most closely related to the contract will apply. Article 128 also carries forward provisions of the FECL permitting contract parties to foreign-related contracts to select the method and forum for resolving disputes.

Contracts may take oral, written or other forms (UCL Art. 10), although in many instances such as foreign trade and investment contracts, the use of a written form will be required by other laws and regulations. Formation of contracts is based on offer and acceptance by the parties (UCL Art. 13), an offer being defined as an expression of interest that is detailed, clearly stated and to which the offeror is bound upon acceptance by the offeree. Acceptance of an offer requires an expression of interest by the offeree, without the requirements for detail and clarity required for the original offer itself (UCL Art. 21). Once acceptance is made, the contract is formed. Acceptance is effective generally upon receipt by the offeror. Lawfully concluded contracts are effective upon conclusion (Art. 44). In a modification of past practice (FECL Art. 7), conclusion of contracts is not delayed until completion of formalities of approval and registration where required by law and administrative regulations. Under the earlier ECL and FECL contract laws, administrative approvals were a requirement for formation of contract, and as a result the parties were often unsure of their legal rights and obligations during the approval process, which often extended for considerable lengths of time. Instead, the new law simply provides that such formalities should be followed:

> Article 44 *Effectiveness of Contract*: A lawfully formed contract becomes effective upon its formation. Where effectiveness of a contract is subject to any procedure such as approval or registration, etc. as required by a relevant law or administrative regulation, such provision applies.

In its first interpretation of the UCL, the Supreme People's Court reiterated this principle:[20]

> In accordance with Paragraph 2 of Article 44 of the Contract Law, where the relevant laws or administrative regulations specify that approval formalities are required for a contract, or approval and registration formalities are required for the effectiveness of a contract, and the parties concerned fail to go through the relevant approval formalities or relevant approval and registration formalities prior to the completion of court debate in the first instance, a people's court shall rule that the contract has not taken effect; if the relevant laws or administrative regulations specify that approval formalities are required for a contract, but without requiring the contract to be registered in order to be effective, failure of the parties concerned to go through registration formalities shall not affect the effectiveness of the contract, provided

that such failure constitutes an impediment to the transfer of ownership or other real rights of the subject matter of the contract.

Thus, the absence of contract approval will not necessarily relieve the
parties of their contractual obligations unless and until the contract is
declared invalid.[21]

While the provisions in the new law on contract formation and
effect give significant attention to the wishes of the parties, there are a
number of exceptions. The principles of freedom of contract are limited
by provisions of the new law governing the effectiveness of contracts.
Under the following circumstances, contracts will be invalid (UCL
Art. 52):

- where one party has concluded a contract through fraud or coercion, which damages State interests;
- where there is malicious collusion, damaging State, collective or
  third party interests;
- where legal means are used to conceal illegal purposes;
- where the public welfare of society is violated; and
- where mandatory provisions of law or administrative regulations
  have been violated.

While the factors of illegal purpose, public welfare, and violation of
law and regulation are unqualified grounds for invalidity of contract,
interpretation of these terms remains ongoing and uncertain. Provisions
of Article 52(5) on contracts being invalid for violation of law and
administrative regulations augment provisions on legality in UCL
Article 7.

Parties are authorized under the law to seek judicial intervention to
modify or revoke contracts in cases of misunderstanding, obvious
unfairness, or where fraud, coercion, or threats are used to induce a
party to conclude a contract that violates honest intentions (UCL Art.

54), thus offering equitable relief to offset the legal effect of formal offer and acceptance. The Supreme People's Court's 2nd Interpretation of the UCL[22] clarifies that unforeseeable changed circumstances may be grounds for seeking judicial amendment or termination of a contract under conditions of manifest unfairness that fall outside the bounds of *force majeure* or commercial risk. Contracts that are deemed invalid or revoked are treated as never having come into effect.

B. Property law

Whereas contract law as it relates to economic development tends to regulate agreements between economic actors about future behavior, property law tends to regulate claims by economic actors to various things, land, ideas, business interests, and so on. Property law concerns not so much the items of property themselves, as the relationships between economic actors about property. Property law in China reflects many of the same policy conflicts between state control and party autonomy that are evident in China's contract law. While the economic reform policies enacted beginning in 1978 and accelerating after 1992 allowed economic enterprises increased autonomy in management and decision making, doctrinal norms continued to emphasize the importance of State interests in the enforcement of property relations. Although the 1982 Constitution extended protection to "lawful property," this allowed the State to make final determinations as to what property rights and relationships would be protected. General constitutional requirements that conditioned the exercise of citizens' rights, including the right to own property, on upholding lawful duties (Constitution, Art. 33), ensured that property claims would not be permitted to conflict with the State or social interests.

Property rights were recognized in the 1986 General Principles of Civil Law (GPCL). Efforts to draft a Civil Code for the PRC had begun during the 1950s but were halted as a result of the "Anti-Rightist

Campaign" of 1958. Efforts were resumed in the early 1960s but came to an end with the political upheavals leading to the Cultural Revolution. Beginning in 1979, the drafting effort was resumed with the establishment of a drafting group that produced its 4th draft in 1982 (coinciding with the revisions to the PRC Constitution). The GPCL was enacted in 1986, reportedly encouraged by CPC Politburo politics and law chair Peng Zhen after his return from Japan where he had been told by a local business association that the absence of a Civil Code was discouraging Japanese investment into China. Subject to general limitations on the need to protect social interests and State plans, the GPCL recognized "legitimate rights and interests" in land, intellectual property, and personal property. The GPCL also contained provisions recognizing the property rights of creditors resulting from contract obligations, highlighting the tension between the economic law dynamics of contracts at the time and the civil law character of the GPCL.

1. Forms of Property Regulation

Protection of property rights was supported by provisions in the GPCL and expanded through specific regulatory regimes for different kinds of property. The continuing role of the state is evident in many areas of property rights, but the examples of land, intellectual property, and corporate property are particularly instructive.

Land. Private ownership of land in not permitted in the PRC. The Constitution of the PRC provides that urban land is owned by the State and rural land by the "collective" (Art. 10). As a result, issues around land rights in China concern the right to use, rather than ownership. Following the highly restrictive policies of the Maoist period, the reforms associated with Deng Xiaoping saw important changes in land policy and law. The 1986 Land Administration Law underscored constitutional principles of public ownership of land, and clarified institutional and jurisdictional arrangements for land administration.

In rural areas, agricultural reform policies have emphasized ideals of collective ownership. The revised Land Administration Law (1999) stressed the importance of socialist public ownership of arable land, such that property rights in land remained limited to land-use rights rather than ownership. Ownership of land by the collective raises questions as to who has authority to make decisions on behalf of the collective and its members, and the procedures related to such decisions. The Rural Land Contracting Law (2002) authorized limited transfers by farmer households of land-use rights received under the so-called "household responsibility system," by which farmer families pursued agricultural and sideline production activities on land assigned to them by the local authorities. Local government approval is required for such secondary transfers, and principles of lawfulness, compensation, and voluntariness that had been included in prior regulations must still be respected.

In an effort to curb local officials from infringing on farmers' land rights by expropriation or by imposed transfers, the Land Administration Law was amended yet again in 2004 to underscore the State's duty to compensate land users for changes to their land-use rights. The Ministry of Agriculture issued new regulations in 2005 containing standards for transfers of land-use contract rights and established "rural land contracting administration agencies" to provide regulatory oversight. The Supreme People's Court's 2005 interpretation on rural land contracting disputes supported adjudication of farmers' legal rights in land contracting, thus bringing judicial institutions to bear on the contested policy issues of public and private rights to land use. A rural land disputes mediation and arbitration mechanism went into effect in 2007, although its effectiveness in resolving conflicts over rural land rights remains uncertain. In October 2008, the 17th CPC National Congress approved a rural reform package that removed the government approval requirements for certain land-use rights transfers.

State ownership of urban land is clearly defined in the Constitution and renders most land-use issues a matter of administrative process. Changing rights to urban land use have been supported by revisions made in 1988 to the PRC Constitution and by the Land Administration Law, which permitted broader land-use rights to be conveyed to private entities. In 1990, China enacted regulations permitting businesses to take long-term interests in land for the purpose of sub-division and development. Local governments began enacting implementing regulations for their own real property markets. China's Law on Urban Real Estate was enacted in 1994, in an effort to expand the possibilities of both private acquisition and management of land-use rights.

The authority of the Land Administration Bureau extends to regulating the range of public and private uses of urban land. China's real estate market has been concentrated primarily in the urban areas and fuelled by constitutional provisions supporting private ownership of buildings and other improvements. While there are few if any debates as to who owns the underlying land, controversies emerge regularly on the regulation of associated buildings and improvements. A particularly sensitive issue has been the question of expropriation of land, either for directly public purposes, such as parks and public buildings, or for private purposes like condominium towers secured through government approvals. Despite provisions in the Constitution and in the General Principles of Civil Law providing rights to compensation, disputes and protests over compensation levels and even the State's authority to expropriate have been common. Several cities, including Beijing and Shanghai, have enacted regulations on expropriation procedures and compensation levels in an effort to manage the issue.

China's rules on land-use tenure continue to undergo significant change. Individuals and groups can secure land-use rights for specified purposes and for specified periods of duration (both of which restrictions remain somewhat flexible).

Problems of corruption and mismanagement, as well as the unregulated conversion of agricultural land to residential purposes (often with the complicity of, and for the profit of, local officials) have led to efforts at reform. In rural areas, land-use issues have come particularly to the fore as development and urbanization efforts intrude on local agricultural communities. While full privatization of land use and land ownership seems unlikely at present, proposals in this direction continue.

Intellectual Property Rights. Rights to intellectual property are emblematic of changing ideas about property rights in knowledge. China's approach to intellectual property rights (IPR) reflects not only the influence of foreign governments and businesses in encouraging China to develop an IPR system, but also the continued dominance of the state in constructing and enforcing property relations. The General Principles of Civil Law (1986) had recognized early on the rights of individuals and legal persons to hold ownership of copyrights, patents, and trademarks. China has also promulgated an impressive array of laws and regulations on intellectual property. Principal legislation includes the Trademark Law (1982, rev. 1993, rev. 2001), Patent Law (1984, rev. 1992, rev. 2000), Copyright Law (1991, 2001), and a Law Against Unfair Competition (1993) protecting trade secrets. China has also joined various international conventions on intellectual property, including the World Intellectual Property Organization convention (1980), the Paris Convention for the Protection of Industrial Property (1984), the Berne Convention for the Protection of Literary and Artistic Works (1992), and the Universal Copyright Convention (1992). In furtherance of its obligations under the WTO Agreement on Trade-Related Aspects of Intellectual Property Rights (TRIPs Agreement), China agreed to strengthen its IPR protection system.

The scope of protection for patents extends to (a) *inventions*, defined as a "new technical solution relating to product, process or improvement thereof;" (b) *utility models*, defined as a "new technical solution relating to share, structure or combination which is fit for practical use;" and (c) *industrial designs*, defined as a "new design of the share, pattern, color or combination of a product, which creates aesthetic feeling and is fit for industrial application." Revisions to the PRC Patent Law and associated regulations were made in 2000 and 2001 in part to comply with the requirements of China's accession to the World Trade Organization. These revisions extended patent protection to chemical formulas, pharmaceuticals, food and beverages, diagnostic procedures, "scientific discoveries," as well as so-called "work for hire" and joint inventions by individuals. The revisions also imposed a duty of confidentiality on China's patent agency and allowed for injunctive relief to be imposed against alleged patent infringers prior to a final administrative or judicial determination on the infringement.

The duration of patent protection is 20 years for inventions and 10 years for utility models and industrial designs. Patent registrations are filed with the China Intellectual Property Office and are subject to processes of filing, public notification, and a period during which contending patent holders can file objections. Foreign patents are protected under a "right of priority" system authorized under the World Intellectual Property Organization (WIPO), which allows patents filed abroad to retain priority in China for 12 months for patents and 6 months for utility models and industrial designs pending registration of the patent in China. China's participation in the "Patent Cooperation Treaty" imposes further registration requirements on foreign patent owners as a condition for protection. Enforcement of patent rights is available through the administrative processes of the China Intellectual Property Office, which generally oversees a negotiated solution or administrative arbitration. Complaints over alleged patent infringement may also be filed with the intellectual property chambers of the

People's Courts. Patent holders who claim unlawful infringement may obtain injunctive relief pending the outcome of their enforcement litigation.

Under the PRC Trademark Law and its Implementing Regulations (2001), trademarks and trade names are protected through a registration system based on the WIPO's 1957 Nice Agreement Concerning the International Classification of Goods and Services. Trademark registrations are made in connection with 34 specified categories of goods and 11 specified categories of services. Thus a trademark registered for footwear would not be protected against a competing trademark registered for headwear. Trademark registration is valid for 10 years and is renewable. Unlike the United States, China follows a "first-to-file" system for trademark protection. Certain images such as national symbols cannot be trademarked.

After an application for registration is filed, competing trademark holders may file notice and protest within a three-month comment period. Foreign registered trademarks are given "right of priority" under the WIPO system. Enforcement is available through the administrative processes of the China Intellectual Property Office and through litigation in the People's Courts. Similarly with the patent system, China's Trademark Law and its Implementing Regulations were revised in 2000/2001 to comply with WTO requirements and expanded protection provisions to include "well-known marks" and to provide stronger compensation and injunctive relief.

Copyright protection is subject to the provisions of the PRC Authorship Rights Law (1990, 2001, rev. 2010) and its Implementing Regulations (2001). Authorship rights extend to authors, translators, compilers, and employees. The scope of coverage includes literature, art, and technical writing, and also extends to protection of computer software. Duration of protection is generally life of the author plus 50 years. Foreign works are protected under provisions of the Berne Copyright Convention. Enforcement is subject to the administrative processes of the National Copyright Administration and also may be pursued through litigation in the People's Courts.

Despite the work of a few courageous judges,[23] however, enforcement of intellectual property rights in China generally remains problematic. Despite periodic public campaigns to improve IPR enforcement, an observed "epidemic" of pervasive intellectual property violations continues. Despite repeated assurances that China will finally begin to enforce rigorously intellectual property rights, the lengthy pattern of non-enforcement raises troubling questions about China's commitment and capacity to comply with WTO disciplines.[24]

Corporate Property. Property rights also extend to questions around the status and performance of corporations. Beginning in the late 1980s and gathering momentum with the establishment of securities exchanges at Shanghai and Shenzhen, efforts to build a legal framework for securities regulation were fraught with conflicts over policy goals. Securities regulation in the PRC gradually extended to the national level in 1992–3, with enactment of uniform standards for the issue and trading of stock. These standards were formalized yet further in the Company Law (1993, rev. 2006) and the Securities Law (1998, rev. 2005). The Company Law was "formulated for the purposes of regulating the organization and operation of companies, protecting the legitimate rights and interests of companies, shareholders and creditors, maintaining the socialist economic order, and promoting the development of the socialist market economy" (Art. 1).[25] Specific attention is given in the law to questions of legal compliance, as well as the responsibilities of shareholders and directors to attend to priorities of social morality, good faith, and social responsibility. Various fiduciary duties of shareholders and directors are also noted:

Article 5: When undertaking business operations, a company shall comply with the laws and administrative regulations, social morality and business morality. It shall act in good faith, accept the supervision of the government and the general public, and bear social responsibilities. The legitimate rights and interests of a company shall be protected by laws and may not be infringed.

. . .

Article 20: The shareholders of a company shall comply with the laws, administrative regulations and articles of association, and shall exercise the shareholder's rights according to law. None of them may injure any of the interests of the company or of other shareholders by abusing the shareholder's rights, or injure the interests of any creditor of the company by abusing the independent status of juridical person or the shareholder's limited liabilities.

. . .

Article 21: Neither the controlling shareholder, nor the actual controller, any of the directors, supervisors or senior managers of the company may injure the interests of the company by taking advantage of its connection relationship. Anyone who has caused any loss to the company due to violation of the preceding paragraph shall be subject to compensation.

The Securities Law was "enacted in order to standardize the issuing and trading of securities, protect the lawful rights and interests of investors, safeguard the economic order and public interests of society and promote the development of the socialist market economy (Art. 1).[26] Particular attention is given to regulation of the issue and trading of securities, emphasizing principles of voluntariness and good faith, as well as the imperative to avoid abusive practices such as insider dealings:

Article 3: Securities shall be issued and traded in line with the principles of openness, fairness and equitability.

Article 4: The parties involved in the issuing and trading of securities shall have equal legal status and adhere to the principles of voluntariness, compensation and good faith.

Article 5: Securities shall be issued and traded in accordance with laws and administrative regulations. Fraudulent and insider trading and manipulation of the securities trading market are prohibited.

China's securities regulatory apparatus reflects an ongoing commitment to maintaining state control over corporate property through processes of approval, registration, and oversight of securities dealers and underwriters.

Both the Company Law and the Securities Law accord to state agencies, particularly the China Securities Regulatory Commission, supervisory authority over securities and securities markets. China's reassertion of sovereignty over Hong Kong has furthered cooperation between China's securities exchanges and the Hong Kong Stock Exchange. Each of these areas of corporate finance has been characterized generally by expanded regulatory authority, increased international market and regulatory linkages, and ever-growing investor interest.

Policy and practice in securities regulation is heavily influenced by the State Council, which exercises regulatory and policy guidance over the drafting of laws and regulations; formulation of principles, policies, and rules; and the establishment of plans and proposals. The People's Bank of China has been a dominant regulator and, despite an ambitious program of banking reform exemplified by the Commercial Banking Law (1995, rev. 2004) and the Law on the People's Bank of China (1995, rev. 2004), continues to use its regulatory authority in pursuit of its interpretation of national development goals. Local regulations also establish a high degree of State control over the issuance and trading of securities on the Shenzhen and Shanghai securities markets.

2. Enactment of the Property Rights Law of the PRC

Efforts to draft a comprehensive property law emerged following various constitutional amendments recognizing expanded private property rights. In 1995, a semi-official proposal on property legislation suggested that conventional boundaries for property rights as set forth in the General Principles of Civil Law might be expanded.[27] In October 1997, President Jiang Zemin's speech to the CPC 15th National Congress called for development of property rights for businesses. Efforts to draft a code of property law resumed in 1998 under the aegis of a Civil Code drafting team. The drafting process revealed ongoing disagreements over the proper scope of private property rights, which in turn echoed broader questions about the respective roles of economic law and civil law models in China's contract law initiatives. On one hand, by clarifying property as a civil law relationship, the drafters emphasized the importance of limiting state intrusion and enlarged the possibilities for private rights. Thus, an early draft of the property law code contained a principle that property rights could not be interfered with by third parties (including government organs).[28] On the other hand, the draft also contained basic economic law principles of protecting "lawful" rights and interests, safeguarding social and economic order and socialist modernization, and prohibiting property rights harming the public interest.

In 1999, the PRC Constitution was amended to expand protection of lawful property, through a provision that self-employed, private and other non-public sectors constituted an important component of the socialist market economy, whose lawful rights and interests would be protected by the State. The Constitution was amended yet again in 2004 to provide in Article 13 that lawful private property shall not be violated. The language on private property rights fell somewhat short of the protections offered in Article 12 that "socialist public property is sacrosanct and inviolable," underscoring the continued dominance of public property. Nonetheless, these constitutional developments in turn paved the way for completion of a draft property law, work on which had begun in the early 1990s.

Enabled in part by the 2004 revisions to the PRC Constitution that enshrined a right to own private property, the preparation of a property law code accelerated with a public release of a draft statute in July 2005. While intended originally to provide greater protection for private property and to lend greater certainty to financing arrangements, the draft law was subject to late-coming criticism from traditionalist intellectuals who challenged its apparent departure from socialist principles. The draft was withdrawn in mid-2006 and underwent significant revisions that entrenched the importance of protecting public and state property and protecting rural land-use rights by restraining the authority of officials to engage in or approve property transfers (including land acquisition and re-allocation). The draft was reconsidered by the NPC Standing Committee throughout late 2006 and submitted to the full NPC for approval in early 2007.

The Property Rights Law of the PRC (PRL) came into force on October 1, 2007. The PRL is described as a "basic civil law," and acknowledges increased autonomy for property relations between private social and economic actors.[29] Yet the economic law regulatory model remains evident in the PRL's policy goals to "uphold the basic socialist economic system" and to "regulate the order of the socialist market economy." Subject to this ongoing policy tension, the PRL's commitment to providing "equal protection to the property of the state, the collective, and the individual," signaled further support for private property rights in the PRC's socialist market economy. The PRL clarifies the rights and obligations attendant to a wide range of property relationships involving real property, movable property and intangibles. While the PRL does not purport to create new property rights, it does clarify the powers of rights holders in matters such as usufruct and condominium relationships. Property security is dealt with at some length, such that mortgages, liens, and charges are now more likely to be clearer and more enforceable, and hence more acceptable to lenders.

Thus, through debates around drafting and enactment of the PRL, legislation that was aimed initially at expanding property rights generally, and private property rights in particular, evolved to include measures to control property rights and curb abuses. PRL provisions limiting the authority of local officials to expropriate land without lawful process and compensation (Art. 42) have become particularly important in cases of expropriation of agricultural land and relocation of urban residents. The PRL also affirms state interests in natural resources (land, water, minerals, etc.), imposing on local officials penalties for unlawful transfer of state assets, while also providing for procedural limits on transfer of collective property, which includes rural land.

3. Provisions of the Property Rights Law

While the PRL provides a basic foundation for property relations in China's changing political economy, it also reflects policy tensions around the protection of public and private rights. Provisions on the civil nature of property relationships underscore the rights and autonomy of property holders, while references to public ownership and state interests reflect the continued attention to ideological tenets of socialism:

> *Article 1*: This Law is enacted in accordance with the Constitution for the purpose of upholding the basic economic system of the State, maintaining the order of the socialist market economy, defining the attribution of things, giving play to the usefulness of things and protecting the property right of obligees.

Article 2: This Law shall be applicable to civil relationships stemming from attribution and use of things.

For the purposes of this Law, things include the immovables and the movables. Where laws stipulate that rights are taken as objects of the property right, the provisions of such laws shall prevail.

The property right mentioned in this Law means the exclusive right enjoyed by the obligee to directly dominate a given thing according to law, which consists of the right of ownership, the usufruct and the security interest on property.

Article 3: In the primary stage of socialism, the State upholds the basic economic system under which public ownership is dominant and the economic sectors of diverse forms of ownership develop side by side.

The State consolidates and develops the public sectors of the economy, and encourages, supports and guides the development of the non-public sectors of the economy.

The State maintains a socialist market economy and guarantees the equal legal status and the right to development of all the mainstays of the market.

Article 4: The property right of the State, the collectives, the individual persons and other obligees are protected by law, and no units or individuals shall encroach on it.

The PRL applies to real estate (combining public rights in land with private rights in buildings and improvements) and personal property, although much of the statute focuses on public land and resources. The PRL underscores the role of public regulation over property relations – allowing in Article 2 for additional kinds of property rights to be brought within the protection of the PRL and ensuring in Article 5 that the types and content of property rights shall be stipulated by law rather than the dictates of the parties. Like the UCL for contracts, the

PRL serves essentially as a "gap-filler" to augment provisions of other legislation on issues such as land, intellectual property, and securities (Art. 8).

The PRL reflects the dynamic of policy conflict and compromise that characterizes many of China's legislative efforts. Key issues involve the relationships between public and private property rights and their role in China's socialist market economy. Thus, Article 1 provides that the law is drafted to safeguard the fundamental economic system of the country and protect the socialist market economic order. Yet Article 1 also speaks to ownership of things and protecting the rights of property holders. For the moment, during China's "primary stage of socialism," the fundamental economic system gives public ownership the dominant role, but acknowledges parallel development of private ownership. Thus, the state adopts the socialist market economy but also ensures equal legal status and the right for development of non-state and non-public actors in the economy (Art. 3). The public interest dimensions of the PRL are also evident in Article 7, which provides that the attainment and exercise of property right must comply with the law and social morals and may not infringe upon the public interest or the lawful rights and interests of others.

The PRL distinguishes between the State, the collective, and private persons (natural and legal persons) as property rights holders (Art. 4). State-owned property (particularly natural resources and land) is affirmed in Chapter V of the law. Individual property includes legal income, houses, household goods, production tools, and raw materials, as well as savings investment and returns and the rights of inheritance. These provisions are consistent with provisions in Articles 75 and 76 of the 1986 General Principles of Civil Law. Property rights extend to corporate property such that the State, the collective, and individuals may make capital contributions to establish limited liability companies, joint stock limited companies or other enterprises (Art. 67). Enterprise legal persons and other legal persons may also have legal rights to real property and things/chattels (Art. 68). The PRL summarizes provisions of existing regulations by requiring that the establishment, modification, transfer, and lapse of rights in real property require registration procedures.[30]

The PRL grants property owners the right to possess, use, dispose of, and obtain profits from real property and things/chattels (Art. 39). Income from property rights (referred to as "usufructuary rights") is protected, as are security interests in property such as pledges, mortgages, liens, and the like that are used to secure repayment of debt. The state retains rights of expropriation for the purposes of public interest (Art. 42), although the interpretation and application of the "public interest" standard remains contested. In rural areas, tensions between interpretations of the public interest used to justify expropriation by local governments and the private interests of individual property holders have emerged around family production contracting and land use. The PRL also provides for special protections for agricultural land, limiting the conversion of agricultural land to construction land – an issue that has led to significant conflict in rural and semi-urban areas of China (Art. 43).

Chapter V of the PRL underscores constitutional provisions and decisions under the General Principles of Civil Law that natural resources, minerals, waters, and sea areas are owned by the State and cannot be transferred through private contacts.[31]

Urban land is also owned by the State in accordance with the Constitution, although the PRL provides that rural land and land on the outskirts of cities may also be owned by the State. The PRL provides that collectively owned lands (as well as forests, mountain areas, grasslands, wasteland, and beaches) are administered on behalf of the collective by village committees and township organizations (Art. 60). This arrangement has led to significant tensions in the past, as officials operating in the name of village committees have conveyed land-use rights to developers over the objections or often without the knowledge of affected villagers. To address this problem, Article 62 requires that local authorities notify members of the collective of conditions of collective property based on national and local laws, regulations, and bylaws. Article 63 provides that decisions by collective economic organizations, village committees, and other principals may be challenged in court where they infringe on legal rights and interests of individual members of the collective.[32]

In response to China's booming real estate market – particularly in the area of condominium development – the PRL provides in Chapter VI for distinctive ownership of exclusive parts within buildings. Condominium owners enjoy exclusive ownership of their assigned exclusive component as well as co-ownership and common management rights to commonly owned property (Art. 70). Common spaces include parking spaces and garages as well as green spaces and other public sites, facilities, and rooms for public service purposes (Arts. 73 and 74). Condominium owners are required to comply with state law on environmental protection and pollution control and adhere to the principle of doing no harm to neighbors' properties in the course of installing water supply drainage and other infrastructure (Art. 92). A Supreme People's Court interpretation in 2009 on disputes between condominium owners and property management agencies stresses the centrality of maintenance contracts in determining the rights and interests of owners and property management firms and opens the way for increased judicial scrutiny in the event of abuses.[33] Real property rights transactions require registration in order to be lawfully valid.

IV. MANAGING DEVELOPMENT: TAXATION AND REGIONAL DEVELOPMENT

China's transition to a socialist market economy has meant in large part that the political incentives which characterized the Maoist, state-planning era have given way to economic incentives. Yet the institutions of the Party/State have not yet fully kept pace, such that management of the undesirable consequences of rapid economic development – particularly income disparities and corruption – remains imperfect. Nonetheless, the government has attempted to strengthen management of development through the tax system and through regimes for regional development.

A. *Taxation*

Since 1978, China's economic reform policies have been aimed generally at effecting a transition from planning to markets as the basis for economic decision making. As part of this process, taxation replaced the direct remittance of profits as the mechanism for government extraction of revenue from economic actors and their transactions. Under the state planning system, state-owned factories and other economic enterprises received budgetary allocations from the government and then remitted all of their income to the State. To the extent that economic enterprises generated surpluses, these were transferred to the state for further redistribution across the society and economy. The decline in the state planning system saw efforts to replace this system with one grounded in taxation of income. The 1994 Tax Sharing Reform adjusted fiscal relations between the center and the provinces to stabilize revenue by expanding the Value Added Tax and ensuring proper revenue sharing between the central government and the provinces.[34] Taxation has become a major source of government revenue, and also has become an important instrument for achieving policy goals of the Party/State, whether in terms of directing investment toward or away from particular sectors and activities and in terms of balancing disparities of income and wealth.

1. Business Taxation

Business taxation is carried out primarily through the Enterprise Income Tax Law (EITL), enacted in 2007. The EITL unified the treatment of domestic and foreign-owned enterprises by distinguishing for tax purposes between resident or non-resident regardless of ownership:

> *Article 1*: Enterprises and other organizations that are located within the People's Republic of China and earn income (hereinafter generally referred to as enterprises) are payers of enterprise income tax, which shall be paid in accordance with the provisions of this Law.
>
> . . .
>
> *Article 3*: Enterprises are divided into resident enterprises and non-resident enterprises.
>
> For the purposes of this Law, resident enterprises are enterprises which are set up in China in accordance with law, or which are set up in accordance with the law of a foreign country (region) but which are actually under the administration of institutions in China.
>
> For the purposes of this Law, non-resident enterprises are enterprises which are set up in accordance with the law of a foreign country (region) and whose actual administrative institution is not in China, but which have institutions or establishments in China, or which have no such institutions or establishments but have income generated from inside China.
>
> . . .
>
> *Article 4*: The rate of enterprise income tax shall be 25 per cent. On the income earned by non-resident enterprises, as specified in the third paragraph of Article 3 of this Law, the applicable tax rate shall be 20 per cent.

Originally, foreign businesses had been subject to different rates of tax for joint ventures (taxed at 33%) and other foreign enterprises (taxed on a sliding scale ranging from 20 to 40%). This disparity was corrected by the 1991 "Income Tax Law of the People's Republic of China Concerning Enterprises with Foreign Investment and Foreign Enterprises," which unified the tax rates for all foreign companies at 33%. The 1991 unification of taxation of foreign firms was due in part to the perceived inequity of taxing equity joint ventures at 33% and contractual joint ventures as foreign enterprises at the foreign enterprise varying rate of 20–40%, as well as to the surge in wholly foreign-owned enterprises (WFOEs) that were also taxed as foreign enterprises. Domestic Chinese enterprises were taxed at 33% under the 1993 "Provisional Regulations on Enterprise Income Tax."

Under pressure to lower tax rates for foreign business, Chinese tax officials also needed to avoid disadvantaging local enterprises. As well, unification of tax rates for domestic and foreign firms conformed to the operational reality that financial globalization has blurred the distinctions between local and foreign ownership, in part through the internationalization of securities markets and financial transfers. By switching to a residence standard, the EITL attempted to unify the tax treatment of all companies operating in China, avoiding tax arbitrage, falsification and concealment of ownership, and inequities of disparate tax treatment for similarly situated enterprises.[35]

The taxation principle underlying the EITL is the taxation of net income, hence the critical issues of administration tend to center on calculation of income and expenses. There are also a number of "turnover" taxes on commercial transactions that affect both foreign and domestic and resident and non-resident firms, such as the Business Tax, Value Added Tax, and various resource- and transport-related taxes, that remain in place.

2. Taxation of Individuals

Taxation of individuals in the PRC is subject to the Individual Income Tax Law (IITL) of the PRC and its Implementing Regulations, both enacted initially in 1980. Although couched in general language, these early measures were aimed primarily at foreign nationals. By virtue of the IITL-1980's generous monthly standard deduction, the IITL-1980 had little relevance for most Chinese individuals. Income of Chinese nationals was taxed mainly under the Individual Income Adjustment Tax (IIAT), which imposed tax based on the extent to which the taxpayer's income exceeded a given local median income. Thus, it was not unexpected that China should enact measures to unify the tax treatment of Chinese and foreign individuals.

In January 1994, the revised Individual Income Tax Law (hereafter, IITL), and its Implementing Regulations (hereafter, IITL Implementing Regulations) were enacted as part of a wide-ranging program of tax reform and applied to both foreign and Chinese nationals. The revised IITL went into effect on January 1, 1994, with Implementing Rules effective from January 28, 1994. Since then, the Individual Income Tax Law has been revised four times. Changes in 1993 and 1999 addressed primarily issues of standard deduction and tax calculations. Revisions in 2005 and 2007 adjusted the standard deduction again and added new provisions on tax administration – particularly the process for self-reporting of tax.

3. Tax Administration

Tax administration in China is generally subject to the Tax Administration Law. The Tax Administration Law grants Chinese tax authorities broad discretionary authority to conduct investigations regarding tax compliance and impose sanctions in events of non-compliance with the tax laws and regulations:

Article 1: This Law is enacted for the purpose of standardizing tax collection and payment, ensuring the tax revenues of the State, protecting the legitimate rights and interests of taxpayers and promoting economic and social development.

Article 2: The administration of tax collection in respect of all taxes to be collected by the tax authorities in accordance with law shall be governed by this Law.

Article 5: The competent department for taxation under the State Council shall be in charge of the administration of tax collection throughout the country. The national tax bureaus and the local tax bureaus in various places shall administer tax collection respectively within the limits set by the State Council.

The local people's governments at various levels shall strengthen their leadership over or coordination of the administration of tax collection within their respective administrative regions, and support the tax authorities in performing their duties in accordance with law, calculating the amounts of taxes to be paid according to the statutory tax rates and collecting taxes in accordance with law.

The departments and units concerned shall support and assist the tax authorities in performing their duties in accordance with law.

No units or individuals may obstruct the tax authorities from performing their duties in accordance with law.

In practical terms, tax enforcement tends to involve protracted negotiations over the amount and sourcing of income and the details of payment and enforcement. Penalties for failure to comply with tax regulations range from specific fines of 2,000–10,000 yuan or more, fines in the amount of up to five times the tax deficiency, confiscation of illegal earnings, and more serious criminal and administrative penalties.

Taxation in China is affected by various bilateral tax treaties that aim to prevent double taxation and tax avoidance.[36] China's bilateral tax treaties generally allocate tax jurisdiction between home and host countries, permitting the host country to tax business income that is "effectively connected" to a home country company's "permanent establishment" located in the host country. Tax treaties typically allow for local taxation of foreign individuals who reside for periods in aggregate of longer than 183 days in the host country. During the early period of China's opening to international investment, China was virtually always the host country and its foreign treaty partners the home country for businesses whose income was subject to bilateral tax treaties. This has changed in recent years with the burgeoning growth of foreign investment by Chinese companies. China's bilateral tax treaties also limit the tax rate applicable on foreign investment income (e.g. interest, dividends, royalties) derived in host economies. Double taxation is avoided through treaty provisions for tax credits in the home country to offset foreign taxes paid in the host economy. Tax treaties generally applied only to income tax, and generally do not cover sales and transaction taxes that are imposed on foreign businesses operating in China. China's bilateral tax treaties also provide for communication between China's tax regulatory authorities and those of its trading partners.

B. Regional development

China has long faced the challenge of building economic development in the inland regions. Despite impressive economic and social development in the coastal areas, China's inner and western regions have long lagged behind. China's "Western Development Program" (WDP) has been developed to augment regional cooperation in economic and security matters. The WDP was announced in 1999, and the leading small group established early in 2000. The State Council gradually formalized the WDP regulatory regime through a series of administrative edicts on economic development priorities and processes. The State Council's notice on WDP implementation issued in 2000 focused on development priorities in the areas of infrastructure; ecology and environment; agriculture; industry; tourism; and technology, education, culture, and public health:[37]

> *Key Tasks and Strategic Objectives*: For the present and the years to come, the key tasks of carrying out the development of China's vast western regions are: speeding up the construction of infrastructure facilities; improving the protection and development of environment; consolidating the basic status of agriculture, adjusting the structure of industry, and developing characteristic tourism; developing undertakings of science and technology, education, culture and sanitation. To work hard for the breakthrough progress in the construction of infrastructure facilities and environment of the western regions and to make a good beginning of the development of the western regions in 5 to 10 years. The western regions shall be built into a new one with prosperous economy, advanced society, stable living, united nationalities and beautiful sceneries at the middle period of the 21st century.

Reflecting the broad relationship between national legal and economic reform programs in the post-Mao period, the WDP is an important factor in efforts to establish legal regulatory regimes for the nationality autonomous regions. The WDP provides impetus for efforts to strengthen civil and economic law regimes on issues such as contracts, property, and administrative process to support economic development. Yet the State Council's WDP policy priorities reflect national rather than local development concerns in areas of construction investment, finance, taxation, and land use. Environmental restrictions on WDP programs also give priority to ensuring local compliance with state policies and regulations. Support for legal development under the

WDP is the responsibility of state organs and departments, while enterprises in nationalities areas are accorded the lawful rights and responsibilities of legal persons under the national legal system, and members of minority nationalities themselves are to be protected as consumers under fair competition regimes and to receive special accommodations for the cultural requirements of their nationality status.

China's Xinjiang Uighur Nationality Autonomous Region offers useful examples of the interplay between central government initiatives on local development and local regulation of social and economic issues. Local regulations on economic development authorized under the NRAL remain subject to national priorities. Xinjiang's regulatory regime for encouraging foreign investment, for example, is confined by provisions of national law and regulation and by the policy requirements of the Western Development Program. Xinjiang's collective contract rules address issues of employment and labor conditions subject to the provisions of national labor contract and trade union legislation. Even rather mundane local regulations, in areas of staff maternity insurance for example, provide benefits for costs of delivery and maternity care according to standards set forth in national regulations as interpreted according to local conditions.

In Xinjiang, national laws for foreign economic relations were given particular attention, as local foreign trade enterprises were directed to attend to contract performance and to attract foreign investment and technology transfer through the "foreign invested enterprise" system envisioned under legal regimes for joint ventures, cooperative enterprises, and wholly foreign-owned enterprises. Regulations on tax preferences as inducements for western development investment projects emphasize the application of tax preference for transportation, electric, and hydropower, posts and telecommunications, agriculture processing, and tourism. Efforts to simplify administrative processes on such matters as taxation suggest efforts by central authorities to respond to local needs, although the effects on economic behavior remain uncertain. Law and policy on economy and development in Xinjiang reflect tensions between efforts to develop agricultural, petroleum, and mineral resources on the one hand, and security programs aimed at suppressing local dissident and separatist movements on the other.

SUMMARY

China's legal regime is aimed in significant part at promoting economic prosperity. Since the 1978 Third Plenum of the 11th CPC Central Committee, Party policy initiatives on economic and legal reform have been closely intertwined. Building on conclusions about the decline of class struggle and the importance of promoting the "forces of production," the PRC regime has enacted a steady stream of laws and regulations aimed at promoting economic growth. Central to these efforts have been legislative initiatives on contract relations and property rights. In furtherance of changing policy priorities supporting ever more autonomous commercial relationships and activities, China's contract law and property law regimes have steadily expanded the private rights of legal actors. However, a strong commitment to public interest remains in both contract and property law. The balancing between public and private interests, expressed imperfectly in legislation, remains a key challenge in the management of China's economy. Challenges of wealth disparity that have accompanied China's rapid economic growth (a familiar pattern in other emerging market economies globally) have led to policy initiatives in the areas of taxation, as well as regional development efforts. Taken together, China's legal regime for economic development offers a remarkable picture of policy-driven law making. China faces ongoing challenges to balance national interests with the requirements of compliance with local and international legal institutions and processes.

DISCUSSION QUESTIONS

1. How does contract law support the policy objectives of the Party/State on economic development?

2. How does property law support the policy objectives of the Party/State on economic development?

3. How does China's tax system balance the rights of individuals and firms with the collective rights of society?

4. How does China's legal system address issues of regional development?

SUGGESTIONS FOR FURTHER READING

Huang Yasheng, *Capitalism with Chinese Characteristics: Entrepreneurship and the State* (Cambridge: Cambridge University Press, 2008).

Mosher, Michael and Fu Yu, eds, *Doing Business in China* (New York: International Juris, looseleaf).

Organization for Economic Cooperation and Development (OECD), *China in the World Economy: The Domestic Policy Challenges* (Paris: Organization for Economic Cooperation and Development, 2002).

Peerenboom Randall, *China Modernizes: Threat to the West or Model for the Rest?* (Oxford: Oxford University Press, 2007).

Potter, Pitman B., *Law, Policy, and Practice in China's Periphery* (London: Routledge, 2010).

United Nations Development Programme, *China Human Development Report 2009/10: China and a Sustainable Future: Towards a Low Carbon Economy and Society* (Beijing: China Translation and Publishing Corporation, 2010).

4   Social Development ————————

As with other sectors, in the area of social development the PRC legal regime serves as an instrument to support the policies of the Party/State. These policies have often been conflicted, however. In the aftermath of the Cultural Revolution, the reformist government of Deng Xiaoping promoted economic development within the collectivist confines of "socialism with Chinese characteristics." As we have seen in chapter 3, economic development priorities came to the fore once again after Deng's 1992 Southern Tour. Under the post-Deng regime of Jiang Zemin, expansion of the economy and privatization of public services became a recurrent policy theme that saw steady economic growth, but reduction in social wellbeing. Responding to growing public discontent over deteriorating conditions for education, labor, and healthcare, Hu Jintao's government attempted to reintroduce priorities of social development under the rubric of "harmonious society." The balancing of economic and social development will continue to be a policy priority for the new government leadership team under Xi Jinping appointed at the 18th CPC Congress in late 2012.

This chapter reviews the ways in which China's legal regime addresses the challenge of social development under changing socio-economic and political conditions. We first examine issues of labor relations, healthcare, education, women's rights, and the treatment of minority nationalities in light of their importance as traditional priorities for the PRC Party/State. This chapter then addresses issues that have become priorities more recently, such as media and the Internet, environmental protection, and corporate social responsibility.

I. TRADITIONAL PARTY/STATE PRIORITIES

Social development has long been a policy theme for the CPC. A major segment of the CPC revolutionary leadership emerged out of the underground union movement that attempted to organize workers in the factories, mines, and railroads of Republican China. Party edicts and regulations issued for the revolutionary Base Areas in Jiangxi in the southeast and in Jin Cha Ji and Shaan Gan Ning Border Areas in the north prior to 1949 emphasized workers' rights (including farm workers) as well as social development priorities in healthcare and education.[1] After the 1949 revolution and throughout the Maoist period, Party policy continued to focus on labor relations (managed under the Party's leadership through the All China Federation of Trade Unions), healthcare (through the campaign of "barefoot doctors"), and education (often pursued through the *xiafang* program of sending educated youth to the countryside as teachers).[2] Social development goals also see law mobilized in the service of women's rights and the treatment of minorities through a range of preferential policies.

The post-Mao leadership under Deng Xiaoping continued to emphasize these aspects of social development, funding them increasingly from income generated by state and private enterprises, whose growth was supported by Deng's economic reform policies. During the 1990s, however, declining central government revenues (often the result of ineffective tax enforcement), along with changing priorities that directed government support toward economic growth, led to a steady deterioration of public services in healthcare and education, as well as declining labor conditions. Under Hu Jintao's leadership beginning in 2002, efforts were made to redress this imbalance, under the rubric of "harmonious society." As with other sectors, China's legal regime has played a key role in articulating and implementing social development policies.

A. Labor relations

As we saw in chapter 1, the CPC has pursued ideals of labor rights since long before the establishment of the PRC, and continually thereafter. However, under the post-Deng regime of Jiang Zemin, policy attention to the relations of production such as labor rights were overshadowed by attention to building the forces of production through economic development. As we examine China's labor relations system, it is helpful to bear in mind the importance of control by the Party/ State and the relationship to the imperative of stability as a precondition for economic development.

Labor relations in China today are governed primarily by the PRC Labor Law and the PRC Labor Contract Law. Numerous additional regulations address a wide array of operational issues such as working conditions, worker training, occupational health and safety, and so on.[3] The Labor Law of the PRC (1995) remains the basic legal expression of labor policy and labor rights, and reveals policy tensions between protecting workers' rights and maintaining their subservience to state control:

> *Article 1*: This Law is formulated in accordance with the Constitution in order to protect the legitimate rights and interests of workers, regulate labor relationships, establish and safeguard a labor system suited to the socialist market economy, and promote economic development and social progress.

> *Article 3*: Workers shall have equal rights to employment and choice of occupation, the right to remuneration for labor, to rest and vacations,

to protection of occupational safety and health, to training in vocational skills, to social insurance and welfare, to submission of labor disputes for settlement and other rights relating to labor stipulated by law.

Laborers shall fulfill their labor tasks, improve their vocational skills, follow rules on occupational safety and health, and observe labor discipline and professional ethics.

While recognizing a range of "guarantees" of equal opportunity, compensation, safety and healthcare, the Labor Law also imposes on workers a number of obligations, including fulfilling work requirements and observing labor discipline. Thus, similarly with the conditional granting of civil and political rights under the PRC Constitution, the Labor Law conditions the rights of workers on their submission to the authority of the Party/State. The role of the Party/State as the main guarantor of workers' rights and interests involves numerous conflicts of interest between workers and local Party officials, contributing to concerns about lax enforcement.

The Labor Law's provisions on labor unions, collective bargaining, and dispute resolution underscore the authority of the Party/State.[4] While the Labor Law provides for union membership, it does not permit independent labor unions or collective bargaining as these are understood under international treaties.

Article 7: Laborers shall have the right to participate in, and organize, trade unions in accordance with the law. Trade unions shall represent and safeguard the legitimate rights and interests of laborers, and independently carry out their activities in accordance with the law.

Under the Trade Union Law of the PRC (1992, rev. 2001),[5] state-sponsored trade unions have exclusive authority to represent staff and workers in concluding collective contracts with enterprises and institutions.

Article 2: Trade unions are mass organizations of the working class formed by the workers and staff members on a voluntary basis.

The All-China Federation of Trade Unions and all the trade union organizations under it represent the interests of the workers and staff members and safeguard the legitimate rights and interests of the workers and staff members according to law.

Article 4: Trade unions shall observe and safeguard the Constitution, take it as the fundamental criterion for their activities, take economic development as the central task, uphold the socialist road, the people's democratic dictatorship, leadership by the Communist Party of China, and Marxist-Leninism, Mao Zedong Thought and Deng Xiaoping Theory, persevere in reform and the open policy, and conduct their work independently in accordance with the Constitution of trade unions.

Article 10: . . . The All-China Federation of Trade Unions shall be established as the unified national organization.

All local trade unions are subject under PRC Trade Union Law to the overall authority of the All-China Federation of Trade Unions (ACFTU), a CPC United Front organization. Independent labor unions are prohibited as illegal organizations. The Trade Union Law also authorizes CPC cadres to take leadership positions in trade unions, which raises conflict of interest issues, since these same cadres often have management positions with employing factories and enterprises.

The Labor Contract Law of the PRC (2008) attempted to remedy concerns over enforcement of the Labor Law, by requiring written labor contracts enforcing Labor Law requirements on conditions of work:

Article 2: This Law is applicable where organizations such as enterprises, self-employed economic organizations and private non-enterprise units within the territory of the People's Republic of China (hereinafter referred to as employing units) establish labor relationships with workers through concluding, performing, modifying, revoking or terminating labor contracts with them.

State organs, institutions and public organizations and the workers with whom they are to establish labor relationships shall conclude, perform, modify, revoke or terminate labor contracts in accordance with this Law.

Article 3: Labor contracts shall be concluded in adherence to the principles of lawfulness, fairness, equality, voluntariness, consensus through consultation, and good faith.

A labor contract concluded in accordance with law shall have binding force. Both the employing unit and the worker shall fulfill the obligations stipulated in the labor contract.

The Labor Contract Law also provides remedies such as compensation as well as fines for failures to comply. While challenges of implementation remain, the Labor Contract Law expresses a renewed commitment by the Party/State to protect the rights of workers. As well, the Labor Disputes Mediation and Arbitration Law of the PRC (2007) established a national arbitration and mediation system for resolving labor disputes on the basis of the substantive provisions of the Labor Law and the Labor Contract Law.

The challenges of managing labor relations and protecting workers' rights were evident in the sharp increase in worker protests during the late 1990s and early 2000s. These arose largely in reaction to the failure by enterprise employers to pay their employees, or otherwise to comply with agreed-upon standards for work. Protests during this period did not seem to challenge the fairness or legality of agreed-upon wages and conditions. Following China's WTO accession in 2001 and more intense international trade competition, working conditions in export factories remained deplorable.[6] For migrant workers in particular, who lacked local residency permits and whose numbers grew steadily throughout the 1990s and 2000s, working conditions were often worse than for local residents. The Foxconn electronics plants in Longhua, Shenzhen, and Wuhan, for example, have seen a raft of worker suicides and threats of suicide protesting working conditions. In these cases, we see general challenges raised against agreed working conditions, even though some of these may have complied with China's labor law regime. Protests against the legitimacy of agreed-upon wage rates have also emerged, as exemplified by the lengthy strike at the Honda auto plant in Foshan, Guangdong in early 2010, demanding higher wages.

B. Healthcare

During the Maoist period, China's public health system seemed a model for developing economies. The "barefoot doctor" system brought to unprecedented numbers of people in rural areas healthcare services that, while very basic (mostly provision of aspirin and rudimentary first aid), was nonetheless a significant improvement over past practices. However, during the post-Mao age, China's economic growth policies and attendant problems of income disparity, declining public budgets, and corruption, undermined public access to healthcare. Privatization policies led to greater emphasis being placed on capital-intensive high-tech healthcare for those who could afford it (mostly in the cities), while basic care for the poor and for isolated areas of the countryside was increasingly neglected.[7] General shifts in placing the funding burden on individual consumers and from the central to the local level governments exacerbated problems of equitable access. Obstacles to public access to healthcare continue, born of market policies and accompanying costs of medicines, equipment, and treatment. These dilemmas reflect the depth of operational challenges facing China's current efforts to reform its healthcare delivery systems.

While China does not have a national health law, legislation has been enacted on a variety of specific health issues, often in response to particular health policy crises.[8] The HIV crisis in central Henan province revealed the degree to which health issues intersect with local socio-economic conditions, as impoverished rural residents gave blood to earn income, only to be infected as a result of poor sterilization protocols and other management failures.[9] China's handling of the 2002–3 SARS crisis illustrated the capacity of the Party/State to mobilize resources for public health, while also revealing the extent to which issues of political and personal interests can interfere with health policy decisions.[10] However, the HIV and SARS crises also revealed the harm that can result from the Party/State's tight restrictions on information.

The PRC Blood Donation Law was enacted in 1997 – largely in response to the Henan AIDS crisis. A law on professional medical practitioners was enacted in 1998, in part to impose licensing and regulatory requirements on the medical profession and to weed out purveyors of folk remedies. The Occupational Health Law was enacted in 2001, mainly to establish standards for prevention of occupational illnesses, which were becoming increasingly prevalent in China's industrialization process. The PRC Infectious Disease Law was enacted in 2004, building on the Ministry of Health's 2003 regulations on reporting of infectious disease, issued in response to the SARS crisis. A draft Mental Health Law was circulated for comment and discussion in 2011 and enacted in 2012. As well, the State Council has enacted various policy edicts and administrative regulations, such as the State Council's 1998 strategic AIDS plan and 2001 AIDS action plan. The decision of the Central Committee and the State Council on Progressively Strengthening Rural Health Work (October 29, 2002) set forth goals for rural health cooperatives and infectious disease control.

In January 2009, the government announced a new Public Health Reform Plan, in response to a report by the State Council Development Research Center that criticized health sector reforms and noted the steady increase of patient contributions to medical fees.[11] The health-care reform plan was aimed in part at providing state subsidies for personal medical expenses and to support universal coverage of basic healthcare costs by the end of 2020.[12] Such coverage will involve complete subsidization of "essential public health care" as well as expanding social health insurance with the goal to achieve 90% coverage for rural and urban residents by the end of 2011. Rural migrants and other at-risk populations will be particularly targeted. The plan also involves reform of the pharmaceutical system (which has been used as a revenue generator by hospitals and clinics) through assured access for patients to an "essential medicine system." A strategic plan for hospital construction was issued in 2011 by the Ministry of Health, in support of the goals of the plan.

China's healthcare policies and law extend to matters of consumer product safety. The Ministry of Health and the State Food and Drug Administration oversee an extensive array of laws and regulations addressing issues of product safety. China's rapid economic growth has seen many of the standards and procedures required for ensuring product health and safety sadly neglected. The Product Quality Law of the PRC (rev. 2000) set forth standards for health and safety in consumer products and provided penalties (including possible criminal prosecution) for violations. As well, the 1994 Consumer Protection Law imposed on businesses a range of obligations including the duty to provide accurate information and disclosure about consumer products. The law was to have been revised in 2009, but formal amendments have not yet been announced.

A Pharmaceutical Safety Law (later termed the "Drug Control Law") and a Food Safety Law were enacted in 2009 in response to crises such as the Melamine milk poisoning scandal and the rising incidents of illness and injury from faulty medications (often using imperfectly pirated pharmaceutical formulas). The Drug Control Law was "enacted to tighten drug control, to ensure drug quality and safety for human beings, to protect the health of people and their legitimate rights and interests in the use of drugs" (Art. 1), while the Food Safety Law was "formulated for the purposes of ensuring food safety and safeguarding public health and life safety." The effectiveness of these laws remains uncertain as factors of local corruption and weak institutional capacity remain obstacles to full enforcement.

Law and regulation on health policy also extends to questions about social security protection. The Constitution of the PRC provides that "The livelihood of retired personnel is ensured by the state and society" (Art. 44). Under the Maoist state planned economy, virtually all of China's population enjoyed cradle-to-grave public security benefits, although their quality varied across regions and between urban and rural areas. With the advent of market transition and the gradual decline in the role of state enterprises in the post-Mao period, however, unemployment insurance, social welfare (involving the *dibao* system for minimum livelihood stipends), and retirement benefits came to be administered under the Ministry of Civil Affairs.[13] In 1997 the pension system was established for enterprise employees in urban areas, and a CPC Central Committee decision on establishing a cadre retirement system was issued the following year. In 2000 a national social security fund was established, primarily for urban areas. Retirement protection in the rural areas remains a challenge, although the Rural Development Reform Policy begun in 2008 and the 2009 Public Health Policy Reform discussed above both aim to address some of these issues. The Ministry of Civil Affairs' law and policy plan for 2010 included the aim to develop laws and regulations to implement social protection, as well as increased administrative oversight of social insurance programs. As yet, major national legislation on social security protection for employment, poverty, and retirement remains a work in progress.

As discussed in the State Council White Paper on Social Security, however, the PRC government remains committed to establishing an effective social security system.[14] Yet the instrumentalist goals of preserving stability and supporting economic development are also evident:

> Social security is one of the most important socio-economic systems for a country in modern times. To establish and improve a social security system corresponding to the level of economic development is a logical requirement for coordinated economic and social development. It is also an important guarantee for the social stability and the long-term political stability of a country.
>
> ... In light of China's actual situation and adhering to the principle of "putting people first," the Chinese Government attaches great importance and devotes every effort to establishing and improving its social security system.
>
> ... China's social security system includes social insurance, social welfare, the special care and placement system, social relief and housing services. As the core of the social security system, social insurance includes old-age insurance, unemployment insurance, medical insurance, work-related injury insurance, and maternity insurance.

C. Education rights

Education is essential to China's development project.[15] With the establishment of the People's Republic, education was a major feature in the social transformation policies of the new regime. While expanding basic education to the rural areas and reforming urban schools away from traditional Confucian models of moral education toward dissemination of practical knowledge, the PRC government also used curriculum reforms to ensure dissemination of the ideals of the Party/State. Herein lay many of the challenges that arose during the Maoist era, as ideological debates within the leadership resulted in inconsistent policies. The Maoist "red vs. expert" debate spilled over into education such that Maoist programs challenged the perceived "elitism" of traditional education, emphasizing instead ideological training and encouraging enrollment by the often unprepared children of the "good classes" of workers, peasants, and soldiers over the better prepared offspring of so-called "bad classes" such as landlords and capitalists. During the Cultural Revolution, colleges and universities were closed as a result of ideological and political tumult. With the post-Mao reforms beginning in 1978, education policy began to emphasize training for economic development. Universities were reopened and subject to national entrance examinations for admission, while primary and secondary schools saw important curriculum reforms supporting increased attention to practical knowledge. These policy changes were reflected in formal laws and regulations.

Education policies are expressed in the Compulsory Education Law of the PRC (1986), emphasizing the role of education in China's development project:

Article 1: This Law is enacted in accordance with the Constitution and the Education Law, for the purpose of ensuring the right of school-age children and adolescents to compulsory education, guaranteeing provision of compulsory education and improving the qualities of the entire nation.

Article 2: The State implements a system of nine-year compulsory education.

Compulsory education means education which is uniformly provided by the State and which all the school-age children and adolescents must receive, and constitutes a public welfare undertaking which must be guaranteed by the State.

. . .

Article 3: In compulsory education, the State policy on education shall be implemented by providing qualities-oriented education, to improve the quality of instruction, with a view to enabling school-age children and adolescents to achieve all-round development – morally, intellectually and physically, so as to lay the foundation for bringing up well-educated and self-disciplined builders and successors of socialism imbued with lofty ideals and moral integrity.

Article 4: All school-age children and adolescents of the nationality of the People's Republic of China shall, in accordance with law, enjoy the equal right, and fulfill the obligation, to receive compulsory education, regardless of sex, ethnic status or race, family financial conditions, religious belief, etc.

The law mandates a nine-year period of compulsory education generally beginning at age six, but imposes funding burdens on local governments. During the past 20 years, education budgets have continually shrunk as a proportion of GDP, while in rural areas particularly, funding structures have disadvantaged low-income people. Nonetheless, China has achieved significantly high levels of primary education. Alongside the public school system, there has emerged a budding network of private schools in China, many of which receive foreign investment and provide curriculum offerings leading to admission to foreign universities.

Higher education is subject to the Higher Education Law of the PRC (1995), which reflects tensions between developing technical expertise, creativity, and intellectual capacity of students on the one hand, and fulfilling priorities of the Party/State around political orthodoxy and economic development on the other:

Article 1: This Law is enacted in accordance with the Constitution and the Education Law with a view to developing higher education, implementing the strategy of developing the country by relying on science and education, and promoting socialist material and ethical progress.

Article 3: In developing socialist higher education, the State adheres to Marxism-Leninism, Mao Zedong Thought and Deng Xiaoping Theory as its guide and follows the basic principles laid down in the Constitution.

Article 4: Higher education shall be conducted in adherence to the educational principles of the State, in the service of the socialist modernization drive and in combination with productive labor, in order that those receiving education shall become builders and successors for the socialist cause, who are developed in an all-round way – morally, intellectually, and physically.

Article 5: The task of higher education is to train people to become senior specialists imbued with the spirit of creativeness and the ability of practice, to develop science, technology and culture and to promote the socialist modernization drive.

The law mandates post-secondary education to serve the goals of "socialist modernization." Rapid expansion of universities and technical schools has been matched by increased competition for admissions through performance in the higher education examination system. Many of China's universities support world-leading research and engage in a wide range of international collaborations, although plagiarism in academic publishing has become increasingly problematic as material and institutional incentives to publish come to outweigh disciplinary rigor and academic ethics. While economic challenges during the global recession beginning in 2008 led to significant difficulties in college graduates finding jobs, education continues to be seen as an essential step toward prosperity.

D. Rights of women

Emancipation of women has been a key policy priority since before the 1949 Revolution. The 1950 Marriage Law and its legal antecedents (see table 1.1) challenged traditions of patriarchy as part of the CPC's revolutionary program of social transformation. Key improvements in areas of property rights and rights to inheritance were noteworthy achievements, although practical enforcement remained inconsistent. Expanded access to education and health services called for in the Marriage Law remained an important component of Party/ State policies, overseen by the CPC United Front organ, the All China Women's Federation (ACWF). The ACWF also worked to expand employment opportunities for women, often encouraging women to pursue independent entrepreneurial opportunities rather than wage-based employment. The 2001 revision to the Marriage Law included proscriptions against domestic violence, once again challenging well-entrenched social norms. While challenges of enforcement have long been evident, the ideals of expanding and protecting the rights of women have been essential elements of the orthodoxy of the Party/State.

In addition to the Marriage Law, the PRC Law on the Protection of Rights and Interests of Women was enacted in 1992 to supplement the indirect protections available in legislation on marriage, education, and labor. The Women's Rights Law recognized rights to equality in social and economic life, underscoring the requirement of equal access to work, school, and healthcare. These ideals echoed long-standing policy goals of the Party/State, but were not accompanied by a specific definition of discrimination that would provide a standard for enforcement.

China has participated in numerous multilateral and bilateral conferences and technical exchanges on women's rights, including hosting the Fourth World Conference on Women held in Beijing in 1995.

China is a member of the UN Committee on the Elimination of Discrimination against Women. China has drawn on the Convention on Elimination of All Forms of Discrimination Against Women (CEDAW) as a basis for drafting local law and regulation on the protection of the rights of women.

The Women's Rights Law was revised in 2005 to take into account provisions in the CEDAW treaty, and to express commitments on government action to support women's rights:'

Article 1: In accordance with the Constitution and the actual conditions of the country, this Law is formulated to protect women's lawful rights and interests, promote equality between men and women and allow full play to women's role in socialist modernization.

Article 2: Women shall enjoy equal rights with men in all aspects of political, economic, cultural, social, and family life.

Equality between men and women is a basic State policy. The State takes the necessary measures to gradually improve the systems for protecting the rights and interests of women, in order to eliminate all forms of discrimination against women.

The State protects the special rights and interests enjoyed by women according to law.

Discriminating against, maltreating, abandoning, and physically abusing women are prohibited.

. . .

Article 4: The protection of women's lawful rights and interests is a common responsibility of the whole society. State organs, public organizations, enterprises and institutions, as well as urban and rural mass organizations of self-government at the grass-roots level shall, in accordance with the provisions of this Law and other relevant laws, protect women's rights and interests.

The State takes effective measures to provide necessary conditions for women to exercise their rights according to law.

The Law provides for gender equality in all aspects of political, economic, cultural, and family life (Art. 2). This extends to political rights, where women are to enjoy equal political rights with men, as the PRC State takes responsibility to encourage training and appointment of female cadres. Gender equality in culture and education includes commitments to ensuring that female school-age children and adolescents receive compulsory education, and to promoting literacy and vocational training for women, especially in rural areas. Addressing the "last to be hired, first to be fired" dilemma affecting women in the workforce, the Women's Rights Law affirms gender equality in work and the principle of equal pay and benefits for women, with special provision for maternity and childcare benefits. Challenging long-standing prejudices, the Law entrenches the provisions for gender equality with regard to property ownership. Echoing ongoing revisions to the Marriage Law, the Women's Rights Law purports to protect women's rights to marital property. The Women's Law also attends to issues of physical security – prohibiting domestic violence and committing state agencies to preventing and punishing it.

Despite these efforts, protection of women's rights in practice remains problematic.[16] The Women's Rights Law does not include the CEDAW treaty's definition of "discrimination," undermining standards for protection. Problems of income disparity between men and women continue, while challenges of human trafficking, disparities in access to education and healthcare, and domestic violence remain serious. The continued failure to define "discrimination" in Chinese law enables unequal treatment between men and women to continue. Problems with transparency and accountability of officials has further impeded efforts to protect women's human rights.

Women have also borne the brunt of regime policies on family planning. The PRC regime has used family law as a mechanism for pursuing population control policies under the rubric of "one child per family." Thus, the age of consent for marriage was raised from 20 years to 22 years for men and 18 years to 20 years for women. As well, the revised Marriage Law and associated marriage registration regulations impose an express duty to pursue family-planning practices. Enforcement has tended to be concentrated on women, imposing forced abortions and sterilization, with few parallel efforts imposed on men.

E. Minority nationalities

Building on the CPC's experience during the civil war with the complexities of relations with minority groups, the PRC Party/State has extolled ideals of cooperative relations with China's minority nationalities. Yet programs of development and assistance have been combined with policies of co-aptation and assimilation. Preferential policies on such issues as taxation, family planning standards, language usage, and education reflected ideals of assisting development for minorities but were aimed as well at inducing local communities to support the Party/State. Establishment of the Minorities University (*Minzu Daxue*) in Beijing, for example, reflected ideals of co-aptation and assimilation through education. Indeed, much of the tension between Han Chinese and minority nationalities stems from conflicted perspectives about these programs – many Han believing minorities to be ungrateful for all the effort spent on them by the Party/State, while many minorities chafe against imposition of the values and priorities of the dominant Han culture.

While criticisms abound over China's abuse of minorities in Inner Mongolia, Tibet, Xinjiang and other areas, the regime continues to defend its orthodoxy on minority nationalities.[17] The PRC Constitution and the Nationality Region Autonomy Law of the PRC (NRAL) provide basic principles on minority nationality matters. The Constitution expressed general ideals about rights of minority nationalities, qualified by insistence on national unity and submission to the central Party/State:

> *Article 4*: All nationalities in the People's Republic of China are equal. The State protects the lawful rights and interests of the minority nationalities and upholds and develops the relationship of equality, unity, and mutual assistance among all of China's nationalities. Discrimination against and oppression of any nationality are prohibited; any acts that undermine the unity of the nationalities or instigate their secession are prohibited. The State helps the areas inhabited by minority nationalities speed up their economic and cultural development in accordance with the peculiarities and needs of the different minority nationalities. Regional autonomy is practiced in areas where people of minority nationalities live in compact communities; in these areas, organs of self-government are established for the exercise of the right of autonomy. All the national autonomous areas are inalienable parts of the People's Republic of China. The people of all nationalities have the freedom to use and develop their own spoken and written languages, and to preserve or reform their own ways and customs.

Constitution Article 4.1 provides that all nationalities in China are equal, although this suggests a formalistic approach to equality, connoting equality of status rather than equality of actual conditions. Article 4.2 affirms that the State protects the lawful rights and interests of minorities and upholds and develops relationships of equality, unity, and mutual assistance among all nationalities. The rights and interests referred to in this provision must be lawful in order to be protected, meaning that these may not contravene provisions for Party supremacy, the socialist system, state interests and other privileged domains, whose protection is the prerequisite to "lawfulness." Article 4.3 prohibits discrimination against and oppression of any nationality, and prohibits acts undermining the unity of nationalities or instigating their secession, although the term "any nationality" includes the dominant Han Chinese and so works to undermine restrictions on Han Chinese activities in minority areas. Article 4.5 provides for the carrying out of regional autonomy and the establishment of organs of self-government, but affirms that all nationality autonomous areas are inalienable parts of China. Article 4.6 provides for local language usage and protection of local cultures, although practical implementation remains problematic as Mandarin (*putonghua*) remains the dominant language in China's minority nationality areas.

The Nationality Region Autonomy Law (NRAL) affirms the importance of the basic Constitutional structure for implementing Party/State policies on ethnic issues and stresses the centrality of the unified Chinese State (NRAL, Art. 5). The NRAL summarizes China's national policies and historical experience in managing relations with its minority nationalities. Enacted initially in 1984, the law was amended in 2001 to account primarily for inclusion of issues related to economic development. The NRAL is aimed expressly at resolving contradictions in the relationships between central and local authority. The NRAL delegates to Autonomous Region Governments limited autonomy to handle civic affairs that are deemed by the Party/State to be a legitimate focus of local governance, even as Article 15 of the NRAL requires submission to central government leadership and central legal and regulatory provisions. NRAL Article 19 specifies central approval for such local regulatory measures. Decisions and edicts enacted by "higher state organs" (*shangji guojia jiguan*) deemed inappropriate to local conditions may be adjusted or suspended, but this requires local autonomy area organs to seek prior approval from the issuing bodies (NRAL Art. 20). Economic and financial policies enacted by nationality autonomous areas, while supposedly based on local conditions and requirements, remain subject to the leadership of state planning (NRAL Art. 25).

The underlying principles informing the NRAL underscore the dominance of central control. Revisions to the NRAL in 2001 were made in part to acknowledge the expanded role accorded China's socialist legal system generally, as well as to support increased investment and development in minority areas, and ensure coordination with other regulatory regimes in China. The unitary state principle dictates that local laws and regulations conform to central Party/State policies, conform to the limits on jurisdiction conferred to the localities, and conform to laws enacted at the national level. Thus, the NRAL reiterates constitutional provisions on securing NPC Standing Committee approval for local autonomy regulations and special regulations before they go into effect. While the NRAL purportedly recognizes local autonomy, requirements for central approvals and the subordination of local economic programs to national supervision suggest that autonomy remains highly constrained.

China's 2009 White Paper on Ethnic Policy[18] affirms the basic policy priorities of central control voiced through discourses of equality, unity, autonomy, and development:

18. Full equality among ethnic groups is a constitutional principle of China. The Constitution of the People's Republic of China (hereinafter referred to as the "Constitution") stipulates: "All ethnic groups in the People's Republic of China are equal." Based on this principle, the Law of the People's Republic of China on Regional Ethnic Autonomy (hereinafter referred to as the "Law on Regional Ethnic Autonomy") [this reference is to the NRAL] and other laws and regulations make clear and detailed stipulations about equality among ethnic groups.

19. In China, the definition of full equality among ethnic groups includes three aspects: first, regardless of their population size,

length of history, area of residence, level of economic and social development, differences in spoken and written languages, religious beliefs, folkways and customs, every ethnic group has equal political status; second, all ethnic groups in China have not only political and legal equality, but also economic, cultural, and social equality; third, citizens of all ethnic groups are equal before the law, enjoying the same rights and performing the same duties.

The White Paper reasserts the principle of equality among ethnic groups, regardless of their population, size, history, and level of social and economic development (Section II). The doctrine of formal equality limits efforts to overcome disparities of wealth and development between Han and local minorities, thus undermining efforts to provide structural benefits and preferences for marginalized groups. The White Paper acknowledges the importance of poverty alleviation and improved healthcare in minority areas, subject to central control over alleged separatism and minority nationalism (Sections III and V). The White Paper emphasizes principles of ethnic unity, emphasizing the efforts to punish local minorities for challenging Party/State orthodoxy on matters of minority policy or human rights and governance in minority areas – tantamount to an official admission that repression will be used to ensure Han control of minority communities in minority areas.

China purports to incorporate international law standards into its minority policies, yet avoids their mandatory application. A party to the International Convention on Elimination of All Forms of Racial Discrimination, China has imposed a reservation against the binding jurisdiction of the International Court of Justice to hear disputes raised under the treaty.

However, independent analysts have concluded that China's treatment of minority nationalities remains inconsistent with both local and international standards:[19]

Government policy in Tibetan areas and in Xinjiang most often contravenes the Chinese Constitution and law . . . Since 2000, China's autonomous regions have experienced increased economic output and improved transportation and communication networks, but central control over development policy and financial resources has weakened economic autonomy in minority areas and disproportionately favored Han Chinese in Tibetan, Uighur, and other border areas.

As indicated by the violence that broke out in Tibet and in Tibetan regions in Gansu, Sichuan, and Qinghai in March 2008, Party and government policies aimed at building stability and development have resulted in ongoing resentment.[20] In Xinjiang, the outbreak of violence in Urumqi in July 2009 signaled further failures of China's policies of control.[21] In Inner Mongolia, local protests over perceived mistreatment of the legacy of Genghis Khan reflected ongoing tensions over Party/State policies on local culture.[22]

II. EMERGING PRIORITIES IN SOCIAL DEVELOPMENT

Aside from traditional priorities for China in the area of social development, the Party/State uses the PRC legal system to confront new challenges born of China's economic transformation. Control of information has long been a matter of concern for the Party/State as it has attempted to ensure popular support for its leadership and programs. Environmental protection has become an emerging feature of government policy in response to the degradation that has occurred over many decades of economic development. Corporate social responsibility has become a rapidly emerging area of policy discourse that attempts to harness the energies of economic growth for the service of social development.

A. Media and the internet

Control of information remains a high priority. Influenced by a traditional political culture in the CPC of hostility to competing sources of authority, the PRC government has imposed censorship routinely on information domestic and foreign. During the Maoist period, mundane information, such as weather reporting as well as concerning a wide range of socio-economic and political events, was routinely suppressed, while international news was carefully managed to ensure that China's own conditions were portrayed in a favorable light. During the post-Mao reform period under Deng Xiaoping, there was considerable relaxation of censorship, although this tended to follow the cycles of *fang* and *shou* (relaxation and restriction) that characterize political and policy life. For example, during the 1989 student democracy demonstrations across China, many news outlets, inspired by reformist political patrons, defied attempts at censorship and publicized student demands and activities, although after the June 4 crackdown intense censorship returned, reflecting the degree to which the political leadership reaffirmed a commitment to orthodoxy.

Administrative measures continue to be used to ensure control over information and expression:[23]

> The Chinese government has long tried to keep a tight rein on traditional and new media to prevent any challenges to its political authority. This has often entailed, watchdog groups say, strict media controls using monitoring systems, shutting down publications or websites, and jailing of dissident journalists and blogger/activists. China's censorship of its media again grabbed headlines in early 2011, when, following an online appeal for Chinese citizens to emulate the revolutions in the Middle East, the government clamped down on foreign media (AP), arrested dissidents, and mobilized thousands of policemen. Google's battle with the Chinese government over Internet censorship in China

and the awarding of the 2010 Nobel Peace Prize to jailed Chinese activist Liu Xiaobo have also drawn increased international attention to media censorship in China. At the same time, the country's burgeoning economy has allowed for greater diversity in China's media coverage, and experts say the growing Chinese demand for information is testing the regime's control over the media.

A variety of Party/State departments, including the Communist Party's Central Propaganda Department, the General Administration of Press and Publication, the State Administration of Radio, Film, and Television, the Public Security Bureau, and the Ministry of State Security all play a role in enforcing censorship over publications. Censorship of print media such as books and newspapers has long been the norm in the PRC, and continues today, ensuring that books printed in China and newspapers do not contain politically objectionable information or opinions.[24] Print censorship is authorized under the State Council's "Regulations on Administration of Publishing" (2001). The State Secrets Law of the PRC (rev. 2010) poses additional restrictions against publishing information deemed a state secret, such as policy decisions; economic and social affairs; and science and technology, as well as information on national security and diplomacy. While certain newspapers such as *Southern Weekend* (*Nanfang zhoumo*) and *Finance* (*Caijing*) have managed to publish politically sensitive articles, many of which challenge government policies and practices, the vast majority of China's official media outlets remain subservient to regime orthodoxy.

The Internet has posed significant challenges for regime efforts to control information, as Chinese micro-blog sites such as *Weibo* and international Chinese language news services such as *Boxun* provide content that often conflicts with official reporting. While many in China support broad access to the Internet, arguing that China's economic growth depends on supporting an "information economy," the

Party/State has focused on controlling unfavorable information. China's Internet regulations reflect this tension between state control and access to information. The "Regulation on Security Protection for Computer Information Systems" (1994) authorizes the Ministry of Public Security to oversee Internet security. The "Provisional Regulations on Management of International Connections for Computer Networks" (1996) provide that Internet service providers (ISPs) must be licensed by the government and that all Internet traffic be routed through government controlled networks. The Ministry of Public Security's "Regulation on Security Management Procedures for Internet Access" (1997) prohibits creating, acquiring, or distributing information deemed "harmful," as including the following:

1. violations of the Constitution, laws, or regulations of China;
2. information inciting overthrow of the government or the socialist system;
3. information promoting separatism or harming national unity;
4. information harming the unity of nationalities;
5. information containing falsehoods or rumors;
6. information that undermines social order;
7. information supporting terrorism;
8. information injuring the reputation of state organizations.

Under the "Computer Information Network and Internet Security, Protection, and Management Regulations" (1997), Internet users are prohibited from a wide range of expression considered in violation of law, challenging to the government or the socialist system, harming national unification, injuring the reputation of government departments, or otherwise deemed objectionable for various enumerated reasons. The Ministry of Information Industry's "Measures for Administration of Internet Information Providers" (2000) controls Internet use through licensing requirements for ISPs and rules on disclosure of information on users. The "Decision on Strengthening the Protection of Online Information" enacted in late 2012 imposed further restrictions against accessing unapproved information.

Taken together, these and other regulatory restrictions, combined with the Ministry of Public Security's ongoing surveillance of Internet traffic, have created the so-called "Great Firewall of China" as an obstacle to open access to information. While some Internet censorship initiatives have been recalled in the face of resistance from international and domestic companies, the government remains committed to ongoing restriction of public access to Internet-based information. The examples of Google and Yahoo attempting to placate government censors exemplified the dilemma facing international media companies doing business in China.[25]

B. Environmental protection

Environmental protection in China has been a challenge throughout the time of the People's Republic.[26] Despite received wisdom about the reverence in traditional China for the natural environment, historical patterns of deforestation and abuse of water resources set a precedent for human degradation of the environment – practices that accelerated under the Maoist ideal of conquering nature in pursuit of industrialization.[27] During the post-Mao period, economic developmental policies further marginalized efforts at preservation and protection.[28]

Environmental law and policy in the PRC today reflect conflicting policy imperatives balancing environmental protection with promotion of economic growth. The government has enacted an extensive array of laws and regulations to support environmental protection. Grounded in provisions of the PRC Constitution specifying state ownership over natural resources (Art. 9), laws and regulations on environmental protection rely on the state's regulatory and supervisory authority. Current laws and regulations find their antecedents in the Environmental Protection Law of the PRC (1990) (EPL) drafted under the aegis of Premier Li Peng, who was later vilified as the architect of the Tiananmen massacre. Drafted in the aftermath of the rush to economic development and industrialization that occurred after 1978, the EPL attempted to secure administrative authority for governmental agencies to oversee environmental protection efforts.

The EPL provides overall direction on environmental protection, while attempting to accommodate the needs of development:

Article 1: This Law is formulated for the purpose of protecting and improving people's environment and the ecological environment, preventing and controlling pollution and other public hazards, safeguarding human health and facilitating the development of socialist modernization.

Article 4: The plans for environmental protection formulated by the state must be incorporated into the national economic and social development plans; the state shall adopt economic and technological policies and measures favorable for environmental protection so as to coordinate the work of environmental protection with economic construction and social development.

Article 6: All units and individuals shall have the obligation to protect the environment and shall have the right to report on or file charges against units or individuals that cause pollution or damage to the environment.

Article 7: The competent department of environmental protection administration under the State Council shall conduct unified supervision and management of the environmental protection work throughout the country.

The law specifies administrative authority of State agencies (now primarily the Ministry of Environmental Protection) over environmental regulation and allocated jurisdiction to local governments to oversee regulation and protection efforts. The EPL also specifies that environmental protection measures should be incorporated into economic planning, thus setting up the possibility of cooperation or competition between environmental agencies and those responsible for economic development policy, such as the National Development and Reform Commission. The EPL specifies the responsibility and potential civil and criminal liability for enterprises found in violation of the pollution and environmental protection provisions in the law and associated regulations. The EPL imposes on local people's governments at various levels responsibility for environmental quality in the areas under their jurisdiction and responsibility to take measures to improve environmental conditions. This extends to prevention and control of pollution and other environmental hazards.

The 2003 PRC Environmental Impact Assessment Law (EIAL) was enacted "in order to implement the sustainable development strategy, to take precautions against adverse effects on the environment after implementation of plans and completion of construction projects, and to promote the coordinated development of the economy, society and environment" (Art. 1). The law requires relevant departments of the State Council as well as local people's governments at the prefecture and provincial levels to develop plans on land use that incorporate environmental impact assessments:

Article 2: Evaluation of environmental effects mentioned in this Law consists of the analysis, prediction, and assessment made of the possible environmental effects after implementation of plans and completion of construction projects, ways put forth and measures for preventing or mitigating the adverse effects on the environment, and the methods and systems applied for follow-up monitoring.

Article 3: When plans within the scope . . . of this Law are formulated, the environmental effects produced by the projects to be constructed within the territory of the People's Republic of China or within the sea areas under the jurisdiction of the People's Republic of China shall be evaluated in accordance with this Law.

Article 4: The environmental effects shall be evaluated in an objective, open and impartial manner, with an all-round consideration given to the possible effects on the various environmental factors and on the ecological system, which is composed of the factors, after a plan is implemented or a project is constructed, providing a scientific basis for decision-making.

The EIAL requires environmental impact assessments to be made for "special programs" in industry, agriculture, forestry, energy, and a range of other sectors, which must include analysis, countermeasures, and a conclusion on environmental impacts. Environmental assessments must be consulted in the course of project approval.

These general provisions are augmented by a range of laws and regulations on specific issues such as conservation, water protection, and pollution control. China's Air Pollution Law (2000) and Water Law (rev. 2002) specify the state's authority (now under the Ministry of Water Resources) to regulate and protect water resources to meet the needs of economic and social development. The state is charged to conduct strategic planning for water usage and development of water resources. Specific laws on water conservation (1991) and pollution prevention and control (1996) combine with regulations on such issues as water use permits and flood prevention to strengthen regulatory authority and authorize punishment of violators.

Despite the wealth of legislation and formal regulations supporting environmental protection, problems remain.[29] Water pollution affects the majority of China's rivers and marine areas. Chemical spills are common – the well-publicized benzene spill into Jilin Province's Songhua River in 2005 was but one example of a widespread problem made worse by worrying evidence of cover-ups by local officials. Despite censoring by the authorities, Chinese blogs were replete with condemnation of the misinformation that characterized official reporting on the spill. A government pollution census released in 2010 found that water pollution was twice as severe as previously recognized, while more than 40 percent of monitored rivers were "unsuitable for human contact."[30] The authorities also conceded that all available water resources will have been exploited by 2030. Air pollution is also severe, as indoor and outdoor pollution are responsible for close to 700,000 premature deaths in China each year. The nine-fold increase in China's fossil fuel emissions has contributed to an air pollution crisis that has resulted in 16 of the world's 20 most polluted cities being in China. Air pollution is not confined to the cities, but is also widely evident in rural areas, presenting a major obstacle to sustainability.

Albeit hampered somewhat by economic growth policies that provide few incentives for government officials to protect environmental conditions at the risk of employment and economic growth levels, the government has expressed increased awareness of the importance of protecting the natural environment. In 2004, the government announced that the "Green GDP" policy would replace the conventional GDP as the measure of China's development. The State Council's 2006 plan for environmental protection focused on sustainable development and called for evaluation of local cadres to include "Green GDP" requirements of environment and sustainability as categories in the cadre evaluation form. Policy commitments to restore water resources, and conserve natural resources and energy suggest important levels of awareness. The 12th Five Year Plan (2011–15) gives specific preference to sustainable development goals linked with environmental protection, while the State Council's 2010 opinion on utilizing foreign investment and the 2011 guiding catalogue for foreign investment offer incentives for environmentally sustainable projects.[31]

Nonetheless, the destructive effects of rapid economic growth continue, as local governments and officials are often complicit in environmental destruction. Imperatives to increase investment, economic growth rates and employment are often given priority by local government agencies and officials over conservation and environmental protection. The increased involvement of local community groups and semi-autonomous NGOs has brought additional voices to the table and begun to challenge the government's long-standing monopoly on environmental protection discourse. This has the potential to undermine the traditional approach that placed primary authority for environmental management with the government.

C. Corporate social responsibility

Efforts to link social development goals with economic growth policies are evident in China's approach to corporate social responsibility (CSR).[32] Chinese regulatory authorities are increasingly suggesting that formal commitments to CSR principles be included as conditions for business license approval. Civil awareness campaigns on CSR are also aimed at building business compliance. These efforts are evident particularly in areas of labor relations, healthcare, and environmental protection. Recognizing perhaps that public sector measures alone will likely be inadequate to address these problems effectively, the government has encouraged greater participation by the private sector.

China's CSR priorities emerge from the discourse of a "Harmonious Society" through which the Hu Jintao leadership has attempted to balance economic growth imperatives with attention to social development.[33] Economic growth priorities are evident in state economic plans, such that the 12th Fifth Year Plan (2011–15) continues to cite

economic growth as the primary objective. Economic growth imperatives are also evident in the foreign investment guide and catalog of
2011 and the State Council's 2010 opinion on foreign investment.
However, each of these measures also contains references to the need
to build sustainability into China's economic development program
– primarily through an emphasis on energy and resource conservation
and environmental production. The social development objectives of
the current government are evident in the Public Health Reform Plan,
which aims to improve universal access to public healthcare; the Rural
Development Program, which aims to invest significant resources in
infrastructure and social services in the rural areas; education reform
efforts aimed at improving access to public education for those who
cannot afford the emerging opportunity of private schools; and the
government's extensive legislative and regulatory efforts on environmental protection.

While many specialists insist that economic growth and social
development can coexist and indeed complement each other, the policy
process in China often poses obstacles. The dominant influence of the
National Development and Reform Commission's economic growth
priorities often works to marginalize the influence of government ministries and agencies charged with such social development imperatives
as labor relations, public health, and environmental protection. As well,
local cadre evaluation and promotion processes continue to privilege
economic indicators such as employment, capital investment, and economic growth rates over attention to working conditions, healthcare,
and environment. These policy distortions, combined with underlying
socio-cultural and political obstacles to enforcement of formal law and
regulation have contributed to the generally weak state of legal performance in areas of labor relations, healthcare, and environmental
protection. China's CSR initiatives should be understood against this
background of policy competition and legal and regulatory enforcement, raising the question whether CSR is a substitute for legal

compliance or a supplement. Many lawyers and law professors in China wonder whether the campaign-style rhetoric of China's CSR programs will undermine formal and consistent enforcement of China's laws and regulations.

Workplace health and safety is a key element in China's CSR policies. China's Ministry of Health and other agencies have enacted regulations and laws aimed at improving workplace health and safety, but violations appear still to be widespread as indicated by the continued phenomenon of mass labor demonstrations. Although minimum wage regulations have been enacted, enforcement remains uneven. China's labor-related CSR campaigns seem aimed at augmenting existing legislative and regulatory requirements and encouraging improved performance by employers. Environmental protection is another CSR priority for China, inviting uncertainty as to the relationship between CSR directives and enforcement of existing environmental laws and regulations. Similarly, education is presented as a CSR priority by which firms are encouraged to provide education and training for their employees – raising questions whether CSR performance is a substitute for the education and vocational training requirements set forth in the Labor Law and the Labor Contract Law.

China's CSR priorities include consumer protection, reflecting in part the absence of consensus on revisions to the 1994 Consumer Protection Law. Consumer protection issues include food and product safety and medical safety, raising questions about the relationship between CSR policies and enforcement of national legislation on food safety, consumer protection, and pharmaceutical safety. Despite existing legislation and regulation, enforcement problems continue to emerge in such areas as food safety inspections, clinical trial approvals for new medicines, and product safety concerns. Whether CSR priorities in these areas will lead to greater enforcement of existing legislation or represent a political alternative to legal enforcement remains uncertain.

Community outreach is another priority in China's CSR efforts. The increased use of public hearings for legislative and regulatory enactments as well as community advisory boards for factories and businesses represent efforts to include greater community involvement in the process of linking economic growth to social development. China's Company Law provides for external (and purportedly independent) directors as well as supervisory committees for certain limited liability companies. These legal provisions are augmented by the CSR initiatives encouraging firms to build in dimensions of community outreach to their operations even when they are not required to do so by specific laws or regulations.

Business corruption represents perhaps the most telling example of the interplay between legal enforcement and CSR policy campaigns. The PRC has struggled since its founding to combat corruption. The so-called, "campaign against counter-revolutionaries" in 1949–50 labeled "officials taking bribes" as a target, while the 1951 "three-anti" (*san fan*) campaign targeted corruption by newly recruited Party cadres as a major target. While the Maoist state planning system limited opportunities for economic corruption, political relationships of patronage and criticism were often abused for personal gain. With the onset of economic reforms, economic corruption returned as a challenge for governance. Indeed, the 1989 student democracy movement began as an anti-corruption effort. After the 1992 "deepening of reform," corruption problems increased such that by 2007, PRC Government reporting identified corruption as the primary concern of people living in the PRC.[34]

The PRC government has attempted numerous efforts to combat corruption – primarily through direct prohibition and highly publicized punishment of officials. The Criminal Law of the PRC contains an entire section on "economic crimes," most of which involve corruption of one sort or another – bribery, price manipulation, speculation, etc. The Administrative Litigation Law (1990) discussed in chapter 2 was enacted in part to curb corrupt behavior by local officials. Providing for judicial review of administrative actions, the ALL allows citizens to sue officials for breaking the law in the course of making administrative decisions on a wide array of licensing and regulatory matters where corruption is often involved. The Anti-Unfair Competition Law (1993) contains prohibitions against abuse of regulatory authority and bribery (Arts. 7 and 8), while the Anti-Money Laundering Law (2011) is aimed to prevent and punish efforts to conceal or transfer proceeds from corruption.

The Company Law represents another systemic effort at combating corruption through regulation of corporate governance. The Company Law applies to state-owned as well as to privately held limited liability companies (LLCs) and publicly-traded companies limited by shares. The Company Law provides that company business operations must comply with PRC law and administrative regulation and also conform to social morality and business morality (Art. 5). Companies must act in good faith, accept the supervision of the government and the general public, and bear social responsibility. Company directors are bound to avoid conflicts of interest that injure the company and otherwise to perform their duties to further the interests of the company (Art. 21). In an effort to strengthen the capacity of boards of directors to conform to standards of fiduciary duty to the company, the 2005 revisions to the Company Law included a provision for appointment of independent directors (Art. 123). A similar provision is under consideration for state-owned enterprises controlled by the central government. Following the German company law model, the Company Law provides for a Supervisory Committee to supervise acts of directors in performance of their duties (Art. 52). Supervisory Boards are mandatory for joint stock limited companies (JSLCs), while they may be established for LLCs (Arts. 52 and 118). Supervisory Committees may complement the use of outside directors, by providing additional independent oversight over company affairs.

As well, high profile trials and punishment of corrupt officials such as former Beijing mayor Chen Xitong, and Shanghai Party Secretary Chen Liangyu have been aimed to deter others under the adage "killing the chicken to scare the monkey." A governmental "central leading group," established in 2006, signified new levels of attention from the Party/State on the problem of corruption, reviewing in part the continued close interplay between legal enforcement and political and policy initiative. As indicated in its 2011 policy White Paper on the subject, the government maintains that it is committed to combating corruption:[35]

> As dramatic changes have been taking place in China's economic system, social structure, the pattern of interests, and people's ideas and concepts, various social contradictions have become increasingly prominent. Since the relevant mechanisms and systems are still incomplete, corruption persists, some cases even involving huge sums of money. Breaches of law and discipline tend to be more covert, intelligent and complicated. The situation in combating corruption is still very serious, and the tasks are still abundant.
>
> The CPC and the Chinese government always keep a clear vision of the long-haul, complicated and arduous nature of the undertaking of combating corruption and building a clean government. They will continue to follow the overall plan to establish and perfect the system of punishment and prevention of corruption, resolutely punish and effectively prevent corruption with more resolutions and powerful measures, so as to win the people's confidence with actual achievements in the anti-corruption campaign.

Unfortunately these efforts do not seem to have much long-term effect, as evidence of corruption expands despite periodic crack-downs, many of which are dismissed by popular opinion as politically motivated and unconcerned with systemic improvements. The purge of Bo

Xilai in 2012 underscored the seriousness of corruption as a nation-wide problem that touches virtually every level of the Party/State. The official China Academy of Social Sciences (CASS) has published the results of an extensive investigation into corrupt financial dealings by company executives and state officials, revealing numerous instances of unlawful capital transfers out of China.[36] In contrast to the rather optimistic tenor of the official White Paper, the CASS report offered a refreshingly, albeit bleakly, candid view of the seriousness of the problem.

The emergence of CSR initiatives and campaigns reflects the government's dilemma of securing social development conditions in the face of policy priorities of economic growth. Much of the development of China's legal system over the past several decades can be attributed to policy decisions favoring economic growth subject to the political control of the Party/State. However, consistent enforcement and performance of the myriad of laws and regulations that have been formally enacted remains problematic. In particular, the government has faced significant difficulties in securing performance of the public interest provisions embedded in most of China's laws and regulations on economic development. China's CSR efforts represent an ironic return to the campaign-style measures of earlier years, in an effort to secure social development in the face of indifferent performance by the engines of economic growth and the continued limits on effective legal regulation.

SUMMARY

Social development remains a key policy priority for the PRC. Traditional priorities of the PRC Party/State in the areas of labor relations, healthcare, education, women's rights, and the treatment of minorities continue to receive attention. Laws and regulations in each of these areas reflect the content and direction of evolving policy decisions. As well, newly emerging policy challenges related to information control and environmental protection have become the focus of legislative and regulatory initiatives. Efforts to link social development with China's economic growth programs are evident in recent initiatives on corporate social responsibility. In each of these areas, policy priorities of the Party/State are expressed in the content of particular laws and regulations. Such instrumentalism suggests both the power of the regime to entrench policy preferences, but also raises questions about the permanence and consistency of the legal regime concerning social development.

DISCUSSION QUESTIONS

1. How does the PRC legal system reflect policy priorities in areas of labor relations, public health, and education?

2. How have policies of the PRC Party/State on women's rights and treatment of minorities been reflected in laws and regulation?

3. How have emerging priorities of the PRC Party/State on information control and environmental protection been reflected in laws and regulation?

4. How has the PRC legal system addressed issues of corruption?

SUGGESTIONS FOR FURTHER READING

China: An International Journal, vol. 8, no. 1, Special Issue on Health Policy (March 2010).

Day, Kristen A., ed., *China's Environment and the Challenge of Sustainable Development* (Armonk, NY: M.E. Sharpe, 2005).

Ho, Virginia E. Harper, "From Contracts to Compliance? An Early Look at Implementation Under China's New Labor Legislation," *Columbia Journal of Asian Law*, vol. 23, no. 1 (2009), pp. 35–107.

Hom, Sharon, "Law, Development, and the Rights of Chinese Women: A Snapshot from the Field," *Columbia Journal of Asian Law*, Special Issue: Celebrating the Work of Stanley Lubman, vol. 19, no. 1 (Spring–Fall, 2005), pp. 345–60.

Mackerras, Colin, *China's Ethnic Minorities and Globalisation* (London: Routledge, 2003).

Reporters Without Borders, "Journey to the Heart of Internet Censorship" (October, 2007), http://www.rsf.org/IMG/pdf/Voyage_au_coeur_de_la_censure_GB.pdf (accessed October 15, 2012).

5	International Engagement

China's legal system supports a wide range of international activities and relationships that have accompanied China's emergence in the world system over the past 30 years. This chapter addresses issues of China's international engagement, including membership in the GATT/WTO, participation in international regimes on human rights and sustainability, and engagement with international treaty regimes affecting China's boundary management policies.

I. CHANGING PERSPECTIVES ON INTERNATIONAL LAW

During the early years of the PRC, official responses to the international legal regime reflected conclusions that the system was created without China's participation and expressed normative positions that conflicted with China's historical conditions and interests.[1] With the establishment of the PRC in 1949, and the removal of the Republic of China to Taiwan, Cold War politics resulted in the exclusion of the People's Republic from most international legal institutions. The PRC's status in international law involved contested issues of state succession and recognition, which in turn affected questions such as UN membership, treaty-making authority, and the legitimacy of the ROC government on Taiwan.

While challenging the authority of "bourgeois international law" and rejecting the historical legacy of "unequal treaties," the PRC nonetheless participated in a range of trade and diplomatic treaty relations throughout the 1950s with states in Europe, the developing world, and within the Soviet Union's realm of influence. During the Cultural Revolution, the PRC's critique of international law as little more than imposed policy preferences of bourgeois imperialism deepened, and was accompanied by challenges to foreign diplomatic missions in China and a short-lived withdrawal of Chinese diplomats from missions abroad. Nonetheless, admission to the United Nations in 1971, coupled with recognition by Canada (1970), Japan (1972), and the United States (1979), confirmed the PRC's emerging international legal status.

During the post-Mao period, expanded PRC participation in the international law regime and increased openness to academic research signaled conflicted acceptance of the international legal order. Academic engagement with international law was reflected in the establishment of international law research centers at Peking and Wuhan Universities as well as the inclusion of international law as a curriculum component in the offerings of China's elite law schools. The expansion of international law research at the Chinese Academy of Social Sciences and at regional social science academies in Shanghai and elsewhere reflected the government's commitment to developing China's policy and research capacity in international law.

During the Deng Xiaoping era, China expanded its participation in bilateral and multilateral cooperation projects with universities and government agencies in Europe, North America, and Japan, aimed at increasing local capacity in various elements of international law performance. The PRC Law on the Process for Concluding International Treaties (1990) confirmed the role of the Ministry of Foreign Affairs in administering the signing of international treaties, subject to supervision and approval of the State Council. While much received wisdom suggested that China was a careful observer of international law norms, this view has been challenged as problems with China's participation in international legal institutions and its treaty performance became clearer.[2] Debates continue on the question of whether international treaties are self-enforcing in China's domestic law regime or whether specific implementing legislation (e.g., PRC Law on the Territorial Sea) or revisions to existing laws (e.g., PRC Civil Aviation Law) is required.[3]

The Chinese government's violent suppression of democracy demonstrations in 1989 created a significant rift in China's relations with the world. Suspension of bilateral cooperation programs with the United States, Europe, Canada and other regions, combined with the chorus of criticism that greeted attendance at international fora by PRC officials, revealed the depth of international revulsion over the Chinese government's violent suppression of calls for political reform. Following Deng Xiaoping's 1992 inspection tour to southern China, the PRC attempted to broaden its engagement with the world community. Aside from closer engagement with international trade and investment systems, China also pursued expanded human rights diplomacy, attempting to influence international substantive discourses on human rights and to deflect attention away from its own human rights abuses. China also expanded its international political and diplomatic activities, participating more fully in UN agencies on health, labor, and arms control and in crisis management in the Middle East and Central Europe. Under the post-Deng leadership of Jiang Zemin and then Hu Jintao, China's participation in the international legal regime has been coupled with pursuit of economic and security interests in the context of processes of globalization.

II. FOREIGN BUSINESS RELATIONS

In keeping with policy priorities in economic development, China's engagement with the international system has given significant priority to international economic relations. Prior to the 1978 economic and legal reforms, China's foreign business relations were conducted mostly with countries allied with the former Soviet Union. Canada's decision to sell wheat to China in 1960 during the great famine despite the US-led embargo was a particularly important exception to the general exclusion of China from the international trade and investment market.

During the first decade of the post-Mao reforms, China opened its doors to foreign investment and began the process of rejoining the General Agreement on Tariffs and Trade (GATT). China's application to join the GATT and its success in joining the World Trade Organization (WTO) represent significant achievements in the process of interaction with international governance systems. While the state-dominated structure of China's foreign trade and investment systems remained significantly at variance from the market-based norms of the GATT, the application process proceeded apace. Another complicating factor was the precise stature of China's application – was the PRC to resume the seat vacated by the Republic of China after its defeat in the revolution and removal to Taiwan, or was it to be treated as a new application that would bring with it various trade concessions accorded new members. In the end, China got a bit of both.

The 1989 Tiananmen crisis delayed consideration of China's GATT application, and China failed to join in time to be considered a founding member of the WTO when it was established in 1995. After further negotiations and considerable debate within China and amongst China's trading partners, the PRC was granted accession to the WTO in 2001. Accession came with conditions, however, that China move rapidly to open markets and improve market-based governance of trade and investment relations. While debate remains as to whether China has fully satisfied the conditions set forth in the Protocol of Accession, entry into the GATT/WTO has had significant effects on China's regulatory regimes for foreign trade and investment.[4]

From the time the Working Party on China's accession to the GATT was established in 1987, through to the establishment of the WTO in

1995, and culminating in the 2001 Final Report on China's accession to the WTO, the Working Party sought to identify points of conflict and commonality between Chinese trade policy and regulatory practice and GATT/WTO standards. Based on a 1997 "Draft Protocol," the 2001 Protocol of Accession confirmed China's agreement to abide by GATT/WTO standards and to further transition its economy to market standards. Concerns over China's ability and willingness to comply with GATT/WTO standards were evident in the Working Party's 2001 Final Report on accession.[5] Among the issues raised were problems of rule of law and judicial review; national treatment; currency and foreign exchange policy; intellectual property protection; and trade in services.

China's accession to the GATT/WTO and to side agreements on trade in services, intellectual property, and trade-related investment raised important challenges for legal and policy reform. Particular attention was paid to the broad themes of "most favoured nation treatment" (GATT, Art. I); "national treatment" (GATT, Article III); and "non-discrimination" (GATT, Art. XIII), as well as the requirements on reducing and eliminating tariffs and trade subsidies. China's accession indicated, formally at least, acceptance of GATT/WTO principles of market autonomy and a willingness to limit state actions of mercantilism and protectionism. This had particular expression in China's acceptance of GATT/WTO principles on transparency and rule of law (GATT Art. X) and its acknowledgement of the responsibility to ensure local compliance (GATT Art. XXIV). China's GATT/WTO accession also brought it within the purview of the WTO Dispute Settlement Body and its Appellate Body, through which binding decisions are made in trade disputes.

Following its accession to the GATT/WTO, China has participated increasingly actively in the world political economy. Increased trade and investment relations with Europe, Japan, and North America saw China increase both its trade flows[6] and share of received foreign direct investment (FDI).[7] China's participation in the GATT/WTO system has also led to participation in a range of trade and investment liberalization agreements with partners such as the Association of Southeast Asian Nations (ASEAN), New Zealand, and Hong Kong, and through which trade preferences are extended in conformity with GATT/WTO rules. China's international commitments on trade and investment provide essential context for the regulatory system on foreign trade and investment.

A. *Trade regulation*

Trade regulation in the PRC is subject to the general authority of the Department of Trade Administration in the PRC Ministry of Commerce. The Ministry of Commerce was created out of the former Ministry of Foreign Trade and Economic Cooperation (MOFTEC) – which had been preceded by the Ministry of Foreign Economic Relations, which itself had brought together the Ministries of Foreign Trade and Foreign Economic Relations and the State Commissions on Foreign Investment and on Imports and Exports. This centralization of authority over trade and investment regulation reflected not only bureaucratic politics of expansion of administrative agency authority and patronage, but also the recognition that trade and investment are intimately related in practice and are integrated closely with domestic economic affairs. The Ministry of Commerce operates at the central level and also through trade commissions established in the provinces and centrally administered cities (Beijing, Tianjin, Shanghai, Chongqing). Augmenting the work of the Ministry of Commerce is the China Council for the Promotion of International Trade (CCPIT), which operates as a trade promotion agency, chamber of commerce, and arbitration institute.

Trade regulation is conducted pursuant to the Foreign Trade Law of the PRC, and a multitude of subordinate and ancillary regulations.

The Foreign Trade Law was "formulated with a view to expanding the opening to the outside world, developing foreign trade, maintaining foreign trade order, protecting the legitimate rights and interests of foreign trade operators and promoting the sound development of the socialist market economy" (Art. 1). As with other legislation, the Foreign Trade Law supports implementation of policies enacted by the Party/State. Although, as a product of China's accession to the GATT/WTO, the Trade Law expresses policies oriented more toward markets than state planning, the law continues to assert the autonomy of the Party/State to regulate foreign trade.

While the range of entities authorized to engage in foreign trade as "foreign trade operators" under the Foreign Trade Law has expanded considerably from the early days of reform, when only state enterprises associated with the large central government trading agencies could conduct foreign trade, state control remains effective through the import and export licensing system. Reflecting China's policy goals of export-led economic growth, administration of licenses to export remains considerably more flexible than import licensing, which must conform to non-competition and technology licensing restrictions. Imports are also subject to "commodity inspection" processes which often involve so-called "non-tariff barriers" – barriers to trade that do not take the form of import tariffs and customs duties.

The PRC Customs Bureau exercises inspection of imports and exports to confirm the validity of required licenses and the results of commodity inspection, and imposes import duties, which vary considerably between products and shipments in response to both broad policy directions and local administrative priorities. Special provisions are made for imports to foreign-invested enterprises for the purpose of producing exports. China's specially designated trade and investment areas (particularly the Special Economic Zones/SEZs, free trade zones, and economic and technology development zones/ETDZs) also enjoy preferential customs treatment.

Table 5.1   WTO Complaints in Comparative Perspective

Country	As Complainant	As Respondent	As Third Party
Argentina	18	21	44
Australia	7	13	73
Brazil	26	14	73
Canada	33	17	83
China	**10**	**29**	**92**
European Union	87	72	124
India	21	21	79
Japan	16	15	127
United States	103	119	97

Source: http://www.wto.org/english/tratop_e/dispu_e/dispu_by_
country_e.htm (accessed October 25, 2012).

China's regulation of import and export trade raises a number of issues around compliance with GATT/WTO standards. For imports, these include questions about the permissibility of import quotas and the potential application of non-tariff barriers. Export licensing issues include questions around export subsidies. In its bilateral agreements with the US, Canada, and the European Union required for accession to the GATT/WTO, China agreed to eliminate import quotas and import substitution requirements; comply with the transparency requirements of the GATT; avoid using standards and testing procedures to restrict imports; and generally reduce tariffs. Although many observers agree that China's regulation of foreign trade has become more regularized and consistent with the standards of the GATT/WTO, China continues to face numerous complaints over issues around subsidies and anti-dumping as well as market-access questions as indicated in table 5.1.

Noting the increased use of trade protection measures by its trade partners, the Foreign Trade Law incorporates GATT/WTO provisions on retaliatory measures:

Article 7: In the event that any country or region applies prohibitive, restrictive or other like measures on a discriminatory basis against the People's Republic of China in respect of trade, the People's Republic of China may, as the case may be, take counter-measures against the country or region in question.

Supported by the WTO/GATT provisions of Article XXIV of the GATT, China has pursued a range of bilateral free trade agreements (FTAs).[8] China has ratified FTAs with Pakistan, Chile, New Zealand, Singapore, Peru, Hong Kong, Macau, and Costa Rica. Additional agreements with Australia, Iceland, and Norway are under negotiation. China has also used the FTA approach to build regional trade arrangements. China has ratified an FTA with the Association of Southeast Asian Nations (ASEAN) and is in FTA negotiations with the South African Customs Union (SACU) and the Gulf Cooperation Council (GCC). While the matter remains subject to debate, influential policy voices have suggested that China is interested in joining (or at least cooperating with) the proposed Trans-Pacific Partnership (TPP).[9] These efforts complement China's trade regulatory system and underscore policies of engagement with the GATT/WTO world trading system.

B. *Foreign investment*

China's accession to the GATT/WTO has also had significant implications for foreign investment. The WTO agreements on trade-related investment measures (TRIMs), trade-related intellectual property (TRIPs) and trade in services (GATS) extend to these sectors protections enshrined in the original GATT treaty on trade in goods. As licenses for use of intellectual property rights and the provision of technical training often comprise components of foreign investment projects, their regulation under the GATT/WTO has a significant impact on foreign investment decisions and practices. As well, GATT/ WTO standards on matters such as transparency and the rule of law have general application to governance and regulation, with implications for trade and investment alike.

China's first law on foreign-invested joint ventures was promulgated in 1980, as part of the legal and economic reform package approved at the 1978 Third Plenum of the 11th CPC Central Committee. The Equity Joint Venture Law of the PRC (EJVL) and its Implementing Regulations applied only to so-called "equity joint ventures," in which Chinese and foreign parties contributed varying proportions of capital as equity contribution to the formation of limited liability companies. Under the EJVL, representation on the joint venture board of directors is allocated according to the proportion of equity contributed by the investing entities, although local regulatory restrictions and the informal realities of bureaucratic and regulatory control mean that the PRC side often has influence exceeding its proportion of capital contribution. Following preliminary discussions and the issuance of a "project commencement letter" that nominally authorizes the PRC side to commence discussions on a particular project, equity joint ventures are formed through an elaborate process of negotiation and approval involving contracts, feasibility studies, articles of association, and registration.[10] The formation process involves approvals by multiple agencies such as the state planning authorities (National Development and Reform Commission), the Ministry of Foreign Trade and Economic Cooperation (MOFTEC and its predecessors), the State Administration for Industry and Commerce (SAIC), and the tax and public security bureaus.

The linkage between proportion of equity contribution and managerial control over foreign-invested enterprises soon became problematic for foreign businesses, which hoped to limit their financial exposure while ensuring better control over their joint ventures in China. As a result, new creative forms of foreign business began to emerge – not always with formal policy acknowledgment, even though receiving the requisite bureaucratic approvals. The 1988 Cooperative Enterprise Law of the PRC (CJVL) formalized arrangements for foreign-invested enterprises in which the responsibilities of the parties and their control over business activities were negotiated through contract rather than being dependent on proportion of equity contribution. Pioneered by the Occidental Petroleum coal-mining project in northwest Shanxi province, cooperative enterprises (also referred to as "cooperative joint ventures") have become a common feature of the foreign investment landscape in China. While the structure of these enterprises was different from their equity joint venture counterparts, the approval process followed very much the same lines of (a) commencement letter; (b) feasibility study; (c) negotiation and approval of contract and articles of association; (d) business license issuance; and (e) tax and public security registrations.

Throughout the 1980s, the joint venture form remained dominant in China's foreign investment landscape. However, problems emerged from conflicting business goals and strategies between the Chinese and foreign partners – encapsulated in the phrase "sleeping in the same bed but having different dreams" (*tong chuang yi meng*). Foreign investors often found that their Chinese joint venture partners did not share their business objectives and long-term strategies. Conflicts between Chinese and foreign joint venture partners became common and pressure arose for permission to establish wholly foreign-owned subsidiaries in China. While this ran counter to long-established policy resistance to foreign control over local economic and market conditions (a legacy of the "semi-colonial" conditions of the late nineteenth and early twentieth centuries when foreigners and foreign business interests enjoyed privileged protection in China), PRC policy efforts at economic reform and particularly around access to the GATT/WTO led to changes in policy and law.

The Wholly Foreign-Owned Enterprise Law of the PRC (WFOEL) was enacted in 2000, updating and formalizing provisions of the 1986 Law on Enterprises Operated Exclusively With Foreign Capital and its Implementing Regulations (1990). While the approval process remains quite similar to that for equity and cooperative joint ventures, the WFOEL does not require the elaborate contract negotiation process involved with joint ventures. Certain business sectors, such as various financial and information industries and activities, natural resource exploration and development projects, and national security and defense industries are outside the permitted scope of WFOEs.

Thus, by the time of China's accession to the GATT/WTO in 2001, foreign investment in the PRC was already being pursued through a variety of foreign invested enterprises (FIEs), including equity joint ventures, cooperative enterprises (contractual joint ventures), and wholly foreign-owned enterprises. The Company Law of the PRC provides additional regulatory standards for these various types of foreign-invested companies (Art. 18). With the development of China's securities markets, new opportunities emerged to establish FIEs limited by shares and to establish foreign-owned investment holding companies. China's accession to the GATT/WTO resulted in further amendments to China's foreign investment laws to conform to market principles and also stimulated changes in the foreign investment regulatory system more broadly.

In anticipation of accession to the GATT/WTO, China enacted regulations that relieved joint ventures and wholly foreign-owned enterprises of the requirement to submit production and operations plans to departments in charge and to give priority to the Chinese market in purchasing supplies. As well, WFOEs were relieved of the obligation to use advanced technology and equipment or to be export-oriented (generally a 60% export quota). Barriers to sales by foreign-invested enterprises into the Chinese domestic market were also gradually eased. Of particular interest was the emerging practice by China's Ministry of Foreign Trade and Economic Cooperation (MOFTEC) of issuing "guidance catalogs" to inform foreign investors as to which sectors of China's economy were permitted, encouraged, restricted, or prohibited for foreign investment. China's WTO accession also stimulated efforts to simplify the process of balancing foreign exchange by foreign-invested enterprises that needed either to convert Chinese currency received from domestic sales into international currencies or to convert international currencies into Chinese currency in order to pay for local staff and materials. As mentioned above, China's tax system was unified in 2008 under the Enterprise Income Tax Law of the PRC, to apply equal tax treatment to FIEs and domestic enterprises.

A key element in China's foreign investment regulatory regime concerns the management of foreign exchange. Chinese currency, the RMB yuan, is not fully and freely convertible into foreign currency, but is subject to state-controlled exchange rates and procedures. Even after the specialized "foreign exchange certificates" required for all foreign-related transactions were abolished in 1994, significant regulatory restrictions were still imposed on both foreign currency transactions and the export of RMB. Pursuant to the "Foreign Exchange Control Regulations" of the PRC (1983), and its numerous ancillary regulations, foreign businesses operating in China were required to obtain government approvals under the authority of the State Administration of Foreign Exchange (SAFE) for exchanges of foreign currency into local RMB. This affected investment projects, particularly since these often involve investments of foreign currency and the generation of business income in RMB. This meant in effect that FIEs must exchange their international receipts (investment contributions, budget allocations, etc.) for local Chinese currency to pay local expenses, and that local Chinese currency receipts (business income) must be converted into foreign currency in order to be remitted abroad.

The PRC "Regulations on Foreign Exchange Control" were revised in 1997 and again in 2008 to liberalize controls on foreign exchange. Presently, foreign exchange transactions for current accounts are not restricted, but restrictions remain on capital accounts and on the import of foreign currency. The Foreign Exchange Regulations still require filing of documentation with Chinese customs authorities and foreign exchange banks for transactions that move foreign exchange in and out of China; and require approvals by SAFE for capital account transactions, securities, and other foreign exchange assets taken out of China. The PRC "Administrative Regulations on Settlements, Sales and Payments in Foreign Exchange" (1996) ("Settlement Regulations") imposed detailed requirements for filings and approvals for foreign exchange transactions, including requirements on the use of designated foreign exchange banks. Opening the market of designated foreign exchange banks to foreign investment was a key negotiating issue in the context of China's accession to the GATT/WTO.

China's regulatory regime for foreign investment was initially concerned almost exclusively with managing in-bound investment. Beginning in 1999, however, the government introduced a policy encouraging Chinese firms to invest abroad, although it took several years before significant impacts were seen. In particular, the new policy required changes to China's foreign exchange policies, which had restricted export of Chinese currency, the RMB yuan, thus inhibiting Chinese firms from investing abroad. With increased international investment opportunities for PRC firms (supported by China's massive foreign exchange surpluses) came further regulatory encouragement for outbound investment. Beginning in 2004, MOFTEC began to issue preferential policies on particular investment sectors, such as natural resource development. In 2009, regulations were issued loosening foreign exchange restrictions on Chinese companies investing abroad. The "Measures for the Administration of Overseas Investment" (2009) expressed broad government approval for expanded Chinese foreign investment abroad, while the SAFE "Regulations on Foreign Exchange Administration of the Overseas Direct Investment of Domestic Institutions" (2009) specified procedures to facilitate foreign exchange transactions by Chinese firms investing abroad.

The "Invest Abroad" program has helped China transition from being a capital importer to becoming a major investment force in the international market. Not surprisingly, China has become increasingly active in concluding Bilateral Investment Treaties (BITs).[11] While for many decades China's BITs had been aimed at protecting foreign business investments in China, China has come to see BITs as important instruments for protecting the interests of PRC investors operating abroad. Whereas in the 1980s, China's BITs were concluded generally with capital exporters like Australia, Japan, Singapore, and members of the European Union (e.g., Denmark, Italy), beginning in the 1990s, China's BIT network extended across the globe with particular emphasis on developing economies in Africa and Latin America.[12] Long-standing delays in concluding BITs with the US and Canada are also being resolved. Negotiations on a US–China BIT, delayed for many years over such issues as transparency of Chinese investment regulations and subrogation of insurance claims in the event of expropriation, have been accelerated.[13] A Foreign Investment Protection and Promotion Agreement with Canada was concluded in 2012 after a lengthy period of negotiation.[14] In addition to its bilateral investment agreements, over 90 ratified by mid-2012, China has also entered into a regional investment framework agreement with ASEAN to supplement the bilateral agreements in place with various ASEAN economies. As well, China's Export-Import Bank supports overseas investments by Chinese firms, linking China's Invest Abroad program with expanding foreign aid initiatives in developing economies.[15]

As with China's accelerated approach to free trade agreements, China's BIT network brings China more fully into the international investment regime – particularly the International Center for the

Settlement of Investment Disputes (ICSID) system for investor–state dispute resolution. This involves commitments to general principles of National Treatment, Most-Favored Nation Treatment, and Minimum Standards of Treatment (fair and equitable treatment, provision of full protection and security) associated with the GATT/WTO system.

C. Dispute resolution

China's international trade and investment relations unavoidably involve issues of dispute resolution. Arbitration of trade and investment disputes has emerged as a workable compromise between the overly informal processes of traditional mediation and the challenges of enforcing judicial decisions. The Arbitration Law of the PRC (1994) provided general rules for arbitration institutions and procedures. Arbitration and conciliation of disputes involving foreigners are often handled by the China International Economic and Trade Arbitration Commission (CIETAC), although the local provincial government arbitration bodies also have jurisdiction to handle these types of cases. Pursuant to the Arbitration Law, local arbitral bodies such as the Shanghai Arbitration Commission have been established under local people's governments to handle a wide array of foreign and domestic economic disputes. Maritime disputes are subject to the China Maritime Arbitration Commission. While rules have been enacted by CIETAC and other arbitral bodies requiring fairness and impartiality by arbitrators, *ex parte* private contacts between arbitrators and appointing parties as well as obstruction and delay in enforcement of awards and evidentiary rulings continue. Bureaucratic politics have also played a role, as Chinese courts often subject arbitral decisions to extensive review prior to enforcement.

Enforcement of arbitral awards is subject to the New York Convention on the Recognition and Enforcement of Foreign Arbitral Awards, which China ratified in 1986. China's compliance with the

New York Convention was called into question by the 1993 Revpower case, in which Revpower was blocked from enforcing an arbitral award in the amount of US$6.6 million plus interest issued by the Arbitration Institute of the Stockholm Chamber of Commerce against Shanghai Far East Aero-Technology Import & Export Corporation (SFAIC).[16] However, a series of Supreme People's Court edicts on enforcement of foreign arbitral awards has strengthened enforcement considerably.[17]

Arbitration of investment disputes is also available to foreign parties through China's participation in the Washington Convention on the Settlement of Investment Disputes. However, China's obligations remain voluntary, and so far no investor claim has been accepted by ICSID against China. China's expanded use of bilateral investment treaties containing ICSID dispute settlement provisions raises the possibility that China will become more active in the ICSID system. China is also a participant in the Hague Conference on Private International Law, which covers issues such as jurisdiction, conflicts of law, and recognition and enforcement of judgments, although the impact of this process on China's legal system so far remains limited.

III. PARTICIPATION IN INTERNATIONAL GOVERNANCE REGIMES

In addition to international economic relations, China's global engagement involves participation in international governance regimes. China should not be viewed as a passive recipient of international standards in this process. The power of the "Beijing Consensus" as a state-centered development model that offers alternatives to the market-oriented "Washington Consensus" speaks volumes about Beijing's increasing power to influence events and policies internationally.[18] As well, China has become increasingly influential in the workings of international governance organizations, while PRC scholars and officials have taken increasingly prominent positions in international organizations. Examples include Peking University economist Justin Yifu Lin, who has served as chief economist at the World Bank; trade ministry legal advisor Zhang Yuejiao, who served as General Counsel to the Asian Development Bank; and law professor Xue Hanqin, who serves on the International Court of Justice. China is certainly influencing the activities and perspectives of the international system.

Yet China continues to draw actively from international legal standards in establishing the contours of its own legal system. China also seeks to build legitimacy both domestically and internationally through its engagement with international legal standards. International governance regimes for human rights and sustainable development present useful examples of engagement with China's legal system.

A. Human rights

While many human rights matters are not new to China – the PRC Party/State has long stood for ideals of promoting the rights of women and workers, for example, China's re-engagement with the world system during the Deng era and afterward has meant engagement with international standards on a broader array of human rights issues. As indicated previously, China has signed both the International Covenant on Economic, Social and Cultural Rights (ICESCR) and the International Covenant on Civil and Political Rights (ICCPR), and has ratified the ICESCR, subject to reservations that preserve China's policy preferences on labor rights. China has ratified many other human rights treaties on such matters as preventing slavery, torture, and organized crime, as well as treaties protecting the rights of women, children, and minorities.[19] Amendments to the PRC Constitution in 2004 included the provision that "the State respects and protects human rights." Yet these efforts remain constrained by policy imperatives of economic development and the preservation of Party supremacy.

Just as ideologies of Marxism-Leninism provided a vernacular for explaining policy decisions by the PRC Party/State to emphasize development (forces of production) over class struggle (relations of production), so too has PRC law and policy on human rights been articulated through neo-Marxist doctrines around the "right to development." As a signatory of, and advocate for, the 1993 Bangkok Declaration on Human Rights,[20] China has placed strong emphasis on the right to development with associated principles on the supremacy of national sovereignty and state choice in the determination of local political systems and on the subordination of civil and political rights.

The Chinese government's views on the right to development have implications for the centrality of the Party/State as the source of rights and as the determinant of the beneficiaries of rights. Human rights are often characterized as either "positive rights" to certain conditions such as health, housing, working conditions, and a clean environment, and "negative rights," which concern protection of various behaviors such as expression, religion, and association against intrusion by the state. China's rights orthodoxy around the right to development tends to support state involvement in protection of a range of "positive rights" such as employment, healthcare, housing, and education, rather than recognition of "negative" civil and political rights against state control. As well, in contrast to natural rights theories that view rights as inalienable and intrinsic to the human condition, the PRC Constitution limits the rights of citizens to those prescribed by the Constitution, which in turn conditions the enjoyment of legal and civil rights on citizens' performing their "duties prescribed by the Constitution and the law" (Art. 33). Under PRC orthodoxy, rights are not inherent to the human condition, but rather are specific benefits conferred and enforced at the discretion of the Party/State, conditional on satisfaction of certain performance standards by members of society.

Through a series of White Papers, the government has articulated its human rights doctrine, emphasizing economic and social development over civil and political rights. The 2000 White Paper noted that China's conditions require "putting the rights to subsistence and development in the first place under conditions of reform, development and stability," while subsequent White Papers list achievements in subsistence and development as having priority over civil and political rights.[21] While acknowledging "there is still much room for improvement in [China's] human rights conditions,"[22] the 2009 human rights White Paper reiterated the priority of the people's rights to subsistence and development as essential priorities in the context of China's response to the global financial crisis. Particular attention is given to poverty alleviation, rural development, and public healthcare.

China's human rights orthodoxy prioritizes the development imperatives of the Party/State while also directing the rule of law toward protection of stability. In some positive rights areas such as labor, education, and public health, legislative and regulatory pronouncements incorporate policy ideals of the Party/State, and resulting laws and regulations serve as the legal foundation for implementation of these policies. In the area of negative rights, by contrast, we often see law serve not as a mechanism for restraint on the Party/State but rather as an instrument of political repression in the name of preserving stability. For example, the trial and imprisonment of Liu Xiaobo for alleged "incitement against state power" may have seemed perfectly rational to cadres in the political-legal regime of the Party/State, even while appearing to outsiders as a grotesque misapplication of law to punish a peaceful (and in many instances, supportive) critic of the regime. These rights orthodoxies provide essential context for understanding China's international human rights behavior.

In light of assertions in the Bangkok Declaration and elsewhere that international human rights standards should be considered as an evolving rather than fixed set of norms, the PRC government has worked diligently to build legitimacy for its official discourses, limiting the extent and conditions for human rights. Facing recurring criticism before the UN Commission on Human Rights for a range of abuses, most prominently in response to the Tiananmen massacre and also regarding suppression in Tibet, China began encouraging efforts to "reform" the UN human rights system. The UN Human Rights Council, established in 2006 to replace the UN Commission on Human Rights, was in part a result of China's human rights diplomacy aimed at reducing the legal effect of international scrutiny and promoting the authority of individual states to evaluate their own human rights conduct.

China's 2009 submission to the Universal Periodic Review (UPR) process under the newly reorganized UN Human Rights Council echoed many of the provisions in the Action Plan, but was also criticized internationally for failing to address outstanding abuses and omissions.[23] While China accepted some recommendations centered on building exchanges and cooperative relations in human rights with other countries, it rejected a wide range of recommendations involving minority nationality policy and opening up of minority areas to foreign journalists, reforming arbitrary detention records and providing greater transparency and information reporting on detention and torture; ratification of the ICPCR; expansion of media freedoms; and protection of the rights of lawyers to defend their clients free from harassment.

In anticipation of its submission to China's first periodic review before the UN Human Rights Council, the State Council issued a National Human Rights Action Plan in 2009.[24] The report covered three main thematic areas: economic, social, and cultural rights; civil and political rights; and the rights of particular groups, including women, ethnic minorities, the elderly, children, and people with disabilities. It outlined plans for actions to be taken during a two-year period to implement human rights "guarantees" in all of these areas, largely involving the implementation of already-existing legal and policy commitments.

The 2009 Action Plan drew heavily on the government's formal statements on human rights contained in previous State Council White Papers, and reiterated that subsistence and development are the primary objectives, trumping international standards on civil/political and economic, social, and cultural rights:[25]

> The realization of human rights in the broadest sense has been a long-cherished ideal of mankind and also a long-pursued goal of the Chinese government and people. . . .
>
> By putting people first, the Chinese government makes sure the constitutional principle that "the state respects and protects the human rights of its citizens" is implemented. While respecting the universal principles of human rights, the Chinese government in the light of the basic realities of China, gives priority to the protection of the people's rights to subsistence and development, and lawfully guarantees the rights of all members of society to equal participation and development on the basis of facilitating sound and rapid economic and social development. . . .
>
> The plan was framed on the following fundamental principles: First, in pursuit of the basic principles prescribed in the Constitution of China, and the essentials of the Universal Declaration of Human Rights and International Covenant on Civil and Political Rights, the plan is aimed at improving laws and regulations upholding human rights and advancing the cause of China's human rights in accordance with the law; second, adhering to the principle that all kinds of human rights are interdependent and inseparable, the plan encourages the coordinated development of economic, social and cultural rights as well as civil and political rights, and the balanced development of individual and collective rights; third, in the light of practicality and China's reality, the plan ensures the feasibility of the proposed goals and measures, and scientifically promotes the development of the cause of human rights in China.

These efforts depict China as protecting human rights and honoring international human rights standards. Whether in the area of civil and political rights where the government claims achievements in "strengthening democracy and the rule of law," or in the realm of economic, social, and cultural rights where the government asserts achievements in "steady and rapid socio-economic development of the country," China's official human rights orthodoxy is one that claims compliance with international standards.[26] Yet, the PRC continues to resist accepting international human rights standards that challenge the power of the Party/State. International civil and political rights standards on matters such as freedom of expression and religion, for example, remain constrained in China by provisions requiring submission to the Party/State. Official orthodoxy extols the virtues of China's "democratic" system over those associated with the "western multiparty system."[27] China rejects international human rights standards on labor, for example, that involve specific provisions on collective bargaining and independent labor unions, because these potentially impinge on the power of the government.

Not surprisingly, independent human rights NGOs have noted continued barriers to full human rights protection in China even after completion of the 2009 Universal Periodic Review and the 2009 Action Plan:[28]

> ... NGOs, UN expert bodies and mechanisms, the media, and China's own citizens have documented and reported on the disparities between the Action Plan on paper and the actual human rights situation on the ground. Some specific examples, including those reflective of the areas highlighted in this note, include:
> + The detention, conviction, and sentencing of Liu Xiaobo, recipient of the 2010 Nobel Peace Prize, to eleven years prison, for activities clearly constituting peaceful exercise of fundamental rights and freedoms;

+ Ongoing crackdowns against lawyers, activists, and rights defenders;
+ The expanded use of torture not only as a means to coerce confessions, but as means of violent intimidation in extra-legal settings;
+ The ongoing and expanded practice of extra-legal detentions, illustrated by the ongoing house arrest and abuses against activist Chen Guangcheng and his family; and
+ The preliminary conclusions of the UN Special Rapporteur on the right to food following his first country visit to China, pointing out the persistence of serious human rights obstacles, especially for rural and migrant populations.

Evidence of human rights violations continues to emerge despite the publication of the 2009 Action Plan:[29]

> What is especially significant is that this harassment comes at the heels of the release of the National Human Rights Action Plan by the Chinese government, which proclaims that "the right of the person is legally protected at every stage of law enforcement and administration of justice." (Sharon Hom, Executive Director of HRIC)

China's assessment of its achievements in human rights are often contradicted in detail by outside human rights observers:[30]

> Against a backdrop of rapid socio-economic change and modernization, China continues to be an authoritarian one-party state that imposes sharp curbs on freedom of expression, association, and religion; openly rejects judicial independence and press freedom; and arbitrarily restricts and suppresses human rights defenders and organizations, often through extra-judicial measures.

Nonetheless, China continues to assert that it has honored its international human rights obligations. The 2011 government White Paper,

"The Socialist System of Laws with Chinese Characteristics," affirmed the commitment to a human rights doctrine centered on subsistence and development.

China's engagement with international human rights standards underscores a normative position giving primacy to the role of the Party/State in furthering development. Official orthodoxy on issues of civil and political rights such as democracy and the rule of law, while appropriating language drawn from international standards, tends to subordinate civil and political rights to the authority of the Party/State. China also rebuts aggressively international human rights standards with which it disagrees. International civil and political rights standards are routinely dismissed as reflecting Western bias and unsuitable to China's needs for stability and development. This approach lends substantive operation to the abstractions of the "socialist rule of law" as they pertain to human rights. The imperative of Party rule mandated by the Four Basic Principles informs the operations of legislative, judicial, and administrative organs involved in human rights protection, and find expression in the privileging of the imperatives and authority of the Party/State through the discourse of the right to development.

B. Sustainable development and climate change

The PRC legal system also reflects the impact of international relationships in the area of sustainable development. China's participation in the China Council on International Cooperation in Environment and Development (CCICED) represents a multilateral effort to draw on international law and policy norms on sustainability as a basis for reforms and improvement in China's domestic environmental protection regime. While sustainability in China continues to be a major challenge, the CCICED effort exemplifies expanded efforts by the Party/State to engage with the international legal regime.[31]

Many of China's laws on environmental protection reflect this engagement.

China's international engagement around sustainable development also involves issues of climate change. China issued a National Climate Change Program in 2007 that focused on resource conservation and adaptation to climate change challenges. China's 2008 Climate Change White Paper in 2008 articulated key perspectives around China's developing country status, resource conservation policies, and an emphasis on adaptation to climate change:[32]

> As a developing country with a large population, a relatively low level of economic development, a complex climate and a fragile ecological environment, China is vulnerable to the adverse effects of climate change, which has posed substantial threats to the natural ecological systems as well as the economic and social development of the country. . . .
>
> China addresses climate change in the context of implementing sustainable development strategy, combined with its accelerated steps to build a resource-conserving and environmental-friendly society and an innovation-oriented country. Taking economic development as the core objective, and placing emphasis on energy conservation, optimization of the energy mix, reinforcement of protection and restoration of ecological system, supported by advancement of science and technology, China strives to control greenhouse gas emissions and continuously enhance its adaptation capability.

The White Paper also included commitments to resource conservation and environmental protection, greenhouse gas emission controls, and energy conservation, although economic development and protection of a socialist harmonious society remained primary objectives. The principles of addressing climate change include acceptance of the framework of sustainable development; attendance to the principle of "common but differentiated responsibilities," which essentially relieves developing countries of the major burdens to ameliorate the costs of climate change; placing equal emphasis on mitigation and adaptation; and reliance on integrated policy approaches, science and technology, and international cooperation. Strategic goals on climate change include controlling greenhouse gas emissions, enhancing the capacity about rotation through infrastructure development and conservation, enhancing research and development to address climate change, and raising public awareness and improving management. Specific policy measures focused on energy conservation, including a 10-year energy conservation plan, as well as conservation and environmental programs for industry, agriculture, and forestry. The White Paper also addressed China's position on key climate change issues, focusing on mitigation of greenhouse gas emissions; adaptation to climate change; technology cooperation and transfer; implementation of commitments under the United Nations Framework Convention on Climate Change and the Kyoto Protocol; and regional cooperation.

China's participation in international climate talks, particularly the Copenhagen conference of 2009, reflected both the trend toward broader participation and also the commitment to use that participation to further China's specific policy interests. China has been concerned particularly that global regulatory regimes on climate change should not prejudice China's own economic growth priorities. Allied with India and other developing economies, China has taken a lead role in insisting that climate change policies impose on developed industrial economies the costs of remediation, while limiting the burden on China and other developing economies to make immediate reforms.

China's State Council issued a second climate change White Paper in late 2011.[33] Mitigating climate change remains a key objective, with particular attention given to industrial reform, energy conservation, developing low carbon energy controlling non-energy-related greenhouse gas emissions, increasing forestry carbon sinks, and promoting low carbon development in the localities. The White Paper addressed issues of adaptation in the context of policies on agricultural reform, protection of water resources, and public health. As well, the White Paper stressed the need to enhance basic capacity for managing climate change through legislative and regulatory initiatives as well as policy reform, expanded public participation, and proactive participation in international negotiations through the UN framework. Reiterating China's adherence to the principle of "common but differentiated responsibilities," the White Paper asserts the primary responsibility of developed economies to take the lead in shouldering the historical responsibility to reduce emissions. Subject to this broad principle, the White Paper addresses China's policy reforms to promote sustainable development.

C. Management of boundary issues

China's engagement with the international legal regime is also evident in the area of boundary management. The reversion of Hong Kong to PRC rule involved the application of China's legal system to postcolonial arrangements. China's relations with Taiwan are intimately related with international law questions about sovereignty and territorial integrity. China's boundary concerns in Central Asia are evident in its participation in the Shanghai Cooperation Organization, with implications for China's western regions. China's maritime boundary policies in the South China Sea also find expression through the PRC legal system.

1. Integration of Hong Kong

The PRC's approach to governance in Hong Kong centers on the "one country, two systems" approach. While the "Hong Kong Basic Law" represents the legal foundation for PRC governance in the Hong Kong Special Administrative Region (SAR), China's control over Hong Kong's political system is also exercised through a range of Party and government units. These include the State Council's Hong Kong-Macao Affairs Office and the Leading Small Group on Hong Kong Affairs, which have worked to ensure that PRC interests are protected and promoted.

Viewed in light of the PRC Constitution upon which it is based, the Basic Law of Hong Kong reflects the perspectives of the central government on how the balance between central control and local autonomy should be achieved. Article 2 of the Basic Law confers on Hong Kong a "high degree of autonomy." Specific provisions of the Hong Kong Basic Law on the relationship between the SAR government and the Central People's Government invite consideration and debate over the meaning of local autonomy. For example, Article 12's provision that Hong Kong shall enjoy a high degree of autonomy confirms Hong Kong's status as a political subdivision of the PRC, subject to the conditions set forth in Articles 31 and 62(13) of the PRC constitution. While the promise of a 'high degree of autonomy' (*gaodu zizhiquan*) remains significant, it also remains subject to constitutional interpretation by China's NPC Standing Committee. As with language describing autonomy for China's minority autonomy areas, the use of *"zizhiquan"* to express the idea of autonomy embraces ideals about self-government that are significantly more limited than terms such as *"zizhuquan"* (sovereignty) and *"zijuequan"* (self-determination).

Hong Kong Basic Law Article 19 provides for independent judicial power, including that of final adjudication. However, as various "right of abode" cases have indicated,[34] China views final adjudication as limited to application of law rather than final interpretation, which under Article 67 of the PRC Constitution remains the province of the NPC Standing Committee. Perspectives on the meaning of adjudication and the role of the courts in the PRC differ significantly from common law perspectives in Hong Kong. In particular, despite shared doctrines of parliamentary sovereignty, PRC perspectives on judicial independence and judicial authority to interpret legislation are significantly more limited than the common law tradition would suggest, and underscore the potential for political limitations on judicial behavior.

China's approach to political authority as an element of governance in Hong Kong has echoed themes of central control and Party dominance evident in PRC policies and practices in the Minority Nationality Areas. Against a backdrop of instrumentalism that directs enactment and interpretation of legal texts to satisfy the policy imperatives of the Party/State, orthodox perspectives on the reach and potential for autonomy in Hong Kong remain limited, as preoccupation with national sovereignty has tended to dominate official discourses on the one country–two systems constitutional model.

2. China's Claims Concerning Taiwan

Conflict between China and Taiwan has been a salient feature of economic, political, social, and security relations in Asia since 1949. China's claim to sovereignty over Taiwan has been grounded in international law principles on state succession, while sovereignty claims are also at the heart of China's efforts to deny Taiwan international personality or treaty rights. China's behavior regarding Taiwan illustrates the ways in which PRC's reception of international law remains contingent on assertions of national self-interest on matters of sovereignty and security.

China's White Paper on Taiwan policy issued in 2000 expressed a paradoxical commitment to international legal standards while also asserting China's rights to use force against Taiwan.[35] Expanding on the principles set forth in the previous 1993 White Paper, the 2000 document asserted China's right to non-peaceful reunification if the Taiwan authorities fail to negotiate a reunification agreement with China promptly and in good faith. The White Paper rejected the "two German states" model associated with German reunification as a basis for cross-strait reconciliation, since this might be taken to support separate sovereignty for Taiwan and the Mainland. Instead, the White Paper reiterated the commitment to "one country–two systems" as a basis for reunification, allowing for a different application than that used in the case of Hong Kong.

The 2000 White Paper presented an international legal argument relying on theories of state succession to justify claims that China–Taiwan issues were wholly domestic and therefore beyond the reach of international law's general prohibition against the use of force between states. While not without controversy, China's use of international law arguments to justify claims to Taiwan indicates the extent to which the PRC Party/State has come increasingly to recognize the utility of engagement with the international legal regime in justifying its sovereignty goals.

China's perspectives on the application of international law to Taiwan were also evident in the PRC "Anti-Secession Law" enacted in March 2005.[36] Drawing on themes from the "one country, two systems" paradigm, the Anti-Secession Law (ASL) promises, "After the country is reunited peacefully, Taiwan may (keyi) practice a system different from that on the Mainland, and enjoy a high degree of autonomy." By requiring agreement to reunification negotiations first, China retains the capacity to determine what will be the "political status of the Taiwan authorities." The Law reiterated that the China–Taiwan relationship will be based in the PRC Constitution (Art. 1), thus extolling principles of national unity and territorial integrity. The ASL suggests that reunification with Taiwan may proceed on the basis of political equality between authorities on both sides of the Taiwan Strait (Art. 7). The political status of the Taiwan government may be a subject for reunification discussions (Art. 7.4). The ASL also allows for discussion of Taiwan's "room for international operations," thus holding out the promise of some sort of international status. In the wake of China's campaign to oppose Taiwan's participation in UN organizations such as the WHO, a grant of authority to participate independently in the international community may be a significant improvement for Taiwan. However, as these are simply issues for discussion, the outcome remains uncertain.

Echoing provisions of the 2000 White Paper, the Anti-Secession Law also provides for non-peaceful reunification of Taiwan with the PRC in the event that "Taiwan independence forces" or outside events result in separation of Taiwan from China, or if all possibility of peaceful reunification is lost:

> *Article 5*: Upholding the principle of one China is the basis of peaceful reunification of the country.
>
> To reunify the country through peaceful means best serves the fundamental interests of the compatriots on both sides of the Taiwan Straits. The state shall do its utmost with maximum sincerity to achieve a peaceful reunification.
>
> . . .
>
> *Article 8*: In the event that the "Taiwan independence" secessionist forces should act under any name or by any means to cause the fact of Taiwan's secession from China, or that major incidents entailing Taiwan's secession from China should occur, or that possibilities for a peaceful reunification should be completely exhausted, the state shall employ non-peaceful means and other necessary measures to protect China's sovereignty and territorial integrity.
>
> The State Council and the Central Military Commission shall decide on and execute the non-peaceful means and other necessary

measures as provided for in the preceding paragraph and shall promptly report to the NPC Standing Committee.

Thus, China's policies on Taiwan reflect the extent to which national security issues have been asserted by reference to international law, but also at times in spite of apparent international law obligations. China's White Papers on Taiwan, as well as the Anti-Secession Law, reflect the influence of international law institutions and norms and may well represent efforts to limit calls for a military solution to the Taiwan issue. On issues such as state succession, conceptions of sovereignty, and protection of territorial integrity, China's reliance on international law discourses on the Taiwan question suggest an effort to adapt international standards to conform with Chinese policy objectives.

3. Shanghai Cooperation Organization and Implication for China's West

China's participation in the Shanghai Cooperation Organization (SCO) represents an important foray into multilateral cooperation that is not exclusively economic in scope.[37] Comprising China, Russia, Kazakhstan, Kyrgyzstan, Tajikistan (the original "Shanghai Five") and Uzbekistan (added in 2001), the organization focuses on security concerns in Central Asia. The Charter of the SCO identifies the goals of the organization:[38]

> *Article 1: Goals and Tasks*
> The main goals and tasks of SCO are:
> to strengthen mutual trust, friendship and goodneighborliness between
>   the member States;
> to consolidate multidisciplinary cooperation in the maintenance and
>   strengthening of peace, security and stability in the region and

promotion of a new democratic, fair and rational political and economic international order;

to jointly counteract terrorism, separatism and extremism in all their manifestations, to fight against illicit narcotics and arms trafficking and other types of criminal activity of a transnational character, and also illegal migration;

to encourage the efficient regional cooperation in such spheres as politics, trade and economy, defense, law enforcement, environment protection, culture, science and technology, education, energy, transport, credit and finance, and also other spheres of common interest;

to facilitate comprehensive and balanced economic growth, social and cultural development in the region through joint action on the basis of equal partnership for the purpose of a steady increase of living standards and improvement of living conditions of the peoples of the member States;

to coordinate approaches to integration into the global economy;

to promote human rights and fundamental freedoms in accordance with the international obligations of the member States and their national legislation;

to maintain and develop relations with other States and international organizations;

to cooperate in the prevention of international conflicts and in their peaceful settlement;

to jointly search for solutions to the problems that would arise in the 21st century.

While issues of "terrorism, separatism and extremism" are given primacy, other issues of economic cooperation (especially in oil and gas exploration and extraction) and counterbalancing the geo-strategic reach of the United States following 9/11 and the Afghan war remain important. The SCO was formed in conjunction with the conclusion of a Sino-Russian treaty on "Good Neighborliness and Friendly

Cooperation," aimed at building "partnership and strategic interaction" that will encompass elements of security, territory, and economic, technical, and trade cooperation.[39]

Conditions of economic cooperation and security in central Asia are matters of particular concern to China in light of the complexities of its governance of Xinjiang Uighur Nationality Autonomous Region. China's policies in Xinjiang reflect the importance of the region to Beijing's conception of national interest.[40] Xinjiang has multiple riches of natural resources, including oil and natural gas, which are essential to China's economic development. Xinjiang's strategic location in central Asia has lent particular importance to China's policies, most recently the Chinese government's attempt to use the US-led anti-terrorism campaign as justification for suppression of Islamic separatists.[41] China has joined numerous international treaties against terrorism, including the International Convention for the Suppression of Terrorist Bombings, the International Convention for the Suppression of the Financing of Terrorism, and the International Convention on Prevention of Acts of Nuclear Terrorism.[42] Acknowledging the opportunities presented by UN Security Council efforts for regional organizations to carry out UN Charter provisions on peace and security,[43] China has supported a broader role for regional security efforts in Central Asia. Through these processes, China has sought to assert leadership in building international legal norms and processes to support local and regional policy goals.[44]

4. Maritime Boundaries

China is party to the 1982 UN Convention on the Law of the Sea (UNCLOS III), which provides the standards on such matters as territorial seas, Exclusive Economic Zones (EEZs), and living and non-living marine resources.[45] The UNCLOS regime supports clarity in determination of territorial boundaries, through the use of "baselines" to define the 12-mile territorial limits and 200-mile EEZs of maritime states. China's participation in the treaty is conditioned by the PRC Law on the Territorial Sea and the Contiguous Zone (1992),[46] which adopts UNCLOS language on territorial limits, the use of baselines, and an additional 24-mile contiguous zone.

The 1992 Law on the Territorial Sea and the Contiguous Zone attempts to legislate China's claims to virtually all disputed islands and seabed in the East and South China Seas. Following a 1997 Joint Statement between China and the Association of Southeast Asian Nations (ASEAN), a "Declaration on the Conduct of the Parties in the South China Sea," emphasizing freedom of navigation and peaceful resolution of disputes, was agreed in 2002.[47] In the wake of increased diplomatic and naval confrontations, negotiations on a joint China–ASEAN "Code of Conduct" began in 2012, but China continues to insist on bilateral negotiations where its size and power confer important negotiating advantages, rather than accepting collective solutions:[48]

> China has always been committed to peacefully resolving our disputes with relevant countries concerning sovereignty over islands and reefs and maritime delimitation in the South China Sea. And we are committed to doing so through direct negotiations and friendly consultations on the basis of respecting historical facts and international law.

China's maritime disputes with Japan, Vietnam, and the littoral states bordering the South China Sea continue. China's maritime disputes with Japan over the Senkaku/Diaoyu islands and regarding broader issues of seabed resources in the East China Sea involve conflicting interpretations of both contemporary and historical boundaries. China's dispute with Vietnam over the Paracel Islands led to military conflict in 1974, after which China has maintained physical control over the islands. Territorial disputes in the South China Sea have become particularly tense in recent years, with control over mineral resources and sea shipping lanes emerging as primary issues.

China's participation in international governance regimes reveals the ways in which the Party/State furthers its interests through the international system rather than in opposition to it, as happened during the Mao era. In areas of human rights and sustainable development, engagement with the international system influences China's perspectives on possibilities and constraints facing the policy preferences of the Party/State and the mechanisms available to manage them. As well, China's legal system is closely implicated in policy enforcement on matters of territorial integrity and boundary management.

SUMMARY

The PRC legal system is influenced considerably by China's participation in global systems of law and policy. Following a lengthy period during which China in effect denounced and abstained from international law institutions, the post-Mao era saw expanded participation. China's international engagement involves significant openings to international trade and investment. As with other sectors, China's trade and investment law and policy seek to balance international commercial imperatives with national interest. Participation in international governance regimes on human rights and sustainable development reveals the extent to which international commitments are conditioned on national interests expressed in laws and regulations of the Party/State. China's international engagement is also evident in areas of territorial integrity and boundary management, involving relations with Hong Kong and Taiwan, participation in the Shanghai Cooperation Organization on Central Asia, and maritime boundary issues. These examples reveal the interplay between international commitments and national interests, which in turn are carried out through the PRC legal system.

Over the past two decades, processes of globalization coupled with local policy initiatives have created opportunities for China's expanded participation in the international legal system. While China's engagement with international legal institutions reflects expectations about the potential for China to exercise greater influence in the international system, questions remain as to the depth of China's commitment to the institutions and norms of the international legal regime. The status of international law as a source of Chinese domestic law remains unclear, while the willingness and ability of Chinese governance institutions to implement international legal standards remain uncertain. The extent to which China's pursuit of national policy goals in areas of trade, human rights, and security will affect compliance with international law standards remains a key question.

DISCUSSION QUESTIONS

1) How has China's historical relationship with the outside world affected the PRC's participation in international legal institutions?

2) How are international trade and investment issues addressed in the PRC legal system?

3) How have international treaties in the areas of human rights and sustainability affected Chinese law and practice?

4) How has the legal system supported the PRC efforts at boundary management in East and Central Asia?

SUGGESTIONS FOR FURTHER READING

Breslin, Shaun, *Handbook of China's International Relations* (London: Routledge, 2010).

Cass, Deborah, Brett G. Williams, and George Barker, eds, *China and the World Trading System: Entering the New Millennium* (Cambridge: Cambridge University Press, 2003).

Chan Lai-Ha, Pak K. Lee, and Gerald Chan, "Rethinking Global Governance: A China Model in the Making?," *Contemporary Politics*, vol. 14, no. 1 (2008), pp. 3–19.

Foot, Rosemary and Andrew Walter, *China, the United States, and the Global Order* (Cambridge: Cambridge University Press, 2010).

Xue Hanqin, *Chinese Perspectives on International Law* (Leiden: Martinus Nijhoff, 2012).

Zheng Yongnian, *China and International Relations: The Chinese View and the Contribution of Wang Gongwu* (London: Routledge, 2010).

Conclusion

The ancient Chinese art of calligraphy involves a combination of form and apparatus, much like the dynamic of law. Like law, forms of calligraphy are expressed through learned discourse, practice, and even dictionaries containing the model expressions of calligraphers going back centuries or more. Like the trappings of the courtroom and the legislative chamber, the calligraphy studio involves material accoutrements (including brushes and brush washers, ink stones and wells, paper and paper holders), each making accommodation to modernity as the computerization of judicial and legislative proceedings is matched by the emergence of calligraphy for ball-point pens and electronic tablets. Both law and calligraphy involve the use of words to express ideas, the calligrapher for example detailing the word *long* (dragon) to express variations on themes of authority and power, just as the jurist uses terms like "rights" to depict variations in socio-economic and political relationships. But while the calligrapher is content with the artistic outcome of expression, the jurist must be mindful that the outcome of her expression affects the community in which she lives. The future of China's legal system depends on whether those involved in drafting, enactment, interpretation and implementation of law in the PRC will be able to draw upon the changing dynamics of legal form and apparatus to express ideals and practices of law which transcend limitations of Party/State rule to build a legal system that genuinely and effectively responds to the needs and aspirations of China's people. This survey hopefully offers a basis for understanding how the PRC legal system responds to this challenge and perspectives for engaging with law in China as it does so.

Proceeding from an understanding of the role of law in China as an instrument of policy, our treatment of the PRC legal system emphasizes the role of the Party/State in setting the conditions for legal behavior. With this in mind, we can appreciate the effects on the PRC legal regime of historical contexts, thematic challenges, and China's place in the world. We began with a discussion of how the historical context of legal antecedents from the Qing Dynasty, the Republic of China, and the Revolutionary Base Areas informed the contours of law not only in the earliest years of the PRC but even today. We turned then to thematic contexts of political stability, economic prosperity, and social development, discussing how the PRC legal system has been developed and deployed by the Party/State to achieve particular policy goals. Finally, we explored China's expanding role in the world and the ways in which the PRC legal system supports this role. Taken together, these five chapters are aimed to enable students and other observers of the PRC legal system to understand the contexts and influences that underpin law in China today, and also to anticipate and respond effectively to future changes.

Looking forward, students of law in China are encouraged to appreciate how current conditions and limitations on the role of law deployed in the service of the Party/State provide a historical context for future developments. For example, current doctrines on political stability and the concomitant features of China's criminal law system and administrative control system provide important historical antecedents for future legislation aimed at securing political stability. While ongoing revisions to the PRC Criminal Law and Criminal Procedure Law may well strengthen protections for criminal defendants and reduce reliance on the death penalty, the role of Party leadership over the relations between and among the Public Security

Ministry, the Procuratorate, and the People's Courts will likely remain constant. Expanding provisions for public input into legislation may well continue, whereas the leading role of the CPC in setting the policy goals for which legislation is enacted will probably remain. Ongoing constitutional change may afford stronger protection for human rights, even as constitutional doctrine privileging the dominance of the Party affects the tension between improving social economic conditions and protecting civil and political rights. Throughout it all, questions about consistent implementation and enforcement of law and regulation will remain.

In the area of economic prosperity, the current provisions for contract and property relations are likely to set the foundation for future developments, even as ongoing challenges of corruption and income disparities may well lead to further changes in the tax regime. China's legal regulation of social development can be expected to respond to changes in local conditions. Policy changes on labor relations, healthcare, education, women's rights and the treatment of minorities may well lead to stronger protections even while the legal and regulatory structure remains dependent on and entrenches political control by the Party/State. Similarly with challenges around media and information, environment, and corporate social responsibility, social development policy goals may well change in response to changing conditions even as the legal regime continues to protect the controlling authority of the Party/State.

In each of these areas of politics, economy, and society, the tension between adjusting policies to suit changing conditions and protecting the political monopoly of the Party/State will remain a fundamental challenge for the PRC legal system. The question remains whether changing conditions in political relations, economic development, and social life will outstrip the governing regime's efforts at control. In the political realm, for example, local demands for greater accountability and responsiveness by government may well outstrip efforts by the Party/State to allow tentative reforms in areas such as elections and transparency. In the economic realm, challenges of resource allocation and general economic opportunity may well constrain efforts by the Party/State to further liberalize the economy. In the area of social relations, expanding demands by the populace for more effective government services and protection of working and living conditions may generate policy responses even as they challenge efforts by the Party/State to maintain its political monopoly.

China's current engagement with the world also serves as a template for future developments. China's foreign trade and investment regimes are likely to continue to expand along the lines established for regulating foreign investment enterprises and furthering participation in the GATT/WTO trading system, although policy priorities may well change. Human rights doctrine may well come to involve more consistent enforcement, but the emphasis on the leadership by the Party/State will likely continue. The PRC's pursuit of boundary management and security will likely find expression in the socialist legal system, but will not likely be constrained by it.

As with conditions in the PRC today, the future of the PRC legal system is uncertain. Yet the norms and institutions of PRC law today will set the context for future changes, just as the historical contexts of Qing, ROC, and Border Region law influenced legal change in the PRC. The challenges of political stability, economic prosperity, and social development will likely continue, just as these themes inform the PRC legal system today. And China's engagement with international legal regimes, begun in earnest with the 2001 GATT/WTO accession and continuing with human rights, sustainability, and boundary management, remain contingent on global and local conditions. As each of these dimensions changes, so too will China's policy responses change with it, and changes in the PRC legal regime will follow close behind. While the decision at the 18th CPC Congress in November 2012 not to extend Politburo Standing Committee membership to Meng Jianzhu, Chair of the CPC Politics and Law Committee, signaled for some an effort to separate politics from the legal system, policy priorities of the Party/State will likely continue to be the foundation for the PRC's socialist legal system for some time to come.

Notes

Introduction

1 Jerome Alan Cohen, *The Criminal Process in the People's Republic of China* (Cambridge, MA: Harvard University Press, 1968); Stanley Lubman, *Bird in a Cage: Legal Reform in China After Mao* (Stanford, CA: Stanford University Press, 1999); R. Randle Edwards, "An Overview of Chinese Law and Legal Education," *Annals of the American Academy of Political and Social Science*, vol. 476: China in Transition (1984), pp. 48–61; William C. Jones, *Basic Principles of Civil Law in China* (Armonk, NY: M.E. Sharpe, 1989). The pioneering work of these scholars has been continued, often by their students, such as Albert Chen, Donald Clarke, Alison Connor, James Feinerman, and many, many others.

2 *See* review by Pitman B. Potter, "Legal Reform in China – Institutions, Culture, and Selective Adaptation," *Law & Social Inquiry*, vol. 2, no. 4 (Spring 2004), pp. 465–95. Also *see* Stanley Lubman, *Bird in a Cage: Legal Reform in China After Mao* (Stanford, CA: Stanford University Press, 1999); R. Randall Peerenboom, *China's Long March Toward Rule of Law* (Cambridge: Cambridge University Press, 2002).

3 *See* e.g., Neil Diamont, Stanley Lubman, and Kevin O'Brien, eds, *Engaging the Law in China: State, Society, and Possibilities for Justice* (Stanford, CA: Stanford University Press, 2005); Eva Pils, "Land Disputes, Rights Assertion, and Social Unrest in China: A Case From Sichuan," *Columbia Journal of Asian Law*, "Special Issue: Celebrating the Work of Stanley Lubman," vol. 19, no. 1 (Spring–Fall, 2005), 235–92; Ethan Michelson, "Justice from Above or Below?" *The China Quarterly*, no. 193 (2008), pp. 43–64; Sida Liu, "Lawyers, State Officials, and Significant Others: Symbiotic Exchange in the Chinese Legal Services Market," *The China Quarterly*, no. 206 (June 1, 2011), pp. 276–93.

4 The list of exemplary work by scholars from Asia, Europe, and North America is too vast to include in this text. However, an appreciation for the breadth and depth of current scholarship on Chinese law can be gained from "Special

Issue: Celebrating the Work of Stanley Lubman," *Columbia Journal of Asian Law*, vol. 19, no. 1 (Spring–Fall, 2005), pp. 1–29; "Special Issue: China's Legal System: New Developments, New Challenges," *The China Quarterly*, no. 191 (September 2007); and Michael Mosher and Fu Yu, eds, *Doing Business in China* (New York: Interjura, looseleaf).

5 A short and woefully incomplete selection of PRC scholars working on issues of contract and property includes Cui Jianyuan, "Tudi shang de quanliqun lungang" [Theoretic outline of the cluster of rights in land], in *Zhongguo faxue* [Chinese legal studies], no. 2 (1998), pp. 14–20; Gong Xiangrui and Jiang Mingan, "Zai lun gongmin caichanquan de xianfa baohu" [Again, on constitutional protection for citizens' property rights], in *Zhongguo faxue* [Chinese legal studies], no. 2 (1998), pp. 70–3; Guo Mingrui, "Guanyu woguo wuquan lifa de san dian sikao" [Three perspectives on our country's property legislation], in *Zhongguo faxue* [Chinese legal studies], no. 2 (1998), pp. 21–6; He Qinhua, "Fa de yizhi yu fa de bentuhua" [Legal transplanting and localization of law], in *Zhongguo faxue* [Chinese legal studies], no. 3 (2002), pp. 3–15; Jiang Ping, "Drafting the Uniform Contract Law in China," *Columbia Journal of Asian Law*, vol. 10, no. 1 (1996), pp. 245–58; Jiang Ping, *Zhonghua renmin gongheguo hetong fa* [Contract law in the People's Republic of China] (Beijing: Red Flag Press, 1999), pp. 735–8; Liang Huixing, "Zhongguo hetong fa qicao guocheng zhong de zhenglun dian" [Points of contention in the process of drafting China's contract law], *Faxue yuekan* [Law Science Monthly], no. 2 (1996), pp. 13–15; Liang Huixing, *Zhongguo wuquanfa caoan jianyi gao* [Outline of opinion on a draft Chinese property law] (Beijing: Social Science Manuscripts Press, 2000), pp. 95–7; Qian Mingxing, *Wuquan fa yuan li* [Principles of Property Law] (Beijing: Peking University Press, 1994); Wang Liming, "Tongyi hetong fa zhiding zhong de ruogan yinan wenti tantao" [Inquiry into various difficult questions in enacting a unified contract law], *Zhengfa luntan* [Political Science and Law Tribune], no. 4 (1996), pp. 49–56 and no. 5 (1996), pp. 52–60; Wang Liming, *Wuquan fa lun* [On property rights law] (Beijing: Chinese University Politics and Law Press, 1997); Zhang Lihong, "The Latest Developments in the Codification of Chinese Civil Law," *Tulane Law Review*, vol. 83 (2009), pp. 999–1039; Zhang Mo, *Chinese Contract Law: Theory and Practice* (Leiden: Brill, 2006).

1: Development of the Socialist Legal System

1 Philip C.C. Huang, *Code, Custom, and Legal Practice in China: The Qing and the Republic Compared* (Stanford, CA: Stanford University Press, 2001); Hugh Scogin, "Between Heaven and Man: Contract and the State

in Han Dynasty China," *Southern California Law Review*, vol. 63, no. 5 (1990), pp. 1325–404 (1990); Derk Bodde and Clarence Morris, *Law in Imperial China* (Philadelphia, PA: University of Pennsylvania Press, 1967).

2 Sybille van der Sprenkel, *Legal Institutions in Manchu China* (London: Athlone Press, 1962).

3 Joseph R. Levenson, *Confucian China and Its Modern Fate* (Berkeley, CA: University of California Press, 1958).

4 Levenson, *supra*, Chapter IV; Jonathan Spence, *The Search for Modern China* (New York: Norton, 1999), pp. 225–6.

5 William E. Butler, ed., *The Legal System of the Chinese Soviet Republic 1931–34* (New York: Transnational Publishers, 1983).

6 http://baike.baidu.com/view/149912.htm#5 (accessed October 14, 2012) (tr. Juan Li, Liu Huan, Liu Yue, and Pitman B. Potter).

7 http://www.lawyee.org/Act/Act_Display.asp?RID=27173 (accessed October 14, 2012) (tr. Juan Li, Liu Huan, Liu Yue, and Pitman B. Potter).

8 "Xianfa 1954" [1954 Constitution], in Chen HeHeHefu, ed., *Zhongguo xianfa leibian* [Varieties of China's constitutions] (Beijing: Academy of Social Sciences Press, 1980), pp. 213–34 (tr. Juan Li, Liu Huan, Liu Yue, and Pitman B. Potter).

9 "Gongtong Gangling" [Common Program], in Chen HeHeHefu, ed., *Zhongguo xianfa leibian* [Varieties of China's constitutions] (Beijing: Academy of Social Sciences Press, 1980), pp. 183–94 (tr. Liu Huan, Juan Li, and Pitman B. Potter).

10 Shao-chuan Leng and Hungdah Chiu, *Criminal Justice in Post-Mao China* (Albany, NY: State University of New York Press, 1985); Victor H. Li, "The Evolution and Development of the Chinese Legal System," in John M. H. Lindbeck, *China: Management of a Revolutionary Society* (Seattle, WA: University of Washington Press, 1971); Jerome Alan Cohen, *The Criminal Process in the People's Republic of China* (Cambridge, MA: Harvard University Press, 1968).

11 Roderick MacFarquhar, *Origins of the Cultural Revolution*, vol. 1 (New York: Columbia University Press, 1974), vol. 2 (New York: Columbia University Press, 1983).

12 "Talks of the Beidaihe Conference (Draft Transcript), August 17–30, 1958," in Roderick MacFarquhar, Timothy Cheek and Eugene Wu, eds, *The Secret Speeches of Chairman Mao: From the Hundred Flowers to the Great Leap Forward* (Cambridge, MA: Council on East Asian Studies, Harvard University, 1989), pp. 423–4.

13 Roderick MacFarquhar, *The Politics of China, 1949–1989* (Cambridge: Cambridge University Press, 1993); Frederick Teiwes, *Politics and Purges*

in China: Rectification and the Decline of Party Norms (Armonk, NY: M.E. Sharpe, 1993).

14 "Resolution of the Central People's Government Ministry of Trade Concerning Conscientiously Signing and Seriously Carrying Out Contracts (Oct. 3, 1950)" and "Notice of the CPC Central Committee and the State Council Concerning Strictly Implementing Basic Construction Procedures and Strictly Carrying Out Economic Contracts (Dec. 10, 1962)," in State Council Economic Law Research Centre General Office, ed., *Jingji hetong fagui xuanbian* [Compilation of Economic Contract Laws and Regulations] (Beiing: Workers Press, 1982) (tr. Pitman B. Potter).

15 Vivienne Shue, *The Reach of the State: Sketches of the Chinese Body Politic* (Stanford, CA: Stanford University Press, 1988).

16 "Regulations on Strengthening Public Security Work in the Great Proletarian Cultural Revolution," in Michael Schoenhals, ed., *The Cultural Revolution, 1966–1969: Not a Dinner Party* (Armonk, NY: M.E. Sharpe, 1996), pp. 49–51.

17 Chen HeHeHefu, ed., *Zhongguo xianfa leibian* [Varieties of China's constitutions] (Beijing: Academy of Social Sciences Press, 1980), pp. 333–43 (tr. Liu Huan, Juan Li, and Pitman B. Potter). Also *see* Jerome A. Cohen, "China's Changing Constitution," *The China Quarterly*, no. 76 (1978), pp. 794–842.

18 Chen HeHeHefu, ed., *Zhongguo xianfa leibian* [Varieties of China's constitutions] (Beijing: Academy of Social Sciences Press, 1980), pp. 1–18 (tr. Liu Huan, Juan Li, and Pitman B. Potter).

19 "Communique of the Third Plenum of the CPC Eleventh Central Committee," http://cpc.people.com.cn/GB/64162/64168/64563/65371/4441902.html (tr. Juan Li, Liu Huan, Yue Liu, and Pitman B. Potter) (accessed September 12, 2012); "Resolution on Certain Questions in the History of Our Party Since the Founding of the People's Republic of China" (June 27, 1981), http://www.marxists.org/subject/china/documents/cpc/history/01.htm (accessed January 29, 2013).

20 "Communique of the Third Plenum of the CPC Eleventh Central Committee (December 22, 1978)" http://cpc.people.com.cn/GB/64162/64168/64563/65371/4441902.html (tr. Juan Li, Liu Huan, Yue Liu, and Pitman B. Potter) (accessed September 12, 2012).

21 Among the many excellent works on the Tiananmen crisis are Deborah Davis and Ezra Vogel, eds, *Chinese Society on the Eve of Tiananmen: The Impact of Reform* (Cambridge, MA: Council on East Asian Studies, Harvard University, 1990); James A. R. Miles, *The Legacy of*

Tiananmen: China in Disarray (Ann Arbor, MI: University of Michigan Press, 1997); Anthony Saich, *The People's Movement: Perspectives on Spring 1989* (Armonk, NY: M.E. Sharpe, 1990); Zhang Liang, Andrew Nathan, Perry Link, and Orville Schell, *The Tiananmen Papers* (New York: Public Affairs, 2001); Zhao Ziyang, *Prisoner of the State: The Secret Journal of Premier Zhao Ziyang* (New York: Simon & Schuster, 2009).

22 For discussion of the Deng Period, see Richard Baum, *Burying Mao: Chinese Politics in the Age of Deng Xiaoping* (Princeton, NJ: Princeton University Press, 1994); Ezra F. Vogel, *Deng Xiaoping and the Transformation of China* (Cambridge, MA: Belknap Press of Harvard University Press, 2011).

23 J. R. McNeill, "China's Environmental History in World Perspective," in Marc Elvin and Liu Ts'ui-jong, eds, *Sediments of Time: Environment and Society in Chinese History* (Cambridge: Cambridge University Press, 1998) pp. 31–49.

24 Judith Shapiro, *Mao's War Against Nature: Politics of Environment in Revolutionary China* (Cambridge: Cambridge University Press, 2001).

25 US Trade Representative's Office, "2011 Report to Congress on China's WTO Compliance" (December 2011), http://www.ustr.gov/about-us/press-office/reports-and-publications/2011/2010-report-congress-china's-wto-compliance (accessed September 3, 2012); Trade Lawyers Advisory Group, "China's Compliance with WTO Commitments and Obligations: 2005–2007 Update" (2007), http://www.uscc.gov/research-papers/2008/TLAG%20Report%20-%20China's%20WTO%20Compliance%20and%20Commitments%202005-2007%20Update.pdf (accessed September 3, 2012).

2: Political Stability

1 Deng Xiaoping, "Jianchi sixiang jiben yuanze" [Uphold the four basic principles], in *Deng Xiaoping wenxuan 1975–1982* [Collected works of Deng Xiaoping 1975–1982], vol. 2, p. 144 (Beijing: People's Press, 1983).

2 Peng Zhen, "Guanyu Zhonghua renmin gongheguo xianfa xiugai caoan de shuoming" [Explanation of the revised draft of the PRC Constitution] (Apr. 22, 1982). *Lun xin shiqi de shehui zhuyi minzhu yu fazhi jianshe* [On establishment of democracy and the legal system during the new era] (Beijing: Central Archives Press, 1989), pp. 100–15 (tr. Juan Li, Liu Huan, Liu Yue, and Pitman B. Potter).

3 http://www.npc.gov.cn/englishnpc/Constitution/node_2830.htm (accessed November 26, 2012).

4 "'Sange daibiao' de kexue hanyi shi shenma?" [What is the scientific meaning of the 'Three Represents'?] http://cpc.people.com.cn/GB/64156/64157/4418474.html (accessed October 29, 2012) (tr. Juan Li, Liu Huan, Liu Yue, and Pitman B. Potter).

5 http://english.people.com.cn/constitution/constitution.html (accessed October 27, 2012).

6 Pitman B. Potter, *From Leninist Discipline to Socialist Legalism: Peng Zhen on Law and Political Authority in the PRC* (Stanford, CA: Stanford University Press, 2003), pp. 117–18.

7 http://english.people.com.cn/constitution/constitution.html (accessed October 27, 2012).

8 National Democratic Institute, Development of Legislative Hearings in China: A Report on NDI's Seminar on Local Legislative Hearings and Local Governance (2003).

9 State Council Information Office, "China's Efforts and Achievements in Promoting the Rule of Law," (February 28, 2008), pp. 4–6.

10 Murray Scot Tanner, "Hu Jintao's Succession: Prospects and Challenges," in David M. Finkelstein and Maryanne Kivlehan, eds, *China's Leadership in the 21st Century: The Rise of the Fourth Generation* (Armonk, NY: M.E. Sharpe, 2003), pp. 45–65 at 58.

11 For complete list, *see* http://www.china.org.cn/e-white (accessed September 3, 2012).

12 Brandon Kirk, "Putting China's Labour Contract Law into Practice," *China Law & Practice*, vol. 22, no. 2 (March 2008), pp. 15–18.

13 State Council Information Office, "China's Efforts and Achievements in Promoting the Rule of Law," (February 28. 2008), p. 6.

14 Carl Minzner, "China's Turn Against Law," *American Journal of Comparative Law*, vol. 59 (2011), pp. 935–84.

15 Xin He, "Black Hole of Responsibility: The Adjudication Committee's Role in a Chinese Court," *Law & Society Review*, vol. 46, no. 4 (December 2012), pp. 681–712.

16 *See* e.g., Interpretation of the Supreme People's Court on Several Issues Related to the Execution of Criminal Procedure Law of the People's Republic of China (Adopted at the 989th Session of Trial Committee of the Supreme People's Court on June 29, 1998) Fashi [1998] no. 23; Interpretation (1st) of the Supreme People's Court on Several Issues Concerning the Application of the "PRC Contract Law," http://app.westlawchina.com.ezproxy.library.ubc.ca/maf/china/app/document?&docguid=i0adf589b0000011e6d83c039d238ab6d&hitguid=i0adf589

b0000011e6d83c039d238ab6d&srguid=ia744c0670000013a8520485f
d87a8eea&spos=7&epos=7&td=8&crumb-action=append&context=
35&lang=en; Interpretation (2nd) of the Supreme People's Court on
Several Issues Concerning the Application of the "PRC Contract Law,"
http://app.westlawchina.com.ezproxy.library.ubc.ca/maf/china/app/doc
ument?&docguid=i3cf76ad3000001213a501d6fe644c56d&hitguid=i3c
f76ad3000001213a501d6fe644c56d&srguid=ia744c0690000013a8521
86d75232f032&spos=2&epos=2&td=8&crumb-action=append&
context=39&lang=en; Interpretation of the Supreme People's Court on
certain questions of the specific application of law to adjudication of
disputes over property management (April 20, 2009), http://app.
westlawchina.com.ezproxy.library.ubc.ca/maf/china/app/document?&
docguid=i3cf76ad300000121781ca6c14569e80b&hitguid=i3cf76ad300
000121781ca6c14569e80b&srguid=ia744dc1e0000013a8f5976456fc
9ed18&spos=1&epos=1&td=5&crumb-action=append&context=9&
lang=en.

17 Keith Hand, "Resolving Constitutional Debates in China," *University of
Pennsylvania East Asia Law Review,* vol. 7, no. 1 (2011), pp. 51–159.

18 Law of the PRC on Lawyers and Legal Representation (October 2007),
http://www.chinanews.com.cn/gn/news/2007/10-28/1061502.shtml;
Human Rights Watch, "China: Curbs on Lawyers Could Intensify Social
Unrest – New Regulations Cast Doubt on Legal Reforms" (December
12, 2006).

19 http://www.chinalawandpractice.com/Article/1692834/
Channel/9934/The-All-China-Lawyers-Association-Lawyers-Code-of-
Practice-Trial-Implementation.html (accessed September 16, 2012).

20 Jonathan Benney, *Defending Rights in Contemporary China* (London:
Routledge, 2012); Fu Hualing and Richard Cullen, "Weiquan (Rights
Protection) lawyering in an authoritarian state: toward critical lawyering,"
The China Journal, vol. 59, no. 111 (2008), http://papers.ssrn.com/so13/
papers.cfm?abstract_id=1083925 (accessed October 31, 2012).

21 Criminal Law of the PRC (1979, rev. 1997), http://www.china.org.cn/
english/government/207320.htm (accessed November 26, 2012).

22 Robin Munro, *Dangerous Minds: Political Psychiatry in China Today
and Its Origins in the Mao Era* (New York: Human Rights Watch,
2002).

23 National People's Congress Reports 1994, no. 8, December 31, 1994.

24 *See* Dui Hua Foundation, "Reducing Death Penalty Crimes in China
More Symbol Than Substance," *Dialogue,* issue 40 (Fall 2010). Also *see*

news.xinhuanet.com, "Capital crimes dropped" (accessed August 15, 2012).

25 See "Criminal Law of the PRC" (1997).

26 Criminal Procedure Law of the PRC (1980, rev. 1996), http://www.china.org.cn/english/government/207334.htm (accessed November 25, 2012).

27 Jerome A. Cohen, "A 'People's Jury' Trial for Criminal Defendants?" US-Asia Law Institute (May 15, 2011), http://www.usasialaw.org/?p=5211 (accessed January 25, 2013).

28 Ian Johnson, "Trial in China Tests Limits of Legal System Reform," *New York Times*, August 19, 2011, http://www.nytimes.com/2011/04/20/world/asia/20china.html (accessed September 3, 2012).

29 "Editorial: 'Big stick 306' and China's contempt for law," *New York Times*, May 5, 2011, http://www.nytimes.com/2011/05/06/opinion/06fri3.html?_r=0 (accessed January 25, 2013).

30 Congressional Executive Committee on China, "Annual Report 2011," p. 83, http://www.cecc.gov/pages/annualRpt/annualRpt11/AR2011final.pdf (accessed April 16, 2012).

31 Congressional Executive Committee on China, "Annual Report 2011," p. 81, http://www.cecc.gov/pages/annualRpt/annualRpt11/AR2011final.pdf (accessed April 16, 2012).

32 See generally, "Criminal Procedure Law of the PRC" (1996). Also see "Commentary: Law Amendments for Better Checks and Balances," Xinhua English Service, Mar. 14, 1996, in *FBIS Daily Report-China*, March 14, 1996, p. 13, and Lawyers Committee for Human Rights, ed., *Opening to Reform? An Analysis of China's Revised Criminal Procedure Law* (1996).

33 See "Zuigao renmin fayuan guanyu zhixing <<Zhonghua renmin gongheguo xingshi susong fa>> ruogan wenti to jieshi" [Interpretation by the Supreme People's Court on certain issues related to the implementation of the <<Criminal Procedure Law of the PRC>>], *Zhongguo fazhi bao* [China legal system gazette], September 9, 1998, p. 2. For discussion of the evolution of this interpretation over the course of two drafts and a joint regulation by the Supreme People's Court and six other central level departments, see "Zuifao fayuan fabu xingshi susong fa sifa jieshi" [Supreme People's Court issues judicial interpretation of the Criminal Procedure Law], *Zhongguo fazhi bao* [China legal system gazette], September 8, 1998, p. 1.

34 See "Zuigao renmin fayuan guanyu zhixing <<Zhonghua renmin gongheguo xingshi susong fa>> ruogan wenti to jieshi" [Interpretation by the

Supreme People's Court on certain issues related to the implementation of the <<Criminal Procedure Law of the PRC>>], *Zhongguo fazhi bao* [China legal system gazette], September 9, 1998, p. 2. Translation by Liu Huan and Pitman B. Potter.

35 Michael McConville et al., *Criminal Justice in China: An Empirical Inquiry* (Cheltenham: Edward Elgar, 2011).

36 Jonathan Watts, "Chinese human rights activist Liu Xiaobo sentenced to 11 years in jail: Anger at harsh treatment of prominent activist found guilty of subversion," *The Guardian*, December 25, 2009, http://www.guardian.co.uk/world/2009/dec/25/china-jails-liu-xiaobo (accessed September 14, 2012); Peter Foster, "China Upholds 11-Year Sentence for Dissident Liu Xiaobo," *The Daily Telegraph*, February 11, 2010; Perry Link, "China's Charter 08," *New York Review of Books*, vol. 56, no. 1 (January 15, 2009) (http://www.nybooks.com/articles/archives/2009/jan/15/chinas-charter-08/) (accessed November 17, 2010).

37 Liu Xiaobo, "I Have No Enemies: My Final Statement" (December 23, 2009), *Foreign Policy*, October 8, 2010 (http://www.foreignpolicy.com/articles/2010/10/08/i_have_no_enemies) (accessed November 23, 2010).

38 Peter Drysdale, "Stern Hu's Trial and its Legal and Economic Implications – Weekly Editorial", East Asian Forum, Economics, Politics and Public Policy in East Asia and the Pacific, March 29, 2010, available at: http://www.eastasiaforum.org/2010/03/29/stern-hus-trial-and-its-legal-and-economic-implications-weekly-editorial/, used by permission.

39 Hefei shi zhongji renmin fanyuan [Intermediate level people's court of Hefei municipality], "Bogu Kailai, Zhang Shaojun guyi sharen an ting shen qingkuang" [Trial Details of Bogu Kailai and Zhang Xiaojun Intentional Homicide Case] (August 9, 2012) http://ww4.sinaimg.cn/bmiddle/6b42db9ejw1dvqm00p21cj.jpg (accessed September 8, 2012) (tr. Juan Li, Liu Huan, Liu Yue, and Pitman B. Potter).

40 Sarah Biddulph, *Legal Reform and Administrative Detention Powers in China* (Cambridge: Cambridge University Press, 2007).

41 State Council Information Office, "White Paper on Criminal Reform in China" (1992) Section V, http://www.china.org.cn/e-white/criminal/8-6.htm (accessed April 16, 2012).

42 "Decision of the State Council on Questions of Re-education and Rehabilitation Through Labour" (1957); "Supplementary Provisions on Re-education and Rehabilitation Through Labour" (1979); "Provisional Measures on Re-Education and Rehabilitation Through Labour" (1982).

43 See "Provisional Measures for Dealing with the Release of Reform through Labor Criminals at the Expiration of their Term of Imprisonment and for Placing Them and Getting Them Employed." Also see CPC General Political Committee, "Suggestions Concerning Strengthening Resettlement and Training Work for Released Labour Reform and Labour Re-education Prisoners," in James D. Seymour and Richard Anderson, *New Ghosts Old Ghosts: Prisons and Labor Reform Camps in China* (New York: M.E. Sharpe, 1995). Subsequent State Council regulations on the handling of reform through labor criminals provided that those who "have not reformed" could be detained under imprisonment at the place of reform. See Decision Regarding the Handling of Offenders Undergoing Reform Through Labour and Persons Undergoing Rehabilitation Through Labour Who Escape or Commit New Crimes (National People's Congress Standing Committee, 1981).

44 See Lawyer's Committee for Human Rights, *Opening to Reform? An Analysis of China's Revised Criminal Procedure Law* (New York: Lawyer's Committee for Human Rights, 1996), p. 25–7.

45 Keith J. Hand, "Using Law for a Righteous Purpose: The Sun Zhigang Incident and Evolving Forms of Citizen Action in the People's Republic of China," *Columbia Journal of Transnational Law*, vol. 45 (Feb. 4, 2007), pp. 114–95; Human Rights Watch, "An Alleyway in Hell," (Nov. 12, 2009), http://www.hrw.org/reports/2009/11/12/alleyway-hell (accessed September 3, 2012).

3: Economic Prosperity

1 Bruce Dickson, "Coaptation and Corporatism in China: The Logic of Party Adaptation," *Political Science Quarterly*, vol. 115, no. 4 (Winter, 2000–2001), pp. 517–40; Jonathan Unger and Anita Chan, "China, Corporatism, and the East Asian Model," *Australian Journal of Chinese Affairs*, vol. 22, no. 1 (January 1995), pp. 29–53.

2 David Wank, "The Institutional Process of Market Clientelism: *Guanxi* and Private Business in a South China City," *The China Quarterly*, no. 147 (September 1996), pp. 820–38; Jean C. Oi, "Communism and Clientilism: Rural Politics in China," *World Politics*, vol. 37, no. 2 (January 1985), pp. 238–66.

3 Philip C.C. Huang, *Code, Custom, and Legal Practice in China: The Qing and the Republic Compared* (Stanford, CA: Stanford University Press, 2001). William P. Alford, "The Inscrutable Occidental? Implications of Roberto Unger's Uses and Abuses of the Chinese Past," *Texas Law Review*, vol. 64

(1986) pp. 915–51; Derk Bodde and Clarence Morris, *Law in Imperial China* (Philadelphia, PA: University of Pennsylvania Press, 1967).

4 Thomas Gold, Doug Guthrie, and David Wank, eds, *Social Connections in China* (Cambridge: Cambridge University Press, 2002).

5 Canadian International Development Agency, *China*, http://www.acdi-cida.gc.ca/china (accessed August 28, 2012); The Ford Foundation, *China* (2011), http://www.fordfoundation.org/pdfs/library/China-brochure-2011.pdf (accessed August 28, 2012).

6 Brian Z. Tamanaha, "The Primacy of Society and the Failures of Law and Development," *Cornell International Law Journal*, vol. 44 (2011) pp. 209–47.

7 UN Development Programme, *Human Development Report* (2011), http://hdr.undp.org/en/reports/global/hdr2011/download/en/ (accessed August 28, 2012); Jose Antonio Ocampo and Juan Martin, *Globalization and Development* (Santiago: UN Economic Commission for Latin America and the Caribbean, 2003).

8 Karl Marx and Freidrich Engels, *The German Ideology* (1845), http://www.marxists.org/archive/marx/works/1845/german-ideology/index.htm (accessed August 28, 2012).

9 For a survey of the dependency literature, *see* Robert A. Packenham, *The Dependency Movement: Scholarship and Politics in Development Studies* (Cambridge, MA: Harvard University Press, 1992).

10 *See* generally, Katherine Pistor and Philip Wellons, eds, *The Role of Law and Legal Institutions in Asian Economic Development* (Oxford: Oxford University Press, 1999). Also *see* Louis Putterman, *Dollars and Change: Economics in Context* (New Haven, CT: Yale University Press, 2001); Charles E. Lindblom, *Politics and Markets* (New York: Basic Books, 1977).

11 This involves perspectives attributed to Max Weber that law lends certainty and predictability to autonomous business transactions. *See* generally, Max Weber, *Economy and Society* (Roth and Wittich, eds) (Berkeley, CA: University of California Press, 1978); Stephen P. Turner and Regis A. Factor, *Max Weber: The Lawyer as Social Thinker* (London: Routledge, 1994).

12 *See* generally, John Hazard, "The Abortive Codes of the Pashukanis School," in Donald D. Barry, F.J. M. Feldbrugge and Dominik Losok, eds, *Codification in the Communist World* (Leiden: A.W. Sijthoff, 1975), pp. 145–75.

13 Wang Liming, ed., *Zhongguo minfa anli yu xueli yanjiu* [Studies in Chinese civil law cases and theory] (Beijing: Law Publishers, 1998).

14 Pitman B. Potter, *The Economic Contract Law of China: Legitimacy and Contract Autonomy in the PRC* (Seattle, WA: University of Washington Press, 1992); James V. Feinerman, "Legal Institution, Administrative Device, or Foreign Import: The Roles of Contract in the People's Republic of China," in Pitman B. Potter, ed., *Domestic Law Reforms* (Armonk, NY: M.E. Sharpe, 1994).

15 *See* generally, Jerome Alan Cohen, "The New Foreign Contract Law," *China Business Review*, July–August 1985 (including a translation of the FECL); Mary Ip, "The Revised Contract Law and Its Implications on Consumerism in China," *International Journal of Business*, vol. 9, no. 1 (2004), pp. 41–58.

16 ""Nongcun chengbao jingying hu qianding de chengbao jingying hetong, shou falü baohu" [A task management contract signed by a rural contractor receives legal safeguard]," Case No. 70, in Chen Youzun, ed., *Minshi jingji jinan anli jiesi* [Interpretation and analysis of difficult civil and economic cases] (Huhehaote: Inner Mongolia University Press, 1990), p. 119 (tr. Juan Li, Liu Huan, Liu Yue, and Pitman B. Potter); Hetong dangshiren yi fang you guocuo, bing zaocheng dui fang jingji sunshi de, yingdang chengdan minshi zeren "[Where one contract party is at fault and also causes economic losses to the other party, it should bear civil liability]," Case No. 106, in Chen Youzun, ed., *Minshi jingji jinan anli jiesi* [Interpretation and analysis of difficult civil and economic cases] (Huhehaote: Inner Mongolia University Press, 1990), p. 187 (tr. Juan Li, Liu Huan, Liu Yue, and Pitman B. Potter).

17 General Principles of Civil Law (1986), http://en.chinacourt.org/public/detail.php?id=2696 (accessed November 26, 2012).

18 "Shao Guoqing yu Jia Zhenbo maimai hetong jiufen yi an" [Dispute case over a sales contract between Shao Guoqing and Jia Zhenbo], Zhengzhou Intermediate Level People's Court Henan, August 10, 2010, www.chinacourt.org (accessed October 25, 2010) (tr. Juan Li, Liu Huan, Liu Yue, and Pitman B. Potter).

19 *See* generally, *Hetong fa xiaochuanshu* [Small compendium on contract law] (Beijing: Law Press China, 2010).

20 Supreme People's Court of the PRC, "Interpretation (1st) on Several Issues Concerning the Application of the 'PRC Contract Law,'" http://app.westlawchina.com.ezproxy.library.ubc.ca/maf/china/app/document?&docguid=i0adf589b0000011e6d83c039d238ab6d&hitguid=i0adf589b0000011e6d83c039d238ab6d&srguid=ia744c0670000013a8520485fd87a8eea&spos=7&epos=7&td=8&crumb-action=append&context=35&lang=en.

21 Luo Wen, "Mai mai fangwu wei banli guohu shouxu de xiaoli" [Validity of home sale absent transfer of ownership], February 9, 2012 http://law.xichu.net/2012/0209/4478.html (accessed October 29, 2012) (tr. Juan Li, Liu Huan, Liu Yue, and Pitman B. Potter).

22 Supreme People's Court of the PRC, "Interpretation (2) on Several Issues Concerning the Application of the 'PRC Contract Law,'" http://app.westlawchina.com.ezproxy.library.ubc.ca/maf/china/app/document?&d ocguid=i3cf76ad3000001213a501d6fe644c56d&hitguid=i3cf76ad3000 001213a501d6fe644c56d&srguid=ia744c0690000013a852186d75232f 032&spos=2&epos=2&td=8&crumb-action=append&context=39 &lang=en.

23 Thomas Moore, "Landmark Judgment for Starbucks in Chinese IPR Case," Ezine Articles (n.d.), http://ezinearticles.com/?Landmark-Judgement-for-Starbucks-in-Chinese-IPR-Case&id=139503 (accessed September 20, 2012).

24 US International Trade Commission, *China: Effects of Intellectual Property Infringement and Indigenous Technology Policies on the U.S. Economy* (May 2011), http://www.usitc.gov/publications/332/pub4226.pdf (accessed May 20, 2011); "Oral Remarks of Robert A. Kapp, President United States–China Business Council to the Trade Policy Staff Committee Hearing on China's Progress in Implementing Its WTO Accession Commitments" (September 23, 2004).

25 Company Law of the PRC (1993, rev. 2006), http://www.csrc.gov.cn/pub/csrc_en/laws/rfdm/statelaws/200904/t20090428_102712.htm.

26 Securities Law of the PRC (1998, rev. 2005), http://www.csrc.gov.cn/pub/csrc_en/laws/rfdm/statelaws/200904/t20090429_102757.htm.

27 *See* Property Law Research Program of CASS Law Institute, "Zhiding Zhongguo wuquanfa de jiben sikao" [Basic perspectives on enacting Chinese property law], in *Faxue yanjiu* [Research in legal studies], no. 3 (1995), pp. 3–10.

28 *See* "Zhongguo wuquan fa (caoan)" [Chinese property law (draft)], Article 2, in Liang Huixing, *Zhongguo wuquanfa caoan jianyi gao* [Outline of opinion on a draft Chinese property law] (Beijing: Social Science Manuscripts Press, 2000), p. 5.

29 Wang Zhaoguo, "Explanation on Draft Property Law" (delivered at the 5th Session of the 10th National People's Congress, March 8, 2007) (http://English.people.com.cn/200703/08/print20070308_355491.html).

30 "Ascertaining the Validity of a Transfer Contract Concerning the Right of Contracted Land Management – Dispute on a Transfer Contract of

the Right of Household Contracted Land Management between Zhan Xiaoming and Han Wende" (July 22, 2009), in Li Xiandong, ed., *Minfa wuquanfa dianxing an li tongyi* [Commentary on typical cases of civil law and property law] (Beijing: Law Press China, 2010), pp. 295–7 (tr. Juan Li, Liu Huan, Liu Yue, and Pitman B. Potter).

31 "Cao Changyou yu Zhang Zhenpu, Li Zhipu, Zhang Xiaoqu hetong jiufen yian" [A contract dispute involving Cao Zhangyou and Zhang Zhenpu, Li Zhipu, and Zhang Xiaoqu], Kongyi Municipal People's Court, Henan, Civil Court Verdict (May 18, 2010) Gongminchuzi No. 590, www.chinacourt.org (accessed August 25, 2010) (tr. Liu Huan, Juan Li, and Pitman B. Potter).

32 "Cunweihui yifa xiangyou jiti tudi shiyongquan" [The village committee has the right to use collective property] (2008). Case report in *Zhonghua renmin gongheguo wuquanfa: Anli zhujie ban* [The Property Rights Law of the PRC: Case and key interpretation edition] (Beijing: China Legal Publishing House, 2009), pp. 40–1 (tr. Liu Huan, Juan Li, and Pitman B. Potter); "Jiti suoyouzhi qiye zhigong hefa quanyi baohu" [The lawful interests of collective ownership system enterprise staff are protected] (2008), Case report in *Zhonghua renmin gongheguo wuquanfa: Anli zhujie ban* [The Property Rights Law of the PRC: Case and key interpretation edition] (Beijing: China Legal Publishing House, 2009), pp. 42–4, tr. Liu Huan, Juan Li, and Pitman B. Potter.

33 "Zuigao renmin fayuan guanyu sheli wuye fuwu jiufen anjian juti yingyong falü ruogan wenti de jieshi" [Interpretation of the Supreme People's Court on certain questions of the specific application of law to adjudication of disputes over property management] (April 20, 2009).

34 Christine Wong, "Central–Local Relations Revisited: the 1994 Tax Sharing Reform and Public Expenditure Management in China," World Bank (2000) (http://citeseerx.ist.psu.edu/viewdoc/download?doi=10.1.1.201.8596&rep=rep1&type=pdf.http://citeseerx.ist.psu.edu/viewdoc/download?doi=10.1.1.201.8596&rep=rep1&type=pdf) (accessed January 25, 2012).

35 *See* Jin Renqing, "Explanation of China's draft enterprise income tax law" (March 8, 2007), http://news.xinhuanet.com/english/2007-03/08/content_6765324.htm (accessed January 26, 2013).

36 *See* e.g., "Agreement Between the Government of Canada and the Government of the People's Republic of China for the Avoidance of Double Taxation and the Prevention of Fiscal Evasion with Respect to Taxes of Income (1986), http://faculty.law.ubc.ca/brooks/treaties/canada/china_e.pdf (accessed August 28, 2012); "UK-China Double

Taxation Agreement" (2011), http://www.hmrc.gov.uk/taxtreaties/ signed/uk-china-dta2011.pdf (acessed August 28, 2012). Also *see* Norman Givant and James Dunlop, "Tax Treaties," in Michael J. Moser and Fu Yu, eds, *Doing Business in China* (New York: Juris, looseleaf), chapter 3.3.

37 "Circular of the State Council Concerning Several Policies on Carrying Out the Development of China's Vast Western Regions" (October 26, 2000), Commercial Clearing House (CCH), ed., *China Laws for Foreign Business.*

4: Social Development

1 *See* generally, *Cambridge History of China*, vol. 13 (Republican China 1912–1949) (Cambridge: Cambridge University Press, 1986), Part II, chapters 12–14. Also *see* Tony Saich, ed., *The Rise to Power of the Chinese Communist Party: Documents and Analysis* (Armonk, NY: M.E. Sharpe, 1996), pp. 974–8; Lan Quanpu, *Jiefangqu fagui gaiyao* [Outline of laws and regulations in the liberated areas] (Beijing: Masses Publishers, 1982).

2 *See* generally, *Cambridge History of China*, vol. 14 (The People's Republic Part I: The Emergence of Revolutionary China 1949–1965) (Cambridge: Cambridge University Press, 1987).

3 For a general introduction, *see* Nathan Jackson, "What are the major aspects of Chinese labor law?," University of Iowa Center for International Finance and Development (April 2011), http://blogs.law.uiowa.edu/ebook/ uicifd-ebook/what-are-relevant-issues-concerning-chinese-labor-and- employment-law (accessed January 30, 2013); Ronald C. Brown, *Understanding Labor and Employment Law in China* (Cambridge: Cambridge University Press, 2009).

4 *See* generally, Feng Chen, "Between the State and Labour: The Conflict of Chinese Trade Unions' Double Identity in Market Reform," *The China Quarterly*, no. 176 (December 2003), pp. 1006–28; Sarah Biddulph and Sean Cooney, "Regulation of Trade Unions in the People's Republic of China," *Melbourne University Law Review*, vol. 19 (December 1993), pp. 255–92.

5 http://english.gov.cn/laws/2005-10/11/content_75948.htm (accessed January 30, 2013).

6 For recent reports, *see* China Labor Bulletin, http://www.clb.org.hk/en/ (accessed January 30, 2013).

7 David Blumenthal and William Hsiao, "Privatization and Its Discontents – The Evolving Chinese Health Care System," *New England Journal of Medicine*, vol. 353, no. 11 (September 15, 2005), pp. 1165–70.

8 *See* list of legislation at PRC Ministry of Health, "Weishenbu zhengfu xinxi gongkai zhuanti" [Ministry of Health News – Public Files], http://www. moh.gov.cn/publicfiles//business/htmlfiles/zwgkzt/pfl/index.htm (accessed August 28, 2012).

9 Jonathan Watts, "Hidden from the world, a village dies of Aids while China refuses to face a growing crisis," *The Guardian*, October 25, 2003, http:// www.guardian.co.uk/world/2003/oct/25/aids.chin (accessed July 5, 2012). Used by permission.

10 World Health Organization, "China's latest SARS outbreak has been contained, but biosafety concerns remain – Update 7" (May 18, 2004), http://www.who.int/csr/don/2004_05_18a/en/ (accessed July 5, 2012). Used by permission.

11 *See China: An International Journal*, vol. 8, no. 1, Special Issue on Health Policy (March 2010).

12 Yuan Ye, Jiang Guocheng, "China unveils health-care reform guidelines," *Xinhua*, http://news.xinhuanet.com/english/2009-04/06/content_ 11138643.htm (accessed September 20, 2012).

13 *See* PRC Ministry of Civil Affairs, "Quanguo minzheng menhu" [National civil affairs gateway], http://www.mca.gov.cn/article/zwgk/fvfg/ (accessed January 25, 2012).

14 State Council Information Office, "White Paper: China's Social Security and Its Policy," http://english.gov.cn/official/2005-07/28/content_ 18024.htm (accessed September 20, 2012).

15 *See* generally, Seren T. Hall, Megan W. Lewis, *Education in China: 21st Century Issues and Challenges* (Hauppauge, NY: Nova Science Publishers, 2008); Rui Yang, *Third Delight: The Internationalization of Higher Education in China* (London: Routledge, 2002); Emily Hannum, "Political Change and the Urban-Rural Gap in Basic Education in China, 1949–1990," in *Comparative Education Review*, vol. 43, no. 2 (May 1999), pp. 193–211; Michael Agelasto and Bob Adamson, eds, *Higher Education in Post-Mao China* (Hong Kong: Hong Kong University Press, 1998); Glenn Peterson, *The Power of Words: Literacy and Revolution in South China 1949–1995* (Vancouver, University of British Columbia Press, 1997); Ruth Hayhoe, *Education and Modernization* (Oxford: Pergamon Press, 1992).

16 Human Rights in China, "Implementation of the Convention on the Elimination of All Forms of Discrimination Against Women in the PRC" (June 2006), http://hrichina.org/content/4124 (accessed January 26, 2013).

17 *See* e.g., Morris Rossabit, *Governing China's Multiethnic Frontiers* (Seattle, WA: University of Washington Press, 2004); International Committee

of Lawyers for Tibet, "Legal Materials on Tibet" (2nd edn) (1997); Amnesty International, *People's Republic of China: Repression in Tibet, 1987–1992* (1992); Amnesty International, *Secret Violence: Human Rights Violations in Xinjiang* (1992); Uradyn E. Bulag, *The Mongols at China's Edge: History and the Politics of National Unity* (Lanham, MD: Rowman and Littlefield, 2002).

18 http://english.gov.cn/official/2009-09/27/content_1427989.htm (accessed October 25, 2012).

19 Congressional Executive Committee on China, *Annual Report 2005*, Shttp://www.cecc.gov/pages/annualRpt/annualRpt05/2005_3a_minorities.php (Section III) (accessed October 15, 2012).

20 Jim Yardley, "Simmering Resentments Led to Tibetan Backlash," *New York Times*, March 18, 2008; Geoffrey York, "Why Tibet is Boiling Over," *Globe and Mail*, March 21, 2008.

21 Congressional Executive Committee on China, *Annual Report 2009* (October 10, 2009) http://www.cecc.gov/pages/annualRpt/annual-Rpt09/CECCannRpt2009.pdf (accessed November 19, 2009), pp. 243–5.

22 "Genghis Khan's Tribe Fears for His Honor," *The Age*, November 13, 2004; "Mongols Resist Government's Plan of Privatizing Chinggis Khaan Mausoluem, Police Impose Curfew on College Campuses in Inner Mongolia," New York Southern Mongolia Human Rights Information Centre (October 31, 2004).

23 Isabella Bennett, "Media Censorship in China," *Council on Foreign Relations*, March 7, 2011, http://www.cfr.org/china/media-censorship-china/p11515 (accessed September 20, 2012); Reporters Without Borders, "Journey to the Heart of Internet Censorship" (October 2007), http://www.rsf.org/IMG/pdf/Voyage_au_coeur_de_la_censure_GB.pdf (accessed October 15, 2012).

24 *See* generally, Congressional Executive Committee on China (CECC), "Freedom of Expression," http://www.cecc.gov/pages/virtualAcad/exp/expcensors.php (accessed April 19, 2012); He Qinglian, *The Fog of Censorship in China* (New York: Human Rights on China, 2008), http://www.hrichina.org/content/4050 (accessed April 19, 2012).

25 Rebecca MacKinnon, "Shi Tao, Yahoo!, and the lessons for corporate social responsibility," (Working paper, December 30, 2007), http://rconversation.blogs.com/YahooShiTaoLessons.pdf (accessed September 20, 2012); Christina Wilson, et al. "Google in China: The Great Firewall." Case study made under the supervision of Prof. Wayne Norman, edited

by Prof Chris MacDonald. Available http://www.duke.edu/web/kenanethics/CaseStudies/GoogleInChina.pdf.

26 Kristen A. Day, ed., *China's Environment and the Challenge of Sustainable Development* (Armonk, NY: M.E. Sharpe, 2005); Elizabeth Economy, *The River Runs Black: The Environmental Challenge to China's Future* (Ithaca, NY: Cornell University Press, 2004).

27 Mark Elvin and Liu Ts'ui-jong, eds, *Sediments of Time: Environment and Society in Chinese History* (Cambridge: Cambridge University Press, 1998).

28 Kristen A. Day, ed., *China's Environment and the Challenge of Sustainable Development* (Armonk, NY: M.E. Sharpe, 2005).

29 Alex L. Wang, "China's Environmental Tipping Point," in Timothy Weston and Lionel Jensen, *China In and Beyond the Headlines* (Lanham, MD: Rowman and Littlefield, 2012), pp. 112–33; Carin Zissin and Jayshree Bajoria, "China's Environmental Crisis," *Council of Foreign Relations*, August 4, 2008, http://www.cfr.org/china/chinas-environmental-crisis/p12608 (accessed September 20, 2012).

30 Jonathan Ansfield and Keith Bradsher, "China Report Shows More Pollution in Waterways," *New York Times*, February 9, 2010, http://www.nytimes.com/2010/02/10/world/asia/10pollute.html?_r=0 (accessed September 8, 2012).

31 Joseph Casey and Katherine Koleski, "Backgrounder: China's 12th Five Year Plan," U.S.–China Economic and Security Review Commission (June 24, 2011), http://www.uscc.gov/researchpapers/2011/12th-Five-YearPlan_062811.pdf (accessed September 20, 2012); State Council, "Several Opinions on Further Improving the Work on the Use of Foreign Investment," *China Law & Practice*, April 6, 2010, http://www.chinalawandpractice.com/Article/2483574/Channel/18489/State-Council-Several-Opinions-on-Further-Improving-the-Work-on-the-Use-of-Foreign-Investment.html (accessed September 20, 2012); National Development and Reform Commission and Ministry of Commerce, "2011 Foreign Investment Guidance Catalogue," December 24, 2011, http://www.ndrc.gov.cn/zcfb/zcfbl/2011ling/W020111122 9379511927834.pdf (accessed September 20, 2012).

32 *See*, for example, the Corporate Social Responsibility website, http://www.chinacsr.com/en/, which extols the virtues of CSR and publicizes efforts by government agencies and business groups to encourage voluntary support.

33 Joseph Sarkis, et al., "Winds of Change: Corporate Social Responsibility in China," *Ivey Business Journal*, January/February 2011, http://www.

iveybusinessjournal.com/topics/social-responsibility/winds-of-change-corporate-social-responsibility-in-china (accessed June 25, 2011).

34 Minxin Pei, "Corruption Threatens China's Future," Carnegie Endowment Policy Brief No. 55, October 2007, http://www.carnegieendowment. org/files/pb55_pei_china_corruption_final.pdf (accessed April 19, 2012).

35 State Council Information Office, "White Paper: China's Efforts to Combat Corruption" (December 29, 2010), http://news.xinhuanet.com/english2010/china/2010-12/29/c_13669383.htm (accessed January 5, 2011).

36 Chinese Academy of Social Sciences, "Wo guo tanwu fenzi xiang jingwai zuanyi zichan de tujing ji jiance fangfa yanjiu" [Research on How the Corrupt Officials in China Transfer Their Assets Abroad and to Monitor Them] (June, 2008) (author's copy) (tr. by Yue Liu and Pitman B. Potter).

5: International Engagement

1 Jerome A. Cohen and Hungdah Chiu, eds, *People's China and International Law: A Documentary Survey* (Princeton, NJ: Princeton University Press, 1974); Jerome A. Cohen, "Chinese Attitudes Toward International Law – and Our Own," in Cohen ed., *Contemporary Chinese Law: Research Problems and Perspectives* (Cambridge, MA: Harvard University Press, 1970), pp. 282–93.

2 James V. Feinerman, "Chinese Participation in the International Legal Order: Rogue Elephant or Team Player?" *The China Quarterly*, no. 141 (March 1995), pp. 186–210.

3 Xue Hanqin and Jin Chian, "International Treaties in the Chinese Domestic Legal System," *Chinese Journal of International Law*, vol. 8, no. 2 (July 2009), pp. 299–322; Albert H. Y. Chen, *An Introduction to the Legal System of the People's Republic of China* (3rd edn) (Hong Kong: Butterworths, 2004), pp. 129–30. Also *see* Sophia Woodman, "Human Rights as 'Foreign Affairs:' China's Reporting Under Human Rights Treaties," in *Hong Kong Law Journal*, vol. 35, Part 1 (2005), pp. 179–204; Zhang Shaodong, "Ye lun guoji tiaoyue zai woguo de shiyong," [Again examining the application of international treaties in China], *Faxue pinglun* [Law Review] no. 6 (2001), pp. 73–9.

4 Among the many works on China's accession to the WTO, the most useful include Deborah Cass, Brett G. Williams, and George Barker, eds, *China and the World Trading System: Entering the New Millennium* (Cambridge: Cambridge University Press, 2003); Donald C. Clarke, "China and the World

Trade Organization," Freshfields, ed., *Doing Business in China* (looseleaf), pp. I-11.1– I-11.30; and Sylvia Ostry, Alan S. Alexandroff, and Raphael Gomez, eds, *China and the Long March to Global Trade: The Accession of China to the World Trade Organization* (New York: Routledge, 2002); Council on Foreign Relations, *Beginning the Journey: China, the United States and the WTO* (New York: Council on Foreign Relations, 2001).

5 http://unpan1.un.org/intradoc/groups/public/documents/apcity/ unpan002144.pdf

6 World Trade Organization, *International Trade Statistics 2011*, http://www. wto.org/english/res_e/statis_e/statis_e.htm (accessed September 13, 2012).

7 The World Bank, "Foreign Direct Investment – the China Story" (July 16, 2010) http://www.worldbank.org/en/news/2010/07/16/foreign-direct-investment-china-story (accessed September 15, 2012).

8 Ljiljana Biukovic, "Hub and Spokes Intertwined: Is There Space for Human Rights Linkages in China's Trade and Investment Network?" in Leslie Jacobs and David Drache, eds, *New Policy Spaces For a Dismal Economic Age: International Trade And Human Rights* (Cambridge; Cambridge University Press, forthcoming). Also *see* "China FTA Network" (PRC Ministry of Commerce), http://fta.mofcom.gov.cn/english/fta_qianshu.shtml (accessed January 25, 2013).

9 Cai Penghong, "The Trans-Pacific Partnership: A Chinese Perspective," http:// www.pecc.org/resources/doc_view/1752-the-trans-pacific-partnership-a-chinese-perspective-ppt (Pacific Economic Cooperation Council) (n.d.) (accessed January 25, 2013); Wen Jin Yuan, "The Trans-Pacific Partnership and China's Corresponding Strategies," Freeman Briefing Report (Washington, DC: Centre for Strategic and International Studies, 2012), http://csis. org/files/publication/120620_Freeman_Brief.pdf (accessed January 25, 2013).

10 State Administration for Industry and Commerce (SAIC), "Guidance on Registration" (2005) http://202.108.90.68/gfr/060104114506-0.htm (accessed September 20, 2012).

11 Axel Berger, "China's new bilateral investment treaty programme: Substance, rational and implications for international investment law making" (ASIL Conference Paper 2008), http://www.asil.org/files/ ielconferencepapers/berger.pdf (accessed January 25, 2013).

12 UN Conference on Trade and Development (UNCTAD), "Total number of Bilateral Investment Agreements concluded, 1 June 2012," http:// unctad.org/sections/dite_pcbb/docs/bits_china.pdf (accessed January 25, 2013). Also *see* UNCTAD 2012 Annual Report, "World Investment Report 2012," http://unctad.org/en/Pages/DIAE/World%

20Investment%20Report/WIR2012_WebFlyer.aspx (accessed January 28, 2013).

13 Kong Qingjiang, "U.S.–China Bilateral Investment Treaty Negotiations: Context, Focus, and Implications," *Journal of WTO and International Health Law and Policy*, vol. 7, no. 1 (March 2012), pp. 181–94.

14 *See* "Full Text of Canada–China FIPPA and Explanatory Memorandum," *The Tyee*, October 14, 2012, http://thetyee.ca/Blogs/TheHook/Federal-Politics/2012/10/14/China-Canada-Agreement/ (accessed January 25, 2013). Also *see* Justin Carter, "The Protracted Bargain: Negotiating the Canada–China Foreign Investment Promotion and Protection Agreement," *Canadian Yearbook of International Law*, vol. 47 (2009), pp. 197–258.

15 The Export-Import Bank of China, *Annual Report 2011*, http://english.eximbank.gov.cn/annual/2011.shtml (accessed January 28, 2013).

16 *See* A. Mora, "The Revpower Dispute: China's Breach of the New York Convention?" in *Dispute Resolution in the PRC: A Practical Guide to Litigation and Arbitration in China* (Hong Kong: China Law & Practice, 1995), p. 151. Also see testimony of R.A. Aronson, CEO of Ross Engineering before the House Ways and Means Trade Subcommittee, May 23, 1995, Federal Information Systems, 1995.

17 Supreme People's Court, "Certain Issues Relating to the People's Courts Enforcement Work Regulation Circular (Trial Implementation)" (July 8, 1998); "Several Issues Relating to the People's Courts' Handling of Foreign-related and Foreign Arbitration Matters Circular" (August 28, 1995); "Relevant Matters Concerning People's Courts Vacating of Foreign-related Arbitral Awards Circular" (March–April 23, 1998); and "Problems of Collecting Fees and Time Limits for Review of Recognition and Enforcement of Foreign Arbitral Awards Circular" (October 21, 1998).

18 Joshua Ramo Cooper, *The Beijing Consensus* (London: The Foreign Policy Centre, 2004).

19 A full list of human rights treaties ratified by the PRC is available at http://www.umn.edu/humanrts/research/ratification-china.html.

20 "Final Declaration of the Regional meeting for Asia of the World Conference on Human /rights" (1991), http://www.law.hku.hk,conlaw/outline/Outline8/Bangkok%20Declaration.htm (accessed September 14, 2012).

21 *See* State Council Information Office, "White Paper: Progress in Human Rights in 2009" Section I, http://www.china.org.cn/government/

whitepaper/2010-09/26/content_21007314.htm (accessed April 16, 2012).

22 State Council Information Office, "Progress in China's Human Rights in 2009" (September 2010), http://english.gov.cn/official/2010-09/26/content_1709982.htm (accessed April 20, 2012).

23 Amnesty International, "Human Rights in China" (2012), http://factsanddetails.com/china.php?itemid=297&catid=8&subcatid=50#100 (accessed August 28, 2012).

24 "National Human Rights Action Plan of China" (2009), http://www.china.org.cn/archive/2009-04/13/content_17595407.htm (accessed August 28, 2012).

25 Information Office of the State Council (April 13, 2009), http://english.gov.cn/official/2009-04/13/content_1284128.htm.

26 State Council Information Office, "Progress in China's Human Rights in 2009" (September 2010), http://english.gov.cn/official/2010-09/26/content_1709982.htm (accessed April 20, 2012).

27 State Council Information Office, "White Paper on Political Democracy" (October 19, 2005), http://www.chinadaily.com.cn/english/doc/2005-10/19/content_486206.htm (accessed September 3, 2012).

28 Human Rights in China, "Note on China's Progress Since the 2009 Universal Periodic Review" (November 2011), http://www.upr-info.org/followup/assessments/session17/china/China-HRIC.pdf.

29 Human Rights in China, "Shanghai Rights Defender Harassed on Heels of National Human Rights Action Plan Release" (April 15, 2009), http://www.hrichina.org/content/293, used by permission.

30 See, e.g., Human Rights Watch, China Country Summary 2012, http://www.hrw.org/sites/default/files/related_material/china_2012_0.pdf (accessed September 13, 2012).

31 "About the CCICED: Overview" (February 26, 2008) http://www.cciced.net/enccicedold/abc/200802/t20080226_146393.htm (accessed July 20, 2012).

32 State Council Information Office, "China's Policies and Actions on Climate Change" (October 29, 2008), http://www.china.org.cn/government/news/2008-10/29/content_16681689.htm (accessed April 20, 2012).

33 Information Office of the State Council, "China's Policies and Actions for Addressing Climate Change" (November 22, 2011), http://news.xinhuanet.com/english2010/china/2011-11/22/c_131262368.htm (accessed April 20, 2012).

34 Ng Ka Ling v. Director of Immigration [1999] (HKLRD 315); Cham Kam Nga and Others v. Director of Immigration [1999] (HKLRD 304).

35 State Council Taiwan Affairs Office and Information Office, "The One-China Principle and the Taiwan Issue" (February 21, 2000), http://www.china.org.cn/english/taiwan/7956.htm (accessed August 28, 2012).

36 "Full Text of Anti-Secession Law," Third Session of the 10th National People's Congress and National Political Consultative Congress, http://www.china.org.cn/english/2005lh/122724.htm (accessed August 28, 2012).

37 Chien-peng Chung, "The Shanghai Co-Operation Organization: China's Changing Influence in Central Asia," *The China Quarterly*, no. 180 (2004), pp. 989–1009.

38 "Shanghai Cooperation Organisation Charter" (2006), http://www.chinadaily.com.cn/china/2006-06/12/content_614628.htm (accessed November 26, 2012).

39 Russian Ministry of Foreign Affairs, "Text of Putin–Hu Jintao Joint Declaration" (FBIS May 28, 2003). A border treaty was concluded in 2004, ending 40 years of negotiations. "Sino-Russian Border Treaty" (Xinhuanet, October 14, 2004).

40 S. Frederick Starr, ed., *Xinjiang: China's Muslim Borderland* (Armonk, NY: M.E. Sharpe, 2004); Nicolas Becquelin, "Xinjiang in the Nineties," *The China Journal*, no. 44 (July 2000), pp. 65–90.

41 Chien-peng Chung, "China's 'War on Terror': September 11 and Uighur Separatism," *Foreign Affairs*, vol. 81, no. 4 (July/August 2002), pp. 8–12; Vivien Pik-Kwan Chan, "War on Terrorism: Local Foes in Mainland's Sights," *South China Morning Post*, September 19, 2001.

42 http://treaties.un.org/Pages/DB.aspx?path=DB/studies/page2_en.xml (accessed August 28, 2012).

43 UN Charter Chapter VIII. Also *see*, e.g., "Security Council Highlights Need to Further Strengthen Cooperation Between UN, Regional Organizations in Maintenance of International Peace, Security" (Security Council Resolution 1631/2005).

44 Woodrow Wilson Center for Scholars, "China's 'Good Neighbor' Diplomacy: A Wolf in Sheep's Clothing?," *Asia Program Special Report*, no. 126 (January 2005).

45 "The United Nations Convention on the Law of the Sea (A Historical Perspective)," http://www.un.org/Depts/los/convention_agreements/convention_historical_perspective.htm (accessed August 28, 2012).

46 "Law of the PRC on the Territorial Sea and the Contiguous Zone" (1992), http://www.un.org/depts/los/LEGISLATIONANDTREATIES/ PDFFILES/CHN_1992_Law.pdf (accessed August 28, 2012).

47 Association of Southeast Asian Nations (ASEAN), "Declaration of the Conduct of the Parties in the South China Sea," http://www.aseansec. org/13163.htm (accessed August 28, 2012).

48 Remarks by Foreign Minister Yang Jiechi at the ARF Foreign Ministers' Meeting (July 24, 2011), http://www.fmprc.gov.cn/eng/zxxx/t842183. htm (accessed November 26, 2012).

References

SELECTED LAWS AND REGULATIONS CITED

12th Five Year Plan of the PRC, http://www.kpmg.com/CN/en/IssuesAndInsights/ArticlesPublications/Publicationseries/5-years-plan/Documents/China-12th-Five-Year-Plan-Overview-201104.pdf

1982 Convention on the Law of the Sea (UNCLOS III), http://www.un.org/Depts/los/convention_agreements/convention_overview_convention.htm

Administrative Licensing Law of the PRC (2004), http://www.lehmanlaw.com/resource-centre/laws-and-regulations/administration/administrative-license-law-of-the-peoples-republic-of-china-2003.html

Administrative Litigation Law of the PRC (1989), http://en.chinacourt.org/public/detail.php?id=2695

Administrative Punishment Law of the PRC (1996), http://www.china.org.cn/english/government/207307.htm

Administrative Reconsideration Law of the PRC, http://www.china.org.cn/china/LegislationsForm2001-2010/2011-02/14/content_21916122.htm

Administrative Regulations of the PRC on Settlements, Sales and Payments in Foreign Exchange (1996), http://www.lehmanlaw.com/resource-centre/laws-and-regulations/banking/regulations-on-the-control-of-foreign-exchange-settlement-sale-and-payment-1996.html

Administrative Supervision Law of the PRC (1997), http://www.asianlii.org/cn/legis/cen/laws/asl339/

Agreement Between the Government of Canada and the Government of the People's Republic of China for the Avoidance of Double Taxation and the Prevention of Fiscal Evasion With Respect to Taxes of Income (1986), http://www.fin.gc.ca/treaties-conventions/china_-eng.asp

Air Pollution Law of the PRC (2000), http://www.china.org.cn/english/environment/34422.htm

Anti-Money Laundering Law (2011), http://www.china.org.cn/china/LegislationsForm2001-2010/2011-02/11/content_21900160.htm

Anti-Secession Law of the PRC (2005), http://www.china.org.cn/english/2005lh/122724.htm

Anti-Unfair Competition Law of the PRC (1994), http://en.chinacourt.org/public/detail.php?id=3306

Authorship Rights Law of the PRC (rev. 2010), http://www.china.org.cn/english/government/207485.htm

Bangkok Declaration on Human Rights (1993), http://www.law.hku.hk/conlawhk/conlaw/outline/Outline8/Bangkok%20Declaration.htm

Berne Convention for the Protection of Literary and Artistic Works, http://www.wipo.int/treaties/en/ip/berne/trtdocs_wo001.html

Blood Donation Law of the PRC (1997), http://www.temple.edu/lawschool/phrhcs/conference/Law_on_Blood_Donation.pdf

Central Committee and State Council Decision on Progressively Strengthening Rural Health Work (2002), http://www.chinavalue.net/wiki/showcontent.aspx?titleid=71154

China-ASEAN Declaration on the Conduct of the Parties in the South China Sea (2002), http://www.aseansec.org/13163.htm

Circular of the State Administration of Foreign Exchange on Issuing the Regulations on Foreign Exchange Administration of the Overseas Direct Investment of Domestic Institutions (2009), http://www.safe.gov.cn/wps/portal/!ut/p/c5/04_SB8K8xLLM9MSSzPy8xBz9CP0os3gPZxdnX293QwP30FAnA8_AEBc3C1NjI3dXE6B8JG55MwMCusNB9uHXD5I3wAEcDfT9PPJzU_Uj9aPMcZnibGquH5mTmp6YXKlfkBthkGUSqggAHuiZXA!!/dl3/d3/L2dJQSEvUUt3QS9ZQnZ3LzZfSENEQ01LRzEwT085RTBJNkE1U1NDRzNMMTDQ!/?WCM_GLOBAL_CONTEXT=/wps/wcm/connect/safe_web_store/state+administration+of+foreign+exchange/rules+and+regulations/0bc7710048661f299560b7362e8d3913

Civil Procedure Law (1980), http://www.china.org.cn/english/government/207339.htm

Civil Procedure Law of the PRC (1991, rev. 2008), http://www.lawinfochina.com/display.aspx?lib=law&id=19

Commercial Banking Law of the PRC (1995, rev. 2004), http://www.china.org.cn/english/DAT/214824.htm

Common Program of the Chinese People's Political Consultative Conference 1949 excerpts (Chen Hefu, ed., *Zhongguo xianfa leibian [Varieties of China's constitutions]* (Beijing: Academy of Social Sciences Press, 1980), pp. 183–94).

Common Program of the Chinese People's Political Consultative Congress (1949), http://e-chaupak.net/database/chicon/1949/1949e.pdf

Communique of the 3rd Plenum of the 11th CPC Central Committee (1978), http://www.bjreview.com.cn/special/third_plenum_17thcpc/txt/2008-10/10/content_156226.htm

Company Law of the PRC (1993, rev. 2006), http://www.csrc.gov.cn/pub/csrc_en/laws/rfdm/statelaws/200904/t20090428_102712.htm

Compulsory Education Law of the PRC (1986), http://www.china.org.cn/government/laws/2007-04/17/content_1207402.htm

Constitution of the PRC (1954), http://e-chaupak.net/database/chicon/1954/1954bilingual.htm

Constitution of the PRC, 1954, excerpts (Chen HeHeHefu, ed., *Zhongguo xianfa leibian [Varieties of China's constitutions]* (Beijing: Academy of Social Sciences Press, 1980), pp. 213–34).

Constitution of the PRC (1975), http://e-chaupak.net/database/chicon/1975/1975e.htm

Constitution of the PRC, 1975 (Chen HeHeHefu, ed., *Zhongguo xianfa leibian [Varieties of China's constitutions]* (Beijing: Academy of Social Sciences Press, 1980), pp. 333–43).

Constitution of the PRC (1978), http://en.wikipedia.org/w/index.php?title=File%3APeople%27s_Republic_of_China_1978_Constitution.pdf&page=1

Constitution of the PRC, 1978 (Chen HeHeHefu, ed., *Zhongguo xianfa leibian [Varieties of China's constitutions]* (Beijing: Academy of Social Sciences Press, 1980), pp. 1–18).

Constitution of the PRC (1982), http://www.npc.gov.cn/englishnpc/Constitution/node_2830.htm

Constitution of the PRC (2004 Revisions), http://www.npc.gov.cn/englishnpc/Constitution/node_2825.htm

Consumer Protection Law of the PRC (1994), http://www.china.org.cn/china/LegislationsForm2001-2010/2011-02/14/content_21917139.htm

Contract Law of the PRC (1999), http://www.fdi.gov.cn/pub/FDI_EN/Laws/law_en_info.jsp?docid=50943

Convention on Elimination of All Forms of Discrimination Against Women (CEDAW), http://www.un.org/womenwatch/daw/cedaw/

Corruption Punishment Regulations in the Jin Cha Ji Border Region (1942) (Han Yanlong and Chang Zhaoru, eds, *Zhongguo xin minzhuzhuyi geming shiqi genju di fazhi wenxian xuanbian [Collection of legal documents from the base areas during China's new democratic revolution]* (Beijing: Chinese Academy of Social Sciences Press, 1981)).

Criminal Law of the PRC (1979, rev. 1997), http://www.china.org.cn/english/government/207320.htm

Criminal Procedure Law of the PRC (1980, rev. 1996), http://www.china.org. cn/english/government/207334.htm

Decision of the State Council on Questions of Re-education and Rehabilitation Through Labor (1957), http://www.asianlii.org/cgi-bin/disp.pl/cn/legis/cen/laws/dotscrtqortl766/dotscrtqortl766.html?stem=0&synonyms=0&query=title

Detailed Implementing Rules on Sino Foreign Cooperative Enterprises (1995), http://sl2.mofcom.gov.cn/aarticle/chinalaw/investment/200412/20041200008127.html

Economic Contract Law (1981), http://app.westlawchina.com/maf/china/app/document?&docguid=i3cf76ad30000011ef35155c8633ee5f0&hitguid=i3cf76ad30000011ef35155c8633ee5f0&srguid=ia744c0670000013a8c00b9289658c250&spos=4&epos=4&td=5&crumb-action=append&context=4&lang=en

Enterprise Income Tax Law of the PRC (2008), http://app.westlawchina.com.ezproxy.library.ubc.ca/maf/china/app/document?&docguid=i0adf589b0000011e6d84a4ccd238ae79&hitguid=i0adf589b0000011e6d84a4ccd238ae79&srguid=ia744dc1e0000013a8f5e9b7b63f24a56&spos=1&epos=1&td=21&crumb-action=append&context=25&lang=en

Environmental Impact Assessment Law of the PRC, http://www.npc.gov.cn/englishnpc/Law/2007-12/06/content_1382122.htm

Environmental Protection Law (1989), http://www.china.org.cn/english/environment/34356.htm

Environmental Protection Law of the PRC (1990), http://www.china.org.cn/english/environment/34356.htm

Food Safety Law of the PRC (2009), http://www.procedurallaw.cn/english/law/200903/t20090320_196425.html

Foreign Trade Law of the PRC (1994, rev. 2004, rev. 2007), http://www.china.org.cn/china/LegislationsForm2001-2010/2011-02/14/content_21917089.htm

General Principles of Civil Law (1986), http://en.chinacourt.org/public/detail.php?id=2696

General Principles of Civil Law of the PRC (1986), http://en.chinacourt.org/public/detail.php?id=2696

Guiding Catalogue on Foreign Investment (2011), http://www.bakermckenzie.com/files/Uploads/Documents/China%20Update%202012/al_china_foreigninvestmentcatalogue_jan12.pdf

Guiding Catalogue of Industries for Foreign Investment (2007), http://www.fdi.gov.cn/pub/FDI_EN/Laws/law_en_info.jsp?docid=87372

Higher Education Law of the PRC (1995), http://www.edu.cn/21st_1407/20060323/t20060323_116528.shtml

Hong Kong Basic Law, http://www.basiclaw.gov.hk/en/basiclawtext/index.html

Human Rights White Paper (2000), http://english.gov.cn/official/2005-07/27/content_17730.htm

Implementing Rules for China's Law on Wholly Foreign-Owned Enterprises (rev. 2001), http://www.fdi.gov.cn/pub/FDI_EN/Laws/law_en_info.jsp?docid=101486

Individual Income Tax Law of the PRC (rev. 1993), http://www.chinatax.gov.cn/n6669073/n6669088/6888498.html

Infectious Disease Law of the PRC (2004), http://www.npc.gov.cn/englishnpc/Law/2007-12/12/content_1383919.htm

International Convention on Elimination of All Forms of Racial Discrimination, http://www2.ohchr.org/english/law/cerd.htm

International Convention on Prevention of Acts of Nuclear Terrorism, http://www.nti.org/treaties-and-regimes/international-convention-suppression-acts-nuclear-terrorism/

International Convention for the Suppression of the Financing of Terrorism, http://www.un.org/law/cod/finterr.htm

International Convention for the Suppression of Terrorist Bombings, http://treaties.un.org/Pages/ViewDetails.aspx?src=TREATY&mtdsg_no=XVIII-9&chapter=18&lang=en

International Covenant on Civil and Political Rights (ICCPR), http://www2.ohchr.org/english/law/ccpr.htm

International Covenant on Economic, Social and Cultural Rights (ICESCR), http://www2.ohchr.org/english/law/cescr.htm

Interpretation of the Supreme People's Court on Several Issues Related to the Execution of Criminal Procedure Law of the People's Republic of China (Adopted at the 989th Session of Trial Committee of the Supreme People's Court on June 29, 1998) Fashi [1998] no. 23).

Judges Law of the PRC (2001), http://app.westlawchina.com.ezproxy.library.ubc.ca/maf/china/app/document?&docguid=i3cf76ad30000011ef3515725633ee81e&hitguid=i3cf76ad30000011ef3515725633ee81e&srguid=ia744dc1e0000013a86c125b363f23ca7&spos=1&epos=1&td=4&crumb-action=append&context=9&lang=en

Labor Contract Law of the PRC (2008), http://www.fdi.gov.cn/pub/FDI_EN/Laws/GeneralLawsandRegulations/BasicLaws/P020070831601380007924.pdf

Labor Disputes Arbitration and Mediation Law of the PRC (2007), http://tradeinservices.mofcom.gov.cn/en/b/2007-12-29/27880.shtml

Labor Law of the PRC (1995), http://www.usmra.com/china/Labour%20Law.htm

Land Administration Law of the PRC, http://www.china.org.cn/english/environment/34345.htm

Land Administration Law of the PRC (1986), http://app.westlawchina.com.ezproxy.library.ubc.ca/maf/china/app/document?&docguid=i3cf76ad30000011ef35155f6633ee646&hitguid=i3cf76ad30000011ef35155f6633ee646&srguid=ia744c0670000013a8210003eed740e03&spos=4&epos=4&td=14&crumb-action=append&context=10&lang=en

Land Law of the Chinese Soviet Republic 1931 (William E. Butler, ed., *The Legal System of the Chinese Soviet Republic 1931–34* (New York: Transnational Publishers, 1983)).

Land Reform Law of the PRC (1950), http://www.npc.gov.cn/wxzl/wxzl/2000-12/10/content_4246.htm

Law Against Unfair Competition of the PRC (1993), http://www.ccpit-patent.com.cn/references/Law_Against_Unfair_Competition_China.htm

Law of the PRC on Lawyers and Legal Representation (October 2007), http://www.csclawyers.org/letters/Lawyers%20Law%202007.pdf

Law of the PRC on Mediation and Arbitration of Disputes Involving Rural Land Contract Management http://www.cietac.org/index/references/Laws/47607b541c012c7f001.cms

Law of the PRC on Medical Practitioners (1998), http://www.fdi.gov.cn/pub/FDI_EN/Laws/GeneralLawsandRegulations/BasicLaws/P020060620320621250390.pdf

Law of the PRC on Minority Nationality Region Autonomy, http://www.china.org.cn/english/government/207138.htm

Law of the PRC on Pollution Prevention and Control (1996), http://www.china.org.cn/government/laws/2007-04/17/content_1207459.htm

Law of the PRC on the Process for Concluding International Treaties (1990), http://www.npc.gov.cn/englishnpc/Law/2007-12/12/content_1383893.htm

Law of the PRC on the Protection of Rights and Interests of Women (rev. 2005), http://www.china.org.cn/english/government/207405.htm

Law of the PRC on Sino-Foreign Joint Equity Enterprises (rev. 2001), http://www.saic.gov.cn/english/lawsregulations/laws/200602/t20060227_55249.html

Law of the PRC on the Territorial Sea and the Contiguous Zone, http://www.fdi.gov.cn/pub/FDI_EN/Laws/GeneralLawsandRegulations/BasicLaws/P020060620318668126917.pdf

Law of the PRC on Water Conservation (1991), http://www.china.org.cn/environment/2007-08/20/content_1034358.htm

Law on Mediation and Arbitration of Labor Disputes (December 29, 2007), http://tradeinservices.mofcom.gov.cn/en/b/2007-12-29/27880.shtml

Law on Sino-Foreign Cooperative Enterprises (rev. 2000), http://www.china.org.cn/english/features/investment/36755.htm

Law on the People's Bank of China (1995, rev. 2004), http://www.china.org.cn/business/laws_regulations/2007-06/22/content_1214826.htm

Law on Urban Real Estate (1994), http://www.asianlii.org/cn/legis/cen/laws/aoturel381/

Legislation Law of the PRC (2000), http://english.gov.cn/laws/2005-08/20/content_29724.htm

Marriage Law of the Chinese Soviet Republic 1931 (William E. Butler, ed., *The Legal System of the Chinese Soviet Republic 1931–34* (New York: Transnational Publishers, 1983)).

Marriage Law of the PRC (rev. 2001), http://www1.chinaculture.org/library/2008-02/14/content_22279.htm

Measures for the Administration of Overseas Investment (2009), http://www.faegrebd.com/9816

Measures for Administration of the Qualification for Contracting Overseas Projects (2009), http://app.westlawchina.com.ezproxy.library.ubc.ca/maf/china/app/document?&docguid=i3cf76ad30000012453973b7c7bc1857c&hitguid=i3cf76ad30000012453973b7c7bc1857c&srguid=ia744d04f0000013aaa47fe8029b96cd3&spos=1&epos=1&td=1&crumb-action=append&context=39&lang=en

Mental Health Law of the PRC (2012), http://www.saponline.org/upload/20121220/special_article.pdf

Ministry of Health Regulations on reporting infectious disease (2003), http://news.sohu.com/17/30/news212783017.shtml

Ministry of Information Industry's "Measures for Administration of Internet Information Providers" (2000), http://www.china.org.cn/business/2010-01/20/content_19274704.htm

National Climate Change Program (2007), http://www.china.org.cn/english/environment/213624.htm

National Human Rights Action Plan (2009), http://www.china.org.cn/archive/2009-04/13/content_17595407.htm

New York Convention on the Recognition and Enforcement of Foreign Arbitral Awards, http://www.uncitral.org/uncitral/en/uncitral_texts/arbitration/NYConvention.html

Nice Agreement Concerning the International Classification of Goods and Services for the Purpose of Registration of Marks, http://www.wipo.int/treaties/en/classification/nice/trtdocs_wo019.html

Notice of Ministry of Commerce on Further Improving Examination and Approval of Foreign Investments (2009), http://sa2.mofcom.gov.cn/aarticle/shangfuting/200904/20090406140607.html

Notice of NDRC on Issues Relating to Improving Administration of Overseas Investment Projects (2009), http://app.westlawchina.com.ezproxy.library.ubc.ca/maf/china/app/document?&docguid=i3cf76ad300000121f8e0e62698245d9e&hitguid=i3cf76ad300000121f8e0e62698245d9e&srguid=ia744dc1e0000013aaa50e1063da7fe0b&spos=1&epos=1&td=1&crumb-action=append&context=59&lang=en

Occupational Health Law of the PRC (2001), http://english.gov.cn/laws/2005-10/10/content_75718.htm

Office of National Leading Group for Promoting Sustainable Development, PRC, *Program of Action for Sustainable Development in China in the Early 21st Century* (n.d.), pp. 12–35, http://en.ndrc.gov.cn/newsrelease/t20070205_115702.htm

Organization Law on the People's Courts (1978), http://app.westlawchina.com.ezproxy.library.ubc.ca/maf/china/app/document?&docguid=i3cf76ad30000011ef35155b9633ee5d8&hitguid=i3cf76ad30000011ef35155b9633ee5d8&srguid=ia744c0690000013aa38aded4fa150efd&spos=3&epos=3&td=6&crumb-action=append&context=79&lang=en

Organization Law on the People's Procuratorate (1979), http://app.westlawchina.com.ezproxy.library.ubc.ca/maf/china/app/document?&src=nr&docguid=i3cf76ad30000011ef35155ba633ee5da&lang=en&crumb-action=append&crumb-label=文件

Outline of China's Land Law 1947 (Tony Saich, *The Rise to Power the Chinese Communist Party: Documents and Analysis* (Armonk, NY: M.E. Sharpe, 1996)).

Paris Convention for the Protection of Industrial Property, http://www.wipo.int/treaties/en/ip/paris/trtdocs_wo020.html#P19_137

Patent Cooperation Treaty, http://www.wipo.int/pct/en/texts/articles/atoc.htm

Patent Law of the PRC (rev. 2008), http://www.chinaipr.gov.cn/lawsarticle/laws/lawsar/patent/201101/1186462_1.html

Pharmaceutical Safety Law of the PRC (2009), http://www.sfda.gov.cn/WS01/CL0617/39865.html

Product Quality Law of the PRC (rev. 2000), http://www.most.gov.cn/eng/policies/regulations/200501/t20050105_18422.htm

Property Rights Law of the PRC (2007), http://www.china.org.cn/china/ LegislationsForm2001-2010/2011-02/11/content_21897791.htm

Protocol on the Accession of the People's Republic of China, World Trade Organization, WT/L/432, November 23, 2001.

Provisional Measures on Re-Education and Rehabilitation Through Labor (1982), http://app.westlawchina.com.ezproxy.library.ubc.ca/maf/china-cn/ app/document?&docguid=i3cf76ad30000011ef35147d0633ed6a7&hitguid =i3cf76ad30000011ef35147d0633ed6a7&srguid=ia744c0670000013aa3f9e 40fd5ce15cb&spos=5&epos=5&td=185&crumb-action=append&context= 197&lang=cn&crumb-label=%E6%96%87%E4%BB%B6

Provisional Regulations of the PRC on Management of International Connections for Computer Networks (1996), http://www.asianlii.org/cn/legis/cen/laws/ ipgtmotcinitproccttin1488/

Provisions on Foreign Exchange Administration of Outward Direct Investment by Domestic Institutions (2009), http://app.westlawchina.com.ezproxy. library.ubc.ca/maf/china/app/document?&docguid=i3cf76ad30000012289 1b84517f382c1d&hitguid=i3cf76ad300000122891b84517f382c1d&srguid =ia744c0670000013aa3465a218837dae9&spos=1&epos=1&td=229&cr umb-action=append&context=9&lang=en

Public Health Reform Plan (2009), http://www.gov.cn/zwgk/2009-04/07/ content_1279256.htm

Regulation on Security Management Procedures for Internet Access (1997), http://www.wipo.int/wipolex/en/details.jsp?id=6571

Regulation on Security Protection for Computer Information Systems (1994), http://www.gov.cn/flfg/2005-08/06/content_20928.htm

Regulations on Foreign Investment Guidelines (2002), http://www.fdi.gov.cn/ pub/FDI_EN/Laws/law_en_info.jsp?docid=51272

Regulations for the Implementation of the Law of the People's Republic of China on Joint Ventures Using Chinese and Foreign Investment (2001), http:// dehengdubai.com/en/libaryDetail.asp?id=19

Regulations of the PRC on Administration of Publishing (2001), http://english. gov.cn/laws/2005-08/23/content_25588.htm

Regulations of the PRC on Administrative Reconsideration, http://www.asianlii. org/cn/legis/cen/laws/roar461/

Regulations of the PRC on Security Administration and Punishment (1957, rev. 1986, rev. 1994), http://www.eduzhai.net/yingyu/615/763/yingyu_ 246322.html

Resolution on Party History (1981), http://www.marxists.org/subject/china/ documents/cpc/history/index.htm

Rules of the PRC on Foreign Exchange Control (1983, rev. 1997, rev. 2008), http://tradeinservices.mofcom.gov.cn/en/b/2008-08-05/58193.shtml

Rural Land Contracting Law (2002) http://english.gov.cn/laws/2005-10/09/content_75300.htm

Securities Law of the PRC (1998, rev. 2005), http://www.csrc.gov.cn/pub/csrc_en/laws/rfdm/statelaws/200904/t20090429_102757.htm

Security Administration Punishment Act (1957), http://www.law-lib.com/law/law_view.asp?id=94225

Several Opinions of the State Council on Further Improving the Work of Using Foreign Investment (2010), http://english.mofcom.gov.cn/aarticle/policyrelease/announcement/201006/20100606982859.html

Sino-Russian Treaty on "Good Neighborliness and Friendly Cooperation," http://www.fmprc.gov.cn/eng/wjdt/2649/t15771.htm

State Compensation Law of the PRC (1994), http://www.giprs.org/en/node/219

State Council AIDS Action Plan (2001), http://www.gov.cn/gongbao/content/2001/content_60908.htm

State Council Information Office, "Environmental Protection in China 1996–2005," http://www.china.org.cn/english/2006/Jun/170355.htm

State Council Information Office, "Human Rights Action Plan for China" (April 13, 2009), http://www.gov.cn/english/official/2009-04/13/content_1284128.htm

State Council Notice on Western Development Program (2000), http://www.asianlii.org/cn/legis/cen/laws/cotsccspocotdocvwr1122/

State Council Opinion on Utilizing Foreign Investment (2010), http://www.fdi.gov.cn/pub/FDI_EN/Laws/GeneralLawsandRegulations/Ministerial Rulings/P020100422347293597538.pdf

State Council Opinion on Western Development Program (2001), http://tw.people.com.cn/GB/14810/14858/872482.html

State Council Regulations on Administration of Publishing (2001), http://english.gov.cn/laws/2005-08/23/content_25588.htm

State Council Strategic AIDS Plan (1998), http://hivaidsclearinghouse.unesco.org/search/resources/NationalPlan1998-2010_HIV_China.pdf

State Council Taiwan Affairs Office and Information Office, "The One-China Principle and the Taiwan Issue" (February 21, 2000), http://english.gov.cn/official/2005-07/27/content_17613.htm

State Council, China National Environmental Protection Plan in the Eleventh Five-Year Plan (2006–2010), http://english.mep.gov.cn/down_load/Documents/200803/P020080306440313293094.pdf

State Secrets Law of the PRC (rev. 2010), http://hrichina.org/sites/default/files/oldsite/PDFs/PressReleases/20101001-StateSecretsLaw-EN.pdf

Strategic Plan for Hospital Construction (2010), http://www.china.com.cn/policy/txt/2010-02/24/content_19464497.htm

Supplementary Provisions on Re-education and Rehabilitation Through Labor (1979), http://www.asianlii.org/cgi-bin/disp.pl/cn/legis/cen/laws/spotscfrtl815/spotscfrtl815.html?stem=0&synonyms=0&query=title(REH ABILITATION THROUGH LABOUR)

Supreme People's Court Interpretation (1st) on Several Issues Concerning the Application of the "PRC Contract Law," http://app.westlawchina.com.ezproxy.library.ubc.ca/maf/china/app/document?&docguid=i0adf589b0000011e6d83c039d238ab6d&hitguid=i0adf589b0000011e6d83c039d238ab6d&srguid=ia744c0670000013a8520485fd87a8eea&spos=7&epos=7&td=8&crumb-action=append&context=35&lang=en

Supreme People's Court Interpretation (2nd) on Several Issues Concerning the Application of the "PRC Contract Law," http://app.westlawchina.com.ezproxy.library.ubc.ca/maf/china/app/document?&docguid=i3cf76ad3000001213a501d6fe644c56d&hitguid=i3cf76ad3000001213a501d6fe644c56d&srguid=ia744c0690000013a852186d75232f032&spos=2&epos=2&td=8&crumb-action=append&context=39&lang=en

Supreme People's Court Interpretation on Certain Questions of the Specific Application of Law to Adjudication of Disputes over Property Management (April 20, 2009), http://app.westlawchina.com.ezproxy.library.ubc.ca/maf/china/app/document?&docguid=i3cf76ad300000121781ca6c14569e80b&hitguid=i3cf76ad300000121781ca6c14569e80b&srguid=ia744dc1e0000013a8f5976456fc9ed18&spos=1&epos=1&td=5&crumb-action=append&context=9&lang=en

Supreme People's Court, "Interpretation on the Application of Law in Adjudication of Cases Involving Rural Land Contracting Disputes" (July 29, 2005), http://app.westlawchina.com.ezproxy.library.ubc.ca/maf/china/app/document?&docguid=i3cf76ad30000011ef34f285f633ba038&hitguid=i3cf76ad30000011ef34f285f633ba038&srguid=ia744c0670000013a852c397ed6d0dcd4&spos=1&epos=1&td=1&crumb-action=append&context=56&lang=en

Supreme People's Court's "Rules on Certain Issues Relating to Jurisdiction over Proceedings of Foreign-Related Civil and Commercial Cases" (2002), http://app.westlawchina.com.ezproxy.library.ubc.ca/maf/china/app/document?&docguid=i3cf76ad30000011ef351557f633ee562&hitguid=i3cf76ad30000011ef351557f633ee562&srguid=ia744c0670000013aa3e9710ac59a3169&spos=1&epos=1&td=1&crumb-action=append&context=143&lang=en

Tashkent Declaration of Heads of Member States of Shanghai Cooperation Organization (June 17, 2004), http://www.ecrats.com/en/normative_documents/2008

Tentative Regulations on the Procedure for Enacting Administrative Laws and Regulations (1987), http://www.law-lib.com/lawhtm/1987/4247.htm

Trademark Law of the PRC, http://www.ccpit-patent.com.cn/references/Trademark_law_China.htm

UK–China Double Taxation Agreement (2011), www.hmrc.gov.uk/taxtreaties/signed/uk-china-dta2011.pdf

United Nations Framework Convention on Climate Change and the Kyoto Protocol, http://unfccc.int/resource/docs/convkp/kpeng.pdf

Universal Copyright Convention, http://portal.unesco.org/en/ev.php-URL_ID=15241&URL_DO=DO_TOPIC&URL_SECTION=201.html

Water Law of the PRC (rev. 2002), http://english.gov.cn/laws/2005-10/09/content_75313.htm

White Paper, "China's Policies and Actions for Addressing Climate Change" (2011), http://english.gov.cn/2008-10/29/content_1134544.htm

White Paper on Ethnic Policy (2010), http://www.china.org.cn/government/whitepaper/node_7078073.htm

White Paper on Labor and Social Security (2002), http://news.xinhuanet.com/english/2002-04/29/content_377416.htm

White Paper, "Progress in China's Human Rights in 2009," http://news.xinhuanet.com/english2010/china/2010-09/26/c_13529921.htm

White Paper, "The Socialist Legal System with Chinese Characteristics," http://www.china.org.cn/government/whitepaper/node_7137666.htm

Wholly Foreign-Owned Enterprise Law of the PRC (rev. 2001), http://english.mofcom.gov.cn/aarticle/lawsdata/chineselaw/200301/20030100062858.html

World Intellectual Property Organization Convention, http://www.wipo.int/treaties/en/convention/trtdocs_wo029.html

WTO Agreement on Trade-Related Aspects of Intellectual Property Rights, http://www.wto.org/english/tratop_e/trips_e/t_agm0_e.htm

WTO, "Protocol on the Accession of the People's Republic of China" (2001), http://unpan1.un.org/intradoc/groups/public/documents/APCITY/UNPAN002123.pdf

SUGGESTIONS FOR FURTHER READING

Alford, William P. and Yuanyuan Shen, "Limits of the Law in Addressing China's Environmental Dilemma," *Stanford Environmental Law Journal*, vol. 16 (1997), pp. 125–48.

Amnesty International, *Country Report – China* (2009) (http://report2009. amnesty.org/en/regions/asia-pacific/china).

Amnesty International, *People's Republic of China: Repression in Tibet, 1987–1992* (London: Amnesty International, 1992).

Amnesty International, *Secret Violence: Human Rights Violations in Xinjiang* (London: Amnesty International, 1992).

Baum, Richard, *Burying Mao: Chinese Politics in the Age of Deng Xiaoping* (Princeton, NJ: Princeton University Press, 1994).

Beehner, Lionel, "The Rise of the Shanghai Cooperation Organization," *Council on Foreign Relations*, (June 12, 2006).

Benney, Jonathan, *Defending Rights in Contemporary China* (London: Routledge, 2012).

Blumenthal, David and William Hsiao, "Privatization and Its Discontents – The Evolving Chinese Health Care System," *New England Journal of Medicine*, vol. 353, no. 11 (Sept. 15, 2005), pp. 1165–70.

Bodde, Derk and Clarence Morris, *Law in Imperial China* (Philadelphia, PA: University of Pennsylvania Press, 1967).

Breslin, Shaun, *Handbook of China's International Relations* (London: Routledge, 2010).

Buhmann, Karin, *Implementing Human Rights through Administrative Law Reforms: The Potential in China and Vietnam* (Copenhagen: Djof Publishing, 2001).

Bulag, Uradyn E., *The Mongols at China's Edge: History and the Politics of National Unity* (Lanham, MD: Rowman and Littlefield, 2002).

Butler, William E., ed., *The Legal System of the Chinese Soviet Republic 1931–1934* (New York: Transnational Publishers, 1983).

Cai Yongshun, *Collective Resistance in China: Why Popular Protests Succeed and Fail* (Stanford, CA: Stanford University Press, 2010).

Cass, Deborah, Brett G. Williams, and George Barker, eds, *China and the World Trading System: Entering the New Millennium* (Cambridge: Cambridge University Press, 2003).

Chan, Anita, *China's Workers Under Assault: The Exploitation of Labor in a Globalizing Economy* (Armonk, NY: M.E. Sharpe, 2001).

Chan Lai-Ha, Pak K. Lee, and Gerald Chan, "Rethinking Global Governance: A China Model in the Making?," *Contemporary Politics*, vol. 14, no. 1 (2008), pp. 3–19.

Chen, Albert H.Y., *An Introduction to the Legal System of the People's Republic of China* (Hong Kong: Butterworths, 2004).

China: An International Journal, vol. 8, no. 1, Special Issue on Health Policy (March 2010).

China Labor Watch, Survey of Chinese Workers Conditions in 2010, March 2011 (http://www.chinalaborwatch.org/news/new-328.html).

China Quarterly, "Developments in Chinese Law: The Past Ten Years," (2007).

Cohen, Jerome A., *The Criminal Process in the People's Republic of China* (Cambridge, MA: Harvard University Press, 1968).

Cohen, Jerome A. and Hungdah Chiu, eds, *People's China and International Law: A Documentary Survey* (Princeton, NJ: Princeton University Press, 1974).

Columbia Journal of Asian Law, "Special Issue: Celebrating the Work of Stanley Lubman," vol. 19, no. 1 (Spring–Fall, 2005), pp. 1–29.

Congressional-Executive Commission on China, *2011 Annual Report* (http://www.cecc.gov/pages/annualRpt/annualRpt11/AR2011final.pdf).

Davis, Deborah and Ezra Vogel, eds, *Chinese Society on the Eve of Tiananmen: The Impact of Reform* (Cambridge, MA: Council on East Asian Studies, Harvard University, 1990).

Day, Kristen A., ed., *China's Environment and the Challenge of Sustainable Development* (Armonk, NY: M.E. Sharpe, 2005).

Diamant, Neil Jeffrey, Stanley B. Lubman, and Kevin J. O'Brien, eds, *Engaging the Law in China: State, Society, and Possibilities for Justice* (Stanford, CA: Stanford University Press, 2005).

Dowdle, Michael, *Building Constitutionalism in China* (New York: Palgrave Macmillan, 2009).

Economy, Elizabeth, *The River Runs Black: The Environmental Challenge to China's Future* (Ithaca, NY: Cornell University Press, 2004).

Elvin, Mark and Liu Ts'ui-jong, eds, *Sediments of Time: Environment and Society in Chinese History* (Cambridge: Cambridge University Press, 1998).

Feinerman, James V., "Chinese Participation in the International Legal Order: Rogue Elephant or Team Player?" *The China Quarterly*, no. 141 (March 1995), pp. 186–210.

Feng Chen, "Between the State and Labor: The Conflict of Chinese Trade Unions' Double Identity in Market Reform," *The China Quarterly*, no. 176 (December 2003).

Foot, Rosemary and Andrew Walter, *China, the United States, and the Global Order* (Cambridge: Cambridge University Press, 2010).

Freeman, Charles W. and Xiaoqing Lu, eds, *China's Capacity to Manage Infectious Diseases* (Washington, DC: Center for Strategic and International Studies, 2009).

Fu Hualing and Richard Cullen, "Weiquan (Rights Protection) Lawyering in an Authoritarian State: Toward Critical Lawyering," *The China Journal*, vol. 59, no. 111 (2008).

Han Nianlong et al., eds, *Diplomacy of Contemporary China* (Hong Kong: New Horizon Press, 1990).

Ho, Virginia E. Harper, "From Contracts to Compliance? An Early Look at Implementation Under China's New Labor Legislation," *Columbia Journal of Asian Law*, vol. 23, no. 1 (2009), pp. 35–107.

Hom, Sharon, "Law, Development, and the Rights of Chinese Women: A Snapshot from the Field," in *Columbia Journal of Asian Law*, "Special Issue: Celebrating the Work of Stanley Lubman," vol. 19, no. 1 (Spring–Fall, 2005), pp. 345–60.

Huang Philip C.C., *Code, Custom, and Legal Practice in China: The Qing and the Republic Compared* (Stanford, CA: Stanford University Press, 2001).

Huang Yasheng, *Capitalism with Chinese Characteristics: Entrepreneurship and the State* (Cambridge: Cambridge University Press, 2008).

Human Rights in China, "China and the Rule of Law," *China Rights Forum*, no. 2 (2003).

Human Rights in China, "Searching for Social Justice," *China Rights Forum*, no. 4 (2005).

Human Rights Watch, "World Report 2012 – China" (http://www.hrw.org/world-report-2012/world-report-2012-china).

International Committee of Lawyers for Tibet, "Legal Materials on Tibet" (2d edn) (1997).

Keith, Ronald C. and Zhiqiu Lin, *Law and Justice in China's New Marketplace* (New York: Palgrave, 2001).

Kent, Ann, *China, the United Nations, and Human Rights: The Limits of Compliance* (Philadelphia, PA: University of Pennsylvania Press, 1999).

Kumiko, Julie, *The Problems of Chinese Labor: Problems in the Implementation of Chinese Human Rights Obligations* (Bloomington, IN: Xlibris, 2010).

Lee, Leah and Kevin M. Rudd, *China's Labor Law Reforms and its Compliance with ILO Conventions on the Protection of Women* (Canberra: Australian National University, 2006)

Li, Victor H., "The Evolution and Development of the Chinese Legal System," in John M.H. Lindbeck, ed., *China: Management of a Revolutionary Society* (Seattle, WA: University of Washington Press, 1971).

Lubman, Stanley B., *Bird in a Cage – Legal Reform in China after Mao* (Stanford, CA: Stanford University Press, 2000).

MacFarquhar, Roderick, ed., *The Politics of China, 1949–1989* (Cambridge: Cambridge University Press, 1993).

McConville, Michael et al., *Criminal Justice in China: An Empirical Inquiry* (Cheltenham: Edward Elgar, 2011).

Mertha, Andrew, *The Politics of Piracy: Intellectual Property in Contemporary China* (Ithaca, NY: Cornell University Press, 2005).

Miles, James A.R., *The Legacy of Tiananmen: China in Disarray* (Ann Arbor, MI: University of Michigan Press, 1997).

Mosher, Michael and Fu Yu, eds, *Doing Business in China* (New York: International Juris, looseleaf).

O'Brien, Kevin J., ed., *Popular Protest in China* (Cambridge, MA: Harvard University Press, 2008).

Organization for Economic Cooperation and Development (OECD), *China in the World Economy: The Domestic Policy Challenges* (Paris: OECD, 2002).

Ostry, Sylvia, Alan S. Alexandroff, and Raphael Gomez, eds, *China and the Long March to Global Trade: The Accession of China to the World Trade Organization* (New York: Routledge, 2002).

Peerenboom Randall, *China Modernizes: Threat to the West or Model for the Rest?* (Oxford: Oxford University Press, 2007).

Peerenboom, Randall, *China's Long March Toward Rule of Law* (Cambridge: Cambridge University Press, 2002).

Potter, Pitman B., *The Chinese Legal System: Globalization and Local Legal Culture* (London: Routledge, 2001).

Potter, Pitman B., "Coordinating Corporate Governance and Corporate Social Responsibility," *Hong Kong University Law Journal*, vol. 39, no. 3 (2009), pp. 675–96. Reprinted in *Tsinghua Faxue* [Tsinghua Law Journal], no. 1 (January 15, 2011) (in Chinese).

Potter, Pitman B., *From Leninist Discipline to Socialist Legalism: Peng Zhen on Law and Political Authority in the PRC* (Stanford, CA: Stanford University Press, 2003).

Potter, Pitman B., *Law, Policy, and Practice in China's Periphery* (London: Routledge, 2010).

Potter, Pitman B. and Li Jianyong, "Regulating Labor Relations on China: The Challenge of Adopting to the Socialist Market Economy," *Cahiers du Droit* (Université Laval, 1996).

Reporters Without Borders, "Journey to the Heart of Internet Censorship" (October, 2007), http://www.rsf.org/IMG/pdf/Voyage_au_coeur_de_la_censure_GB.pdf (accessed October 15, 2012).

Rosett, Arthur, Lucie Cheng, and Margaret Woo, eds, *East Asian Law: Universal Norms and Local Conditions* (London: Routledge/Curzon, 2002).

Rossabit, Morris, *Governing China's Multiethnic Frontiers* (Seattle, WA: University of Washington Press, 2004).

Saich Anthony, *The People's Movement: Perspectives on Spring 1989* (Armonk, NY: M.E. Sharpe, 1990).

Shapiro, Judith, *Mao's War Against Nature: Politics of Environment in Revolutionary China* (Cambridge: Cambridge University Press, 2001).

State Council Information Office, "Assessment Report of the National Human Rights Action Plan of China" (July 14, 2011) (http://www.china.org.cn/china/2011-07/14/content_22989895.htm).

US Department of State, Bureau of Democracy, Human Rights and Labor, "Country Reports on Human Rights Practices: China (includes Tibet, Hong Kong and Macao) 2010" (April 8, 2011) (http://www.state.gov/j/drl/rls/hrrpt/2010/eap/154382.htm).

United Nations Development Programme, *China Human Development Report 2009/10: China and a Sustainable Future: Towards a Low Carbon Economy and Society* (Beijing: China Translation and Publishing Corporation, 2010).

Vogel, Ezra F., *Deng Xiaoping and the Transformation of China* (Cambridge, MA: Belknap Press of Harvard University Press, 2011).

Wang, Alex L., "China's Environmental Tipping Point," in Timothy Weston and Lionel Jensen, eds, *China in and Beyond the Headlines* (Lanham, MD: Rowman and Littlefield, 2012), pp. 112–33.

World Bank, *Cost of Pollution in China: Economic Estimates of Physical Damages*, February 2007 (http://siteresources.worldbank.org/INTEAPREGTOPENVIRONMENT/Resources/China_Cost_of_Pollution.pdf).

WTO Secretariat, *Trade Policy Review: China* (Geneva: World Trade Organization, 2010).

Xue Hanqin, *Chinese Perspectives on International Law* (Leiden: Martinus Nijhoff, 2012).

Zhang Liang, Andrew Nathan, Perry Link, and Orville Schell, *The Tiananmen Papers* (New York: Public Affairs, 2001).

Zhang Xin, *International Trade Regulation in China* (Oxford: Hart Publishing, 2006).

Zhao Litao and Lim Tin Seng, eds, *China's New Social Policy: Initiatives for a Harmonious Society* (Singapore: World Scientific, 2010).

Zhao Ziyang, *Prisoner of the State: The Secret Journal of Premier Zhao Ziyang* (New York: Simon & Schuster, 2009).

Zheng Yongnian, *China and International Relations: The Chinese View and the Contribution of Wang Gongwu* (London: Routledge, 2010).

Index